Fuchsias
The Complete Handbook

Fuchsias

The Complete Handbook

edited by **Miep Nijhuis**
With the Dutch Circle of Fuchsia Lovers

CASSELL

Cassell Publishers Limited
Villiers House, 41/47 Strand
London WC2N 5JE

Copyright © Uitgeverij J. H. Gottmer/H. J. W. Becht 1985
English translation copyright © Cassell Publishers Limited 1994

First published in Great Britain 1994
by arrangement with
Uitgeverij J. H. Gottmer/H. J. W. Becht bv
Bloemendaal, Netherlands

British Library Cataloguing in Publication Data
A catalogue record for this book is available from the British Library

ISBN 0-304-34387-0

Distributed in the United States by Sterling Publishing Co. Inc.
387 Park Avenue South, New York, New York 10016-8810

Distributed in Australia by Capricorn Link (Australia) Pty Ltd
2/13 Carrington Road, Castle Hill, NSW 2154

Typeset by August Filmsetting, St Helens
Printed and bound in Great Britain by Biddles Ltd

English translation by Paul Foulkes
Photographs by: H. Aalhuizen-Nijhuis, S. A. Appel, J. G. van de Beek, C. van Brunschot,
L. Bögemann, P. van der Craats, F. van den Elshout, H. J. de Graaff, M. Grijsen-Sellink,
W. J. Luitse, J. de Nie, J. W. N. W. van der Post, D. Reiman-Dietiker, T. Spakman,
P. C. Venema-Hollestelle and A. van Wijk.

Contents

Publisher's notes

Readers are requested to note that:

1 Measurements in this book are cited in metric units; for those who prefer to think in terms of imperial quantities the following *approximate* conversions may prove helpful:

$2mm = \frac{1}{16}in$ $5mm = \frac{3}{16}in$ $8mm = \frac{5}{16}in$ $10mm\ (1cm) = \frac{3}{8}in$

$1cm = \frac{3}{8}in$	$20cm = 8in$
$2cm = \frac{3}{4}in$	$25cm = 10in$
$3cm = 1\frac{1}{4}in$	$30cm = 12in$
$4cm = 1\frac{9}{16}in$	$35cm = 14in$
$5cm = 2in$	$40cm = 16in$
$6cm = 2\frac{3}{8}in$	$50cm = 20in$
$7cm = 2\frac{3}{4}in$	$60cm = 24in$
$8cm = 3\frac{5}{8}in$	$70cm = 28in$
$9cm = 3\frac{1}{2}in$	$80cm = 32in$
$10cm = 4in$	$90cm = 36in$
$15cm = 6in$	$100cm\ (1m) = 39in$

$1m = 3\frac{1}{4}ft$	$40m = 132ft$	$100m = 330ft$
$2m = 6\frac{1}{2}ft$	$50m = 165ft$	$500m = 1650ft$
$5m = 16\frac{1}{2}ft$	$60m = 196ft$	$1000m = 3300ft$
$10m = 33ft$	$70m = 229ft$	$2000m = 6600ft$
$15m = 49ft$	$80m = 264ft$	$3000m = 9900ft$
$20m = 66ft$	$90m = 295ft$	$4000m = 13200ft$
$30m = 98ft$		

2 The citation of months in the text assumes a readership in the Northern Hemisphere; readers in the Southern Hemisphere should convert the months as follows:

For January, read July
for February, read August
for March, read September
for April, read October
for May, read November
for June, read December

For July, read January
for August, read February
for September, read March
for October, read April
for November, read May
for December, read June

Text credits: A. Bremer (6. Taking Cuttings); F. Brouwer (10. Fuchsias in the Greenhouse – part); E. Brouwers (20. Fuchsia Species – part); J. van Brunschot (10. Fuchsias in the Greenhouse – part); P. van der Craats (9. Winter Care – part); F. van der Elshout (19. Photographing Fuchsias); H. J. de Graaff (2. The Origins and Development of the Genus; 12. Improving Fuchsias; 13. Improving Fuchsias in the Netherlands); M. Grijsen-Sellink (17. Growing Fuchsias for Exhibition); B. A. van der Haven (15. Hardy Fuchsias); A. Hetterscheid (16. Triphylla Hybrids); L. van der Laan-Duyvendak (9. Winter Care – part); J. van Maasakkers (7. Shaping); W. Tinnemans (21. Cultivars – part; Cultivars by Suitability and Colour – part); G. van Veen (8. Pests and Diseases); B. Versantwoort-Brans (21. Cultivars – part; Cultivars by Suitability and Colour – part); L. Vleeshouwer-Overdijkink (18. Using Fuchsias in Nosegays and Corsages); M. van Vugt (5. Soil); A. J. de Waard (14. Fuchsias in the Garden and in Containers); C. H. E. Wagenaar Hummelinck-Berkelbach van der Sprenkel (History of the Dutch Circle of Fuchsia Lovers; 1. The History of the Fuchsia); J. C. van 't Westeinde (11. Grafting); A. van Wijk (4. Pruning); and M. van der Zee-Kruseman (3. The Biology of the Fuchsia; 20. Fuchsia Species – part).

Introduction

Some years ago the Dutch Circle of Fuchsia Lovers sponsored a book on fuchsias that soon came to be regarded as authoritative. As this reprint suggests, this book is still seen as one of the leading texts on the subject, and it has now been translated into English to make the wealth of knowledge and experience contained in the original text available to an English-speaking audience.

Twenty-one experts were asked to contribute a chapter on their particular speciality and their hard work, together with the help of picture researchers and support from the publishers, made possible the production of this definitive volume. Our thanks go to all those who have been involved in this task.

Today fuchsias, in all their wonderful variety in colour and form, are more popular than ever, and it is hoped that this book will encourage still more gardeners to introduce these beautiful plants to their gardens.

P. A. van den Elshout
President
Dutch Circle of Fuchsia Lovers

The Dutch Circle of Fuchsia Lovers

This book was originally published to mark the twentieth anniversary of the Dutch Circle of Fuchsia Lovers, which was founded in Rotterdam in January 1965 by Mrs Meursing, Mr Van Delen and Mr Roks, who took on the roles of President, Secretary and Treasurer respectively. In May of the same year a meeting of all interested parties was held in Utrecht, and the officers of the Circle were formally elected, the constitution was framed and the name was selected.

Some twenty different cultivars were ordered from the UK growers, Wills, and these were planted and tended on behalf of the Circle's members by Mr de Groot of Heerde. This was the beginning. By 1966 the membership had grown to 200. This number doubled after the show in Leiden and increased to 750 after the Elswout show in 1968. By the end of 1991 membership stood at 5,000. Mrs Meursing continued to act as President until she left the Netherlands to live abroad. She was succeeded by Mr N. Aalhuizen and, in 1987, by Mr P. A. van den Elshout, who was still in office when the first edition of this book appeared.

The first of many visits organized by the Circle was to Laken. Members who have been on one of the annual trips to the UK to visit the nurseries there will never forget the experience – hotel rooms with wash-basins overflowing with new acquisitions that required careful tending and the bus filled with newly bought plants of all sizes and colours.

Further shows followed – in Zeist, the 'Floridae', at Appledoorn, Bredevoort, Nueune, Markelo, Lisse, Rotterdam, Echten, Haaren and so on. In view of the worldwide interest in fuchsias, the Circle organized an international congress at Hilversum in 1982, and one result of this was the decision to establish closer links between European fuchsia societies. The umbrella organization Eurofuchsia was set up at this time, and a bi-monthly journal, *Fuchsiana*, is now published. Members in each country meet twice a year, in the spring and autumn, to discuss all aspects of fuchsia culture and to buy and sell seedlings. Regional meetings are also held, including slide shows, and in the summer members' gardens are open to visitors.

Since 1982 groups have been working in plant technology and have formed an association with the Extended Technical Commission. A Dutch group dedicated to plant improvement by amateurs has achieved a high level of expertise, and its members have played an important part in developing approximately 500 new Dutch cultivars.

'Chang'

chapter 1

The History of the Fuchsia

Like the evening primrose and the willow-herb, the fuchsia belongs to the family of Onagraceae. It is fairly easy to grow, and H. Witte has rightly called it a plant for all. It is non-toxic and free from allergens and therefore very popular. Societies of fuchsia enthusiasts have sprung up everywhere.

The fuchsia was named in honour of the German botanist and herbalist Leonard Fuchs (1501–66), although, in fact, Fuchs never saw one. The person who discovered it was Father Plumier. Leonard Fuchs, a botanist and doctor, was born in Wending. At the age of twenty-five he became a professor at Ingolstadt and, later, at Tübingen. In 1542–3 he published his *New Herbarium (De Historia Stirpium Commentarii Insignes)*; this deals with 500 kinds of plants, including 400 that were indigenous to Germany.

Father Charles Plumier (1646–1704), a Jesuit priest in the Order of Minims, was born in Marseilles, France. As botanist to Louis XIV Plumier travelled widely to gather useful plants. In 1689 he visited the Antilles, in 1689–90 he was in Martinique, and in 1696–7 he went to the West Indies. His first publication, which appeared in 1685, was on American plants, and this was followed in 1703 by *Nova Plantarum Americanarum Genera*, which contains the first reference to a fuchsia, which was illustrated, although not well, and which Plumier called *Fuchsia triphylla flore coccinea*. Plumier may have found this fuchsia in Colombia, although this is by no means certain. According to Coutts, the first authentic illustration was published by Feuille in 1725. In 1753 this plant was re-named *Fuchsia triphylla coccinea* by Linnaeus. In 1873 Thomas Hogg, an American, sent seeds of *F. triphylla* to the Botanic Gardens in New York from Santo Domingo.

In Europe in the meantime, a fuchsia was given to Kew Gardens in 1788 by a Captain Firth. This was *F. coccinea* from Brazil, and Firth is usually regarded as being the first person to give a fuchsia to Kew, although some authorities have suggested that Henderson had earlier sent a plant there for identification, which had been grown from seed supplied by Hogg.

It is not known when the first fuchsias were grown in Europe. Coutts says it was in 1786–9, other authorities say it was 1793, that the English nurseryman James Lee saw a plant, probably *F. coccinea*, growing on a windowsill in London and recognized its commercial potential. Joseph Hooker (1817–1911) mentions a plant from Brazil. After that, progress was swift: *F. corymbiflora* (now *F. boliviana*) was first described in 1778–88, *F. lycioides* in 1807, *F. microphylla* in 1823 and *F. arborescens* in 1825. In 1776 and 1839 respectively two New Zealand species, *F. excorticata* and *F. procumbens*, were found, and between 1778 and 1788 and Ruiz and Pavón sent *F. apetala*, *F. decussata* and *F. serratifolia* (now probably *F. denticulata*) from Peru.

Hybridization began in 1825, when *F. coccinea* and *F. macrostema* were crossed with *F. arborescens*. Nothing is known of the results of these early experiments, but in 1835 the first species with reflex petals was obtained. Attempts were made to find a white fuchsia, and the first, an unintentional seedling with a white tube and white sepals, was raised by Gulliver of Hurstmonceaux in 1840. This was 'Venus Victrix', which Youell has called the first important hybrid.

Further hybridization in the 1840s led to the development of a widespread commercial trade and, in the wake of this development, difficulties in the naming of new cultivars. In 1848 Porcher's book on fuchsias appeared, and in 1852 Henderson published a catalogue listing the cultivars then available, which included 'Pumila' and 'Riccartonii'. The names of new hybridizers constantly appeared: in Britain there was W. H. Story, from Newton Abbot in Devon, with the double-flowered 'Queen Victoria' and the first striped fuchsia, 'Striata', and W. Bull and D. Henderson of London. In France the nurseries of Victor Lemoine (1823–1911) produced more than 400 cultivars, while important developments occurred in Austria (Twydry), Belgium (Cornelissen) and the Netherlands. In Germany Carl Bonstedt produced the first important Triphylla hybrids between 1904 and 1906, including 'Thalia' and 'Gartenmeister Bonstedt'. H. Witte's book in the Floralia series was published in the Netherlands in 1872.

Interest waned somewhat after 1914, although it never entirely disappeared, but in 1929 the American Fuchsia Society was established. The Society imported many plants from Europe and began to hybridize to such a degree that, from about 1945, some thirty-five new cultivars have been produced every year.

The British Fuchsia Society was founded in 1938, and societies and groups sprang up throughout Europe, including the Dutch Circle of Fuchsia Lovers in 1965.

In conclusion, two comments. First, Wright, in his book *Fuchsias: A Garden History*, tells us that the fuchsia is fertilized by humming-birds in its natural environment and points out that, being unscented, it is the fuchsia's colour which attracts the birds. Second, Eileen Saunders points out that because *F. magellanica* comes from a dark, cold habitat (the south of South America down to Tierra del Fuego) it is hardy and its descendants are also hardy; *F. fulgens*, on the other hand, comes from a sunny habitat (Mexico), and its descendants prefer a warm site, even thriving in full sun.

Sources

Saunders, E. *Wagtail's Book of Fuchsias*
Witte, J. *Handboekje voor de kennis en het kweken van lievelingsbloemen*
Wood, W. P., *A Fuchsia Survey*
Wright, *Fuchsias: A Garden History*

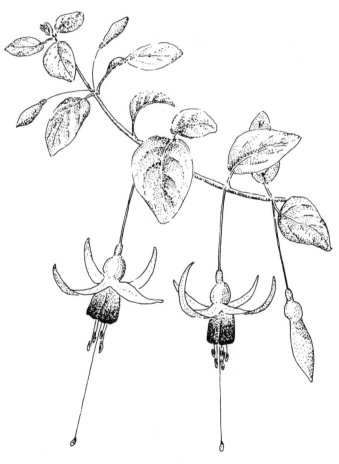

'Hiawatha'

The Origins and Development of the Genus

Some 50 million years ago much of South America was covered with forests. The South Polar region was not yet the ice-cap it is today, and Patagonia had a temperate climate. It was here that the earliest fuchsias grew.

Before dinosaurs had become extinct, a great many flowers, birds and mammals had appeared. The ground was no longer largely covered by ferns and rushes, and although angiosperms were still rare, monocotyledons were beginning to develop. Among these were plants belonging to the family Onagraceae, to which the genus *Fuchsia* belongs.

The only evidence that fuchsias existed then comes from fossilized pollen, which has been dated to 30 million years ago. The oldest fuchsias may be even older. Further evidence comes from discoveries in American, New Zealand and Tahiti. The American biologist Paul Berry thinks that fuchsias spread south, by way of the Antarctic, to New Zealand and, later, across the Pacific to Tahiti, the section Skinnera being found in New Zealand and Tahiti. Birds eat the berries but the seeds, which they also ingest, are not digested and may, therefore, be transported over comparatively wide areas. In the warm, frost-free conditions of the Pacific islands seeds can survive and develop.

Berry also assumes that there was a spread northwards, to Central America and Mexico where the small-flowered, insect-pollinated Encliandra, Jimenezia and Schufia fuchsias are found. A second, subsequent northward development led to the development of the plants in the Ellobium section.

The species within the Quelusia section probably most closely resemble the original fuchsias. They still occur, far to the south, in modern form in the kind of forest in which they must first have grown. The sections that include plants with long, tube-like flowers – Fuchsia and Hemsleyella – are now found in areas of South America where the climate was most favourable, in spite of, or perhaps because of, the rise of the Andes chain: humid mountain forests with moderate temperatures or warmer tropical rain forests. These ideal conditions must partly explain why the greatest number of modern species arose there.

F. lycioides, the only member of the section Kierschlegeria, is different from other species in that it originates from a dry habitat – the Atacama Desert of central Chile – and the leaf stalks, which persist after the leaves have fallen, take the form of small spines.

That fuchsias are found all over the world is largely due to man. Long before travellers such as Plumier supplied European collections with highly prized specimens of tropical plants, we know that South American Indians took plants of *F. boliviana* from the fuchsias' original habitat to new settlements, as can be seen from the motifs used to decorate Inca pottery and wood objects. We do not know if the Incas' fascination with the fuchsia stemmed from the plants' beauty alone, for the plants may have been cultivated for their edible seeds.

Fuchsias that are seen growing wild along the west coast of England and Scotland and in Ireland are garden escapees. The Gulf Stream brings comparatively mild winters to these areas, which allow fuchsias to survive. These hardy forms are mostly of *F. magellanica*, which manage to withstand winters even in northwest Europe, including the Netherlands, although *F. excorticata* and some members of the Encliandra section are also found in the wild.

The sections of the genus *Fuchsia*

The maps that follow show the locations in which fuchsias occur naturally today. The arrows indicate the directions in which the species may have spread from their original habitat.

Quelusia

This section contains five species: *F. bracelinae*, *F. campos-portoi*, *F. coccinea*, *F. magellanica* and *F. regia*.

Distribution
Southeast coast of Brazil, Chile and Argentina.

Characteristics
These plants exhibit the classic form of fuchsia flower with long stamens protruding from the flower and pistil. The flower stalk and calyx are red, and the corolla is blue to violet. There are forty-four chromosomes to each cell. Many of today's cultivars have been hybridized from the species in this section, which is evident not only in the colour of the flowers but also in their form. These fuchsias are largely winter hardy.

Quelusia – Argentina, Brazil and Chile

Fuchsia

This section, which is also sometimes known as Eufuchsia, is the largest, containing sixty-one species: *F. abrupta, F. ampliata, F. andrei, F. austromontana, F. ayavacensis, F. boliviana, F. canescens, F. caucana, F. ceracea, F. cinerea, F. cochabambana, F. concertifolia, F. coriacifolia, F. corollata, F. corymbiflora, F. crassistipula, F. cuatrecasasii, F. decussata, F. denticulata, F. dependens, F. ferreyrae, F. fontinalis, F. furfuracea, F. gehrigeri, F. glaberrima, F. harlingii, F. hartwegii, F. hirtella, F. lehmannii, F. llewelynii, F. loxensis, F. macropetala, F. macrophylla, F. macrostigma, F. magdalenae, F. mathewsii, F. nigricans, F. orientalis, F. ovalis, F. pallescens, F. petiolaris, F. pilosa, F. polyantha, F. pringsheimii, F. putumayensis, F. rivularis, F. sanctae-rosae, F. sanmartina, F. scabriuscula, F. scherffiana, F. sessilifolia, F. simplicicaulis, F. steyermarkii, F. sylvatica, F. tincta, F. triphylla, F. vargasiana, F. venusta, F. verrucosa, F. vulcanica* and *F. wurdackii.*

Distribution
Tropical Andes and Hispaniola.

Characteristics
The fuchsias within this section have very long tubes and comparatively short sepals. The flowers are mostly red to orange, and only very rarely is

there any blue pigmentation. The corolla is clearly marked. There are twenty-two and forty-four chromosomes per cell.

The most important species within this section are *F. denticulata* and *F. triphylla*. The familiar Triphylla hybrids, which arose from crossings with other species, are highly prized because of their coloration. They have a preference for sunlight and warmth, and *F. triphylla* itself originates from the sheltered and low area of the island of Hispaniola in the Caribbean. A new and attractive crossing parent is *F. magdalenae*, with forty-four chromosomes per cell.

Fuchsia – Andes and central South America

Ellobium

There are three species within this section: *F. decidua*, *F. fulgens* and *F. splendens* (syn. *F. cordifolia*).

Distribution
Central America and Mexico (see map on page 23).

Characteristics
The leaves of the fuchsias within this section have broad, heart-shaped or oval leaves, and the plants generally form root tubers. They have twenty-two chromosomes per cell.

The yellowish corolla of *F. splendens*, a typical spring flower, makes it an attractive parent for hybridization purposes. A hybrid of *F. splendens* and *F. fulgens*, 'Speciosa', is widely used for improving other cultivars. The resulting offspring, frequently of deviant colours, often bloom at times of the year when days are short. Unfortunately, they tend to have large leaves.

Hemsleyella

There are fourteen species within this section: *F. apetala*, *F. cestroides*, *F. chloroloba*, *F. garleppiana*, *F. huanucoensis*, *F. inflata*, *F. insignis*, *F. juntasensis*, *F. membranacea*, *F. nana*, *F. pilaloensis*, *F. salicifolia*, *F. tillettiana* and *F. tunariensis*.

Distribution
Tropical Andes.

Characteristics
These fuchsias have a long flower tube, insignificant or no petals, and broad leaves. There are twenty-two chromosomes per cell. The most important species in the group are *F. apetala* and *F. juntasensis*, but none of them is in general cultivation although some have recently been grown in the Netherlands.

Hemsleyella – Andes

Kierschlegeria

There is only one species, *F. lycioides*, in this section.

Distribution
Central Chile.

Characteristics
When the leaves have fallen, the persistent leaf stalks form small, sharp spines. The fruits contain between fourteen and twenty seeds. There are forty-four chromosomes per cell.

Some Dutch growers have started to use *F. lycioides* for hybridization purposes in recent years, but earlier plants with that name are hybrids of *F. magellanica*, while the recent importation under the name *F. rosea* is actually *F. lycioides*.

Kierschlegeria – Chile

Schufia

There are two species within this section: *F. arborescens* and *F. paniculata*.

Distribution
Central American and Mexico (see map on page 23).

Characteristics

The small flowers are rosy purple and are borne in large panicles at the end of each branch. They are sometime dioecious; there are twenty-two chromosomes per cell.

These two species have supplied interesting hybrids in terms of both colour and flowering habit.

Jimenezia

There is one species, *F. jimenezii*, in this section.

Distribution

Panama and Costa Rica.

Characteristics

The inflorescences, with hermaphroditic flowers, are borne at the end of the branches. The small tube and the sepals are red to rose-red, and the stamens are twisted around the tube. There are twenty-two chromosomes per cell.

Jimenezia – Costa Rica and Panama

Encliandra

This section contains six species: *F. encliandra* (syn. *F. encliandra* subsp. *encliandra*), *F. microphylla* (syn. *F. microphylla* subsp. *microphylla*), *F. obconica*, *F. parviflora* (syn. *F. cylindracea*), *F. ravenii* and *F. thymifolia*.

Distribution

Central America and Mexico.

Characteristics

The flowers are borne in the leaf axils; the stamens are twisted around in the flower tube, and there are a few large seeds in each berry. These are dioecious plants, with male and female flowers sometimes looking quite different. There are twenty-two chromosomes per cell.

There are nine sub-species arising from widespread mutual crossing in Britain, and cultivated plants known as *F. cylindracea* are considered to be *F. × bacillaris*. Several attractive cultivars have been bred, especially from crossings with species from the Skinnera and Schufia sections.

Ellobium, Schufia and Encliandra – Central America and Mexico

Skinnera

This section contains four species: *F. cyrtandroides*, *F. excorticata*, *F. perscandens* and *F. procumbens*.

Distribution
New Zealand and Tahiti.

Characteristics
These fuchsias have minute petals and blue pollen; there are single sex and hermaphrodite flowers, sometimes on the same plant; and the leaves are small. There are twenty-two chromosomes per cell. In no other section are the species so diverse in appearance. *F. excorticata* can grow into a large tree, while *F. procumbens* is, as its name suggests, a creeping shrub with lax branches. The colours found in this group are, however, unusual for fuchsias as a whole and they are, therefore, important to hybridizers.

F. colensoi, which is sometimes included in this section, is, in fact, now regarded as a natural hybrid of *F. excorticata* and *F. perscandens*. *F. kirkii*, which is occasionally included as a New Zealand species, is the male form of *F. procumbens*.

Skinnera – New Zealand and Tahiti

Many of the species fuchsias are of little or no importance to amateur growers – some are not particularly decorative and others are difficult to cultivate. However, collections of species, such as that maintained by the botanical section of the Dutch Circle of Fuchsia Lovers, are crucial in the development of new cultivars.

Sources

Berry, P. E. , 'Studies in Fuchsia'
Grzimek, B. , *Enzyklopädie des Tierreiches, Entwicklungsgeschichte der Lebeswesen*
Zee-Kruseman, M. van der, *Recente aantekeningen*

chapter 3

The Biology of the Fuchsia

Although they may look very different, all fuchsias have the same basic constituents.

First, the stems and branches. Some species have stems 10 metres or more high and trunks 1 metre thick. *F. excorticata*, a tree fuchsia from New Zealand, for example, can grow to more than 15 metres high in the right conditions. In its natural habitat *F. boliviana* achieves heights of 4 metres and *F. arborescens* is, as its name suggests, a tree species that, in habitat, can grow to 8 metres. Other species have stems that are only a few millimetres thick, and these are the creeping or prostrate forms. In general it is as well to bear in mind the habitat of the parent species when cultivating fuchsias, but the descriptions of shrub, standard, prostrate, trailing and so on are rather arbitrary. A careful breeder could grow an erect stem from the trailing *F. procumbens* or turn a shrub into a suitable subject for a hanging-basket.

Leaves and the ways in which they are arranged on the stem are important factors in the identification of fuchsias. Many fuchsias, especially cultivars, have leaves that are arranged alternately opposite – that is, the two leaves in one opposite pair point north-south while the next pair point east-west. Many species have from three to six leaves to a shoot, and from each leaf axil a new shoot may grow. Cultivars, too, may have three leaves to a shoot. If you take a cutting from a side shoot you will get a young shrub filled with flowers more quickly and without having to nip it out continually. Eventually, the three-leaved form is usually lost, so it is not a reliable improvement, but it is always worth looking out for it when you come to take cuttings. At the base of the leaf stalk on a cutting you will notice a tiny green spur, the stipule, which is an important factor in the identification of species. The hairs on parts of the plants are also used for identification purposes, but these are usually visible only with the aid of a magnifying glass.

The flowering habit is the next feature. Flowers are borne in terminal or lateral bunches. Small green leaves, or bracteoles, sometimes occur between the flowers. Alternatively, the flowers may be borne from the axils, when they generally hang down on long stalks, and this is usually

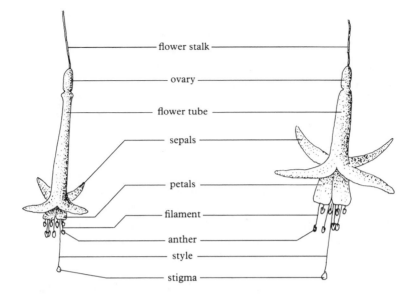

flower stalk

ovary

flower tube

sepals

petals

filament

anther

style

stigma

the case with cultivars. Flowers are borne in panicles on the Triphylla hybrids and on *F. arborescens*, *F. paniculata* and *F. jimenezia*.

Finally, the flowers themselves, which are often the most important feature for many amateur growers. Most flowers are very clearly structured.

The flower is attached to the plant by a pedicel or stalk, which leads to the ovary. On the ovary are the nectaries, or honey glands, which attract the bumble-bees and humming-birds that pollinate the flowers. Each of the ovaries is divided into four sections, which contain the ovules, and when they are fertilized the ovules become seeds. The stamen and pistils are protected in a long tube. The stamen is the male reproductive organ of the flower, and each consists of the flower and two anther lobes, which contain pollen grains. Most fuchsias have four sepals at the end of the tube, and below the sepals is the corolla, which is formed by the petals, the number of which determines whether a cultivar is known as single, semi-double or double. The colour of all these spearate parts can be vital for identifying species. After the flower has bloomed, only the stalk and the ovary remain on the plant.

There are, however, kinds that deviate from the foregoing example. Over the years this has led to much confusion, because the plants were usually gathered and dried by a collector for a herbarium. Then another student some years later might describe and rename these plants. Many errors crept in but have now been resolved by later researchers, who compared herbaria specimens with the new finds.

Some species of wild fuchsia have flowers with pistils and undeveloped stamens without pollen on one plant and flowers with well-developed stamens but undeveloped pistils on another. These plants, therefore, do not produce berries and they are called dioecious. If pistils, flowers and stamen flowers grow on the same plant, it is called monoecious. In some cases all three kinds of flower occur on the same plant, which complicates things for student and amateur alike. This happens generally with Encliandra fuchsias, but also with *F. lycioides* (section Kierschlegeria) and *F. paniculata* (section Schufia). It is, therefore, vital always to check if the pistil and stamens of a single flower are well developed.

Many cultivars have double flowers, but only the petals are more numerous, the other features are the same. Often petaloids are found near the petals but differ in appearance. They stand between sepals and petals and largely differ from petals in shape and colour. This can give the flower an attractive but often untidy appearance. When newly grown double cultivars are being tested, this is always one of the factors that is taken into account.

Finally the fruit. Fuchsia berries are edible, and in South America they are eaten as we eat bramble berries. The berries, which have four compartments in which the seeds grow, are mostly red or violet, although they are black in the Encliandra group. In some cultivars the ripe berries are light green, as for example in the white 'Ting-a-Ling' and in 'Frosted

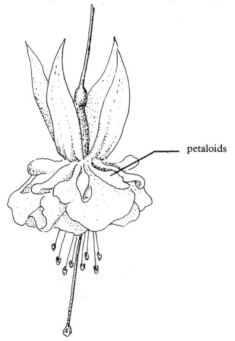

petaloids

Flame', which has a white calyx and a deep red corolla. Apart from being edible, however, fuchsia berries are of little use, except that their sap provided paint for Maori warriors, and the bright blue pollen eye-shadow for the women.

Plant and habit growth

Stem and roots

arbor – tree
bulbus – bulb
caudex – persistent stem of a perennial plant
frutex – bush
radix – root
rhizoma – creeping stem, bearing leaves of aerial shoots from tip and roots from underside
truncus – stem
tuber – short, thickened part of underground stem, from which new plants develop

Stem and root: manner of growth

annuus – annual
biennis – biennial
humifusus – flat over the ground
perennis – perennial
repens – ground hugging, but rooting on buds
scandens – climbing
volubilis – to and fro, or winding in a spiral

Branch

ramulus – side branch
ramus – branch

Direction in which the branch grows

declinatus – overhanging
fastigiatus – straight up
horizontalis – sideways
patens – at an angle of 45° to the stem
pendulus – hanging down

Stalk

caudex – persistent stem of a perennial plant
caulus – stalk
herbaceus – herbaceous; a plant that does not form a persistent, woody
  stem
internodium – length of stalk between two buds
nodus – bud
spina – thorn

Stalk: shape and position

angularis – having angles or corners
dependens – hanging
erectus – upright
laevis – smooth
scandens – climbing
teres – terete; cylindrical; rounded in cross-section

Leaf

axilla – axil; angle between leaf and stem from which further growth
  arises
coriaceus – leathery
folium – leaf
internervum – body of leaf
lamina – flat, expanded part of leaf (distinct from petiole)
margo – leaf rim
nervus – vein in a leaf
petiolus – petiole; leaf stalk
sessilis – sessile; stalkless; leaf or flower that arises direct from stem
stipula – stipule; one of a pair of small leaf-like growth at the base of leaf
  stalk

Leaf position

dispositio foliorum – leaf-position
folia decussata – decussate; two leaves per bud borne at right angles to
  the two pairs of leaves above and below
folia disticha – distichous; arranged in two vertical rows, with leaves on
  opposite sides of a stem
folia sparsa – spread leaves, one per bud in a spiral round the stalk
folia verticillata – verticillate; arranged in a circular formation around
  the stem
oppositus – opposite; growing pairs, but separated by a stem
phyllotaxis – the arrangement of leaves on a stem
sparsus – one leaf to a bud

Leaf form

acuminatus – acuminate; a leaf that tapers to a point
acutus – acute; a leaf ending in sharp point
apex – tip
basis – foot; basal = growing from the base of a stem
cordatus – cordate; heart-shaped
deltoideus – delta-shaped
ellipticus – oval
lamina – flat, expanded part of leaf (distinct from petiole)
lanceolatus – lanceolate; shaped like head of a lance; a narrow leaf,
  broadest at the base and tapering towards the tip
oblongis – oblong; a leaf that has parallel sides; a leaf that is three times
  longer than it is wide
obovatus – obovate; egg-shaped with the broad end at the top
obtusus – obtuse; a leaf that is blunt or rounded
orbicularis – circular; a leaf that is disc-shaped or almost so shaped
ovatus – ovate; egg-shaped with widest part at base
peltatus – peltate; disc-shaped leaf in which the stem is attached at the
  centre
reniformis – reniform; kidney-shaped
rhomboideus – rhomboid
sagittatus – sagittate; arrow-shaped
triangularis – triangular
truncatus – truncate; a leaf that ends abruptly as if the end has been cut off

Ribs or veins

costa – central vein of a leaf
nervus – rib or vein
nervus divergentibus – vein radiating to the rim
nervus lateralis – side vein
venae – fine veins

Leaf margin

dentatus – dentate; with tooth-like notches on the margin
integer – whole; entire
margo – leaf margin
repandus – repand; having a wavy margin
serratus – serrated; like the teeth of a saw

Hairs on leaf and stalk

hirsutus – with rough hair
lanatus – lanate; woolly
pilosus – hairy

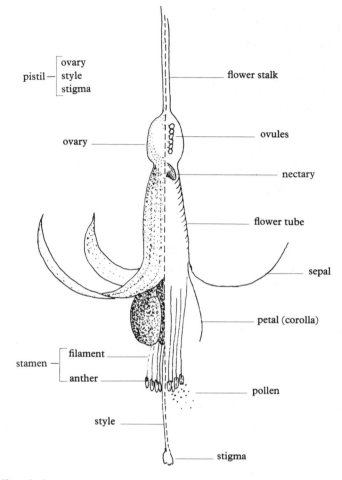

pilus – hair
pubescens – with soft hair
seta – brush
setosus – brush-like
tomentosus – tomentose; densely covered with fine hairs; felt-like
verrucosus – warty
vilosus – with long hair

Flower

anthesis – the state of full bloom of a flower
calix – calyx; outer whorl of protective leaves of a flower, usually green, consisting of sepals fused together, funnel or tube-like structure

1 A standard fuchsia

2 'Mrs W. Rundle'

3 'Space Shuttle'

4 'Beacon Rosa'

5 'Chang'

corolla – corolla; inner protective part of a flower consisting of wholly or
partially fused petals

floris – flower

hypanthium – enlarged cup or rim of tissue supporting the sepals, petals
and stamens

limbus – edge, often of a different colour

nectarium – nectary; part of flower that secretes honey

ovulum – ovule; structure that develops into a seed after fertilization

perianthos – perianth; term used to describe sepals and petals when they
are indistinguishable from each other

petaloides – petaloids; floral organs that resemble petals but are usually
stamens, although they may be sepals

petalum – petal, any of the components, or leaves, of a corolla

pilosus – pilose; covered with hair, especially fine, soft hairs

pistilum – pistil; the complete female organ of a flower (comprising
ovary, stigma and style)

receptaculum – receptacle; the enlarged upper end of the stalk of a
flowering plant on which the flower parts grow; of a cup- or disc-like
structure supporting spores or sex organs

sepalus – sepal; one of outermost whorl of modified leaves composing a
flower, usually green and protecting the petals and sex organs

stamen – stamen; the male reproductive organ of a flower (comprising
filament and anther lobes)

tubus – tube; the lower united part of a gamopetalous corolla or a
gamosepalous calyx

vena – vein

Mode of flowering

actinomorphus or *regularis* – regular or radially symmetrical (divisible
into mirror images in more than one plane)

bractea – bract; modified leaf, usually small and scale-like but
sometimes conspicuous and brightly coloured

bracteola – bracteole; small bract

breacteolula – small leaf at bottom of single flower stalk

corymbus – corymb; broad, flat-topped cluster of flowers, the stalks of
which arise above each other from a vertical stem

cymosus – cymose; a domed, flattened or rounded cluster of flowers, in
which the top or central flowers bloom first, followed by the lower or
outer one

inflorescentia – inflorescence

pedicellus – pedicel; stalk of a single flower

pedunculus – peduncle; main stalk of a flower cluster

racemosus or *botryoide* - raceme; unbranched flower cluster consisting of a single stem along which individual flowers grow on small stems from the base to the apex

Reproductive organs

androecium – the stamens and all the parts belonging to them; the male system of the flower

anther – the part of the stamen containing the pollen grains

filamentum – filament; the stalk of a stamen bearing the anther

gynoecium – the pistil consisting of ovary, seed bud, stalk and stigma (the female part of the flower)

organum reproductivum – reproductive organ

ovarium – ovary; the enlarged hollow part of the pistil or gynoecium containing ovules

ovulum – ovule; structure in seed plants that consists of a mucellus containing an embryo sac and that develops into a seed after fertilization

pistilum – pistil; the seed-bearing organ of a flowering plant; the complete female organ of a flower

placenta – placenta; the part of the lining of an ovary that bear the ovules

pollen – pollen; male sex cells formed in the anthers or pollen sacs of the stamen of a flower

stamen – stamen; the complete male reproductive organs of a flower

staminodium – staminode; a sterile stamen

stigma – stigma; the tip of the female reproductive organ, which secretes a sticky fluid when ready for pollination

stylus – style; the stalk linking the ovary and stigma of a female flower

theca – seed case or sac

Male and female plants

androecium – the male part; the stamens and all the parts belonging to them

dioecious – male (♂) flower on one plant and female (♀) flower on another of the same kind

femineus – female flower; pistil only

gynoecium – the whole of the female reproductive organs

hermaphoditus – double-sex (♂ ♀) flower; stamens and pistil present

masculus – male flower; stamens only

monoecious – male and female single-sex flowers near each other on the same plant

polygamus – double-sex and single-sex flowers on the same plant

unisexualis – single sex

Fruit

bacca – berry; baccate = bearing berries
placenta – placenta; the part of the lining of an ovary that bear the
  ovules
semen – seed

chapter 4

Pruning

Few plants respond so readily to care as fuchsias and growing a handsome specimen can involve a lot of work – stopping, nipping out buds, trimming, watering, fertilizing, potting and repotting – the list is almost endless. Fortunately, a well-tended fuchsia in the right position will more than repay your efforts.

When it comes to pruning, the general rule should be that a spring cutting that has developed roots and that has been potted up will require shaping, while an autumn cutting should be left to rest until the following spring. This guidance is only relative however, for a young plant will continue to grow at temperatures of 8°C and over. Usually, however, autumn cuttings should be overwintered in small pots and watered sparingly to discourage growth. As the days lengthen the cutting can be encouraged to put on more growth by top dressings of leaf mould and more water. As soon as new growth is clearly visible, stop the plant if you have not already done so. From this stage the treatment of spring and autumn cuttings is the same, although autumn cuttings will be several weeks ahead of their spring counterparts.

The root system

The root system, the least visible part of the fuchsia, is, in many ways, as interesting as the part that grows above the ground and it is certainly as important. Without a healthy root system, the plant will not develop, so it is well worth paying a little attention to the roots. It is a good idea to check the soil in the pot regularly, especially where young and developing plants are concerned. Make sure that the soil in the pot is fairly moist so that it does not crumble away when you turn out the plant. Place one hand over the pot, with the main stem between your index and middle fingers, and hold the base of the pot in your other hand. When you turn the pot upside down the soil and root ball should come out altogether. If they are unwilling to move, tap the edge of the pot sharply to loosen the soil. If you have a healthy plant that requires repotting you will see many white roots covered with fine hairs. These are the root hairs, which grow from a cell

Stop autumn cuttings as soon as growth is evident

on the surface of the plant's roots. Root hairs are extremely delicate and new ones are continually formed to replace those that are lost, and they are vital in increasing the surface area available to take up mineral salts and water from the soil.

In an unhealthy plant the white-haired roots will be missing. This may be because the soil is too dry or is too wet; it may be because the soil has become compacted so that air cannot circulate; or it may because there are parasites and grubs in the soil. If the soil is well filled with roots, however, the plant can be repotted. Choose a pot that is 2–3cm larger than the original one and add a layer of new potting compost in the bottom and up the sides. Press the new compost down lightly to remove all air pockets. Place the plant in the pot, firming it down carefully, and perhaps add a little more compost over the top, although you should always leave at least 1cm space below the top edge of the pot. Replace the plant's label. After potting on, allow the plant to rest and keep it out of strong sunlight for a

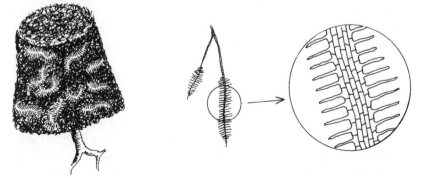

Root hairs should be visible when you repot cuttings

while. You should feed young plants regularly, and it is also beneficial to add leaf mould to the compost from time to time.

Stopping and nipping out

Stopping is the term usually applied to the process of taking out the top of a plant; nipping out is usually done to the side shoots. It is best to use a sharp knife or secateurs so that you do not cause ragged, ugly cuts, which may encourage disease. When it comes to shaping fuchsias, you can take advantage of the fact that when a shoot is stopped, the two axil buds below will send out shoots, so creating two more top shoots.

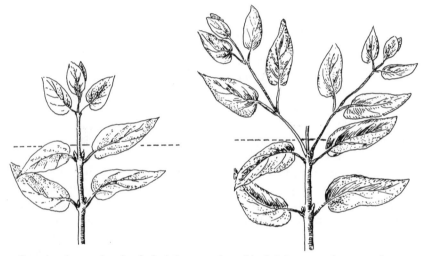

Stopping the growing tip of a fuchsia causes the axil buds below to send out new shoots

Unless they are stopped regularly, a fuchsia's stalks will continue to grow and will eventually bend and perhaps break under the weight of the flowers. This happens mainly in plants that are not self-branching or are reluctant to branch spontaneously. Some cultivars are self-branching – 'Alice Hoffmann', 'Hiawatha' and 'Sugarbush' ('Suikerbossie'), for example – but others, such as 'Party Frock' and 'Lady Boothby', are not, so it is always worth checking the growing habit of the cultivars you acquire.

You should not stop or nip out a plant just before or just after potting on. The first stopping should be done when a rooted cutting has about three pairs of leaves. Thereafter, whenever a stem arising from an axil bud has formed three pairs of leaves, you should nip out the top so that two pairs are left.

Continue to stop shoots whenever three pairs of leaves have grown

If you have trailing fuchsias such as 'Cascade' or 'Trail Blazer' it is advisable to nip out when the shoots have four pairs of leaves, so that three pairs are left.

Trailing species should be stopped after four pairs of leaves

Not all fuchsias, of course, grow in the same way. Sometimes one of the two axil buds does not form a new shoot, and this can produce an irregularly shaped plant. Some plants are more reliable in this respect than others – 'Autumnale' ('Burning Bush'), for instance, is not an easy plant to train into any shape.

Whether you stop shoots at two or three pairs of leaves will also depend to some extent on the distance between pairs of leaves – the closer together the leaves are, the less often will you need to stop the stalks. The distance between leaves can depend on the conditions in which the plants are kept; the better lit the plants, the closer together will be the leaves. However, some cultivars have long joints, whatever conditions they are grow in. 'Lady Boothby', for example, has long joints, while 'Pussy Cat' has very short ones.

Flower buds will arise on the new shoots, so you must not continue to

Cultivars such as 'Lady Boothby', which have
long joints between leaf axils, need to be pinched out
frequently to keep them in shape

pinch out the shoots indiscriminately or you will have a wonderfully branching fuchsia with no flowers. In general, a plant will come into flower from six to nine weeks after the last stopping. The following timings are guidelines only and assume ideal growing conditions, for much will depend on the ambient temperature, the soil and so on:

six weeks – 'Dorothea Flower'
seven weeks – 'Mrs Lovell Swisher'
eight weeks – 'La Campanella'
nine weeks – 'Bon Accorde'

As you work with your plants, you will quickly learn to appreciate what needs to be done when.

The cultivar 'Pussy Cat' has fairly short joints
between leaf joints but still needs to be stopped regularly
to keep it in shape

chapter 5

Soil

In order to understand the soil and the amounts of nutrients that are available and what should be added to promote healthy plant growth, it is necessary to know something about plant physiology: first, the components of the plants themselves (roots, stalks, leaves and so on); second, how much of each element a plant needs for growth and for flowering; and third, what a plant needs from the soil in terms of nutrient reserve, acidity and so forth.

The structure of the fuchsia

A plant is a structure with cellulose walls and complex cells. A large proportion of a plant is actually water, but it is also made up of carbohydrates (sugar, starch and cellulose) and fats, both of which are made from the elements carbon, hydrogen and oxygen; albumens, which contain nitrogen, sulphur and sometimes phosphorus; and other elements, including potassium, phosphorus, calcium, iron and magnesium, as well as the trace elements such as sodium, silicon, chlorine, manganese, aluminium, copper, barium, iodine and fluorine. The nutrients a plant needs are taken up partly from the air (by the assimilation of carbon) and partly from the soil as salts dissolved in water.

Different amounts of the elements listed above are needed for the plants to grow. In order to thrive, the plant needs carbon, hydrogen, oxygen, nitrogen, sulphur, phosphorus, potassium, calcium, magnesium and iron. If one or more of these are lacking, the plant's development is poor and its growth impaired. Carbon is absorbed not from the soil but from the air, and the other nutrients, which taken up in small amounts from the soil, are called subordinate or trace elements. They are generally present in adequate amounts in good soil.

The function of roots

The two most important functions of the roots are to support the plant so that it can stand upright and to enable it to take up nutrients in solution.

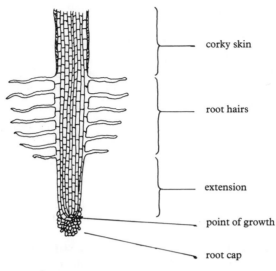

corky skin

root hairs

extension

point of growth

root cap

The structure of a tap root

The solutions are absorbed mainly through root hairs. However, this process can occur only if the temperature of the soil is sufficiently high and if oxygen is present. It is, therefore, essential that the plant is in well-fertilized, loose compost at a temperature that does not inhibit the plant's ability to take in nutrients from the soil.

Not only the plant's growth but the function of roots depends on soil temperature. As the ambient temperature falls, the plant's ability to take up moisture decreases until, when it reaches a certain point, it stops altogether. For many plants this point is quite low; trees (including conifers), shrubs, brassicas and some plants that overwinter with a rosette of leaves, for example, would dry out in winter if they could not continue to take up water.

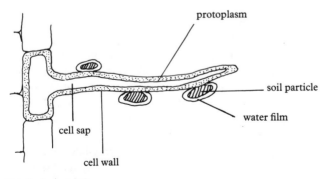

protoplasm

soil particle

water film

cell sap

cell wall

Detail of a root hair

Nutrients from the soil are absorbed through root hairs, via the root's cells. The long, thin cell wall of the root hairs is semi-permeable, and it comes into contact with the moist particles of soil. The moisture contains solutions of the various elements and nutrients that the plant needs, and usually the solutions inside the cell are more concentrated than those in the soil. If the concentration of nutrients in the soil becomes too great, the reverse will be the case, and water will be withdrawn from the root hairs to where the solution is more concentrated, so that the roots eventually die. When this happens the roots are sometimes described as having been burnt, and the same process can happen to leaves.

The function of stems

The main tasks of a plant's stems are to support the plant, to transport and store nutrients and to be a means of propagation.

In the first place, the stem is a propping organ. The stiffness of a plant stem is greatly affected by light. If light is limited, the stem will be long and slack. If it is to be rigid and sturdy, the plant needs an adequate amount of light, even around the base of the stalk.

Nutrient solutions that have been absorbed by the roots are conveyed by vessels in the stems to the leaves, where they combine with carbon dioxide and are transformed into sugar and starch. These two substances travel through fixed tubes along the stems and stalks to where leaves and buds grow.

In many plants the stem is also a nutrient reservoir. What is not needed immediately for growth, will be stored in the stalk and used later, when buds begin to form.

Finally, the stalk is often used for propagation as a cutting or for layering or grafting.

The function of leaves

Leaves are vital in the absorption of the nutrients and transforming them into sugar, starch and other vegetal substances. They are also important for evaporating moisture and for respiration (roots also respire).

Good leaf development is, therefore, vital. If leaves are damaged during the growing period, from being eaten by pests, through disease, or through too much stopping, nipping out or trimming, the plant's development will be impaired. The balance between roots and stalks and the leaves will be disturbed and growth inhibited.

As we have seen, the plant takes in nutrients – carbonic acid from the air and mineral solutions from the soil. To use these substances, the plant must first transform them into other substances that it can use as food.

When it is assimilating carbon, the plant makes carbohydrates from carbon dioxide and water. From carbohydrates and salts, albumens are formed. Assimilation requires light, carbon dioxide in the air, an appropriate temperature and chlorophyll bound to living plasma. In short, carbon assimilation is a process in which chlorophyll particles of the plasma, carbon dioxide from the air and water from the soil combine into carbohydrates formed under the influence of sunlight (or artificial light) at the right temperature, and oxygen (O_2) is given off.

Compost for containers

For optimal growth and flowering, it is important to try to make up a mixture that is as close as possible to the soil in the plant's natural habitat. Many wild fuchsia species occur in the Andes in Central America at heights of some 3,000 metres. They grow in forests that provide dappled shade and high humidity. The leaves falling every year have created a porous soil, rich in humus, containing many micro-organisms, permeable and of a pH between 6 and 7 (slightly acid to neutral).

A good compost for your fuchsia must, therefore, be permeable, able to hold adequate moisture, porous, contain adequate nutrients (although these can be supplied by fertilizers) and be of the right acidity (pH). If you can supply these characteristics, plenty of micro-organisms will be present; otherwise the soil will be dead.

Many of the proprietary composts that are available from garden centres consist mainly of peat products. Peat is almost wholly organic, contains no plant nutrients and is very acid (that is, it has a low pH). Adding organic fertilizers, such as stable manure, compost, chicken manure, dried blood and bone meal, not only provides vital nutrients but also introduces trace elements. This produces good microbiological soil. The pH level of the compost can be adjusted by adding lime, if required, to meet the needs of the plants.

There are many different kinds of compost on the market, and some of these are not suitable for fuchsias – indeed, they are not suitable for container-grown plants at all. Always buy a reputable brand name or, if you prefer to buy one that is made up by your supplier, purchase your supplies from a source you know.

Some growers prefer to mix their own compost by adding home-composted leaf mould to peat or by using a mixture of leaf mould with organic or artificial fertilizers. The most suitable leaf mould derives from beech trees, but you can use other leaves. Oak leaves contain much tannic acid, so you will need to add more lime during the composting. Leaves of willow, poplar, lime, chestnut, alder, cherry, apple, pear and most garden shrubs (except holly) are quickly broken down. Beech and oak leaves take longer, between 18 months and two years, but they will give excellent results if well composted.

The process of composting involves the breaking down of all kinds of leaves (or other healthy organic material), with the addition of stable manure, chicken manure or a proprietary compost activator, through the action of bacteria. Because trees and shrubs remove the most vital nutrients from leaves before shedding them in autumn, leaf compost, like peat, needs added nutrients if it is to be a satisfactory growing medium for other plants.

Opinions differ about the ideal mixture for fuchsias. Over the years, different growers have used different mixes with varying degrees of success. If you live in an area with clay soil, you will need to add some well-composted leaf mould to get a suitable texture. Some fuchsia growers add organic manure, such as dried cow dung or chicken manure. Adding organic material reduces the risk of deficiency diseases as well as increasing bacterial activity. When loam or clay soils are added it is advisable to make the soil more permeable by adding clean sharp sand or perlite or vermiculite.

Proprietary soilless composts consist of a mix of pulverized bark or peat, together with sharp sand, grit or perlite, a fertilizer and, often, chalk. The fertilizer may have many added nutrients – not only the main elements of nitrogen, phosphorus and potassium but also trace elements and calcium. Loam-based composts contain partially sterilized soil, mixed with varying proportions of peat, sand, chalk and, again, a fertilizer.

Most proprietary composts, therefore, contain peat in some degree or other. Peat has the great advantages to fuchsia growers that it contains much air and can hold between eight and ten times its weight of water. A disadvantage is that if the potted root ball dries out it can no longer extract from the soil the necessary moisture containing the dissolved nutrients, so that the ball shrivels and, when it is watered, most of the liquid flows away between the wall of the container and the root ball, which remains dry. It is therefore advisable to add a certain amount of soil or loam so that there is less chance that the medium around the roots dries out. The more loam or clay is added, the more sharp sand, perlite or vermiculite must be added to improve the drainage, for fuchsias do not like being in water-logged soil.

It is, in fact, almost impossible to suggest the perfect medium. Ultimately, everyone finds a mix that suits them and on which whey can rely. Success can be the only yardstick.

Feeding fuchsias

Even when you use a good quality medium, the nutrients present will not usually be sufficient to keep the plants in good condition throughout the growing season. It is, therefore necessary to add inorganic or organic fertilizers regularly.

When you come to select an appropriate fertilizer, you do need to understand the ways in which they affect the plant.

When you come to re-pot after winter, new roots must form first, and adding a fertilizer at this stage is pointless. A good compost will contain sufficient nutrients for the first four or five weeks. Among the substances that the plant requires are nitrogen, phosphorus and potassium. Calcium, magnesium and sulphur are needed, but in smaller amounts, and only very small amounts of iron, manganese, copper, zinc, boron and some other trace elements are required.

Nitrogen

Apart from insectivorous plants, the amount of nitrogen in the atmosphere, approximately 80 per cent, is of little significance to plants.

After phosphorus, sulphur and carbohydrates, nitrogen is required to make the albumens that build up into protoplasm and partly fill the cells. Without nitrogen no new albumen is produced and no growth takes place. When it is present, the plants grow quickly and have a good leaf colour. Most nitrogen-based fertilizers work fast and have a marked effect on the plant's growth. Too much nitrogen, however, causes the plant to become limp and prone to disease.

The formation of flower buds is adversely affected by nitrogen. After the initial phase of growth and at the time when the buds develop, only a small amount of nitrogen need be added. If you always use a fertilizer that is low in nitrogen, in order to stimulate growth in the early stages, you can add a simple nitrate, such as sodium nitrate or potassium nitrate, either of which will work more quickly than ammonium sulphate.

Phosphorus

This element stimulates the formation of flowers buds, and flowering plants are usually given more phosphorus than other plants. In addition, phosphorus encourages the development of roots in young plants and of tubers and seeds in autumn.

Together with nitrogen and sulphur, phosphorus is a constituent of albumens, and the plant takes it in the form in the form of phosphates.

The best known forms are: superphosphate, which is quick acting and contains 19 per cent phosphorus, and a slower acting phosphate with 14–18 per cent, which is not as useful as superphosphate. Growing mediums often contains bone-meal, which consists of calcium and approximately 25 per cent phosphorus.

Potassium

Like nitrogen and phosphorus, potassium is vital for plant growth, and it is important in the formation and transportation of carbohydrates within the plant's cells. Potassium is important for the formation of sturdy stems, which is especially important in plants such as fuchsias, which have woody stems. It is also important in improving a plant's resistance to disease, and a lack of potassium in late summer can lead to problems in winter.

Potassium is important in the formation and fixing of pollen, in the assimilation of carbon during photosynthesis and in the production of chlorophyll. It also has a significant effect on the colours of a fuchsia's flowers, making them brighter.

If too much potassium is present, however, the plant's ability to take in nitrogen is impaired, and growth is retarded, so that the plant becomes prematurely lignified.

Calcium

Calcium is not water soluble. It occurs in the soil in small particles, and its main tasks are to control acidity by neutralizing acids and to improve the soil's structure.

Small amounts of calcium are needed for plant metabolism. It helps to strengthen cell walls and neutralizes poisons and acids in the plant. It is possible to buy special calcium formulations, sometimes based on dolomite (calcium magnesium carbonate).

Trace elements

If the soil or compost within the container contains leaf mould, loam or good garden soil, adequate amounts of trace elements will normally already be present. If you have used a commercial, peat-based compost, to which no trace elements have been added, your plants may suffer from deficiency diseases. Plants can also suffer from an excess of other nutrients to the exclusion of necessary trace elements. If the pH level is too high, lack of iron, manganese or zinc may result; if it is too low, the plant may lack magnesium.

If the nutrients are present in the wrong proportions, the plant may also suffer from deficiencies of various kinds. Too much calcium may lead to lack of potassium, for example; too much phosphorus leads to lack of zinc; too much potassium to a lack of magnesium; and too much iron and aluminium to a lack of phosphorus.

Iron deficiency, better known as chlorosis, arises when too much calcium and phosphorus are present, and its presence revealed when leaves becoming yellow-green, although the veins remain green. Magnesium, a constituent of chlorophyll, plays an important part in the plant's assimilation of carbon and in the transportation of phosphates and carbohydrates. A lack of magnesium is revealed when leaves become discoloured, turning brown or yellow between the veins, and eventually die.

Proprietary fertilizers

In practice, most gardeners uses a proprietary fertilizer of one kind or another. There are several kinds on the market, and many are simply added to water and watered into the compost.

Commercial manufacturers have started to use new formulations in recent years, partly in response to the new growing mediums that have been developed, and if you are using one of these instead of a mix you have made yourself or a commercial product with which you are familiar, you will need to know what proportion the components are present.

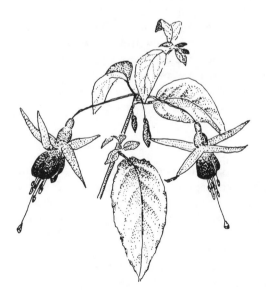

'Petit Point'

Most commercial fertilizers consist largely of nitrogen (N), phosphorus (P) and potassium (K), sometimes with added trace elements, and the composition of each is generally identified on the packet as a ratio of N:P:K. Some are sold in a bio-degradable resin envelope, and how long they continue to act in the soil depends on how thick the resin layer is and on the soil temperature.

Some products are available in a variety of compositions: for example, one manufacturer supplies a range of fertilizers identified as 11N:22P:9K and 6 per cent magnesium oxide; 9N:12P:17K, which would be active for six or seven months; and 14N:9P:18K or 9N:9P:22K, both of which would be active for four or five months. The advantages of these products is that less is needed and they do not drain away. A drawback is that they do not contain trace elements.

Other formulations are available in highly concentrated form. These work fast, may contain many trace elements and leave no residue on the leaves. Look out for packets labelled 20N:20P:20K; 15N:30P:15K; 28N:14P:14K; 10N:52P:10K; 20N-5P-30K and so on. Phostrogen, which is widely available in the UK, is in the proportions 10:10:27 with 2.2 per cent magnesium oxide and 12 per cent sulphur trioxide.

Organic fertilizers may be offered as, for example, 10N:4P:6K with blood-meal and bone-meal. The advantage of an organic fertilizer is that the content promotes organic activity so that the compost stays in better condition.

The plethora of possible combinations of nitrogen, phosphorus and potassium in fertilizers may seem confusing. What is important to remember is that during the summer, when you want to encourage your plants to produce vegetative growth and flowers, you need a formulation that is in the proportion of 2:1:1 or even 3:1:1 – that is, one that is high in nitrogen – while during the spring and autumn, when there is less light, you need to provide more potassium and should be looking for formulations in the proportions 1:1:2 or 1:1:3.

Using fertilizer

As we have seen, fuchsias need soil that is rich in nutrients and they respond readily to the application of fertilizers. However, they are sensitive to excessive concentrations of salts. Using small amounts of a highly concentrated fertilizer has the advantage that fewer carrier substances (salts) are left behind in the pots, and feeding can begin as soon as the root system is well developed.

Before you feed your plants you must make sure that the compost in the container is moist. Never add fertilizer to dry soil. If necessary soak the container with water to which a few drops of a washing-up liquid have been added.

Do not fertilize newly potted cuttings for the first few weeks after potting up. Never fertilize a diseased plant; instead, put it into a smaller pot and remove the old soil. Try to identify the disease and put that right.

Plant growth should be activated by feeding with a fertilizer containing nitrogen to promote the formation of new cells and also phosphorus to promote root formation. As soon as the plants are well developed, you may want to use a fertilizer with a high phosphorus and potassium content but less nitrogen. However, if the level of nitrogen becomes too low, the lower leaves will turn yellow and drop off.

Use a fertilizer regularly – once a fortnight, for example – and always on the same day. Or you may prefer to use lower concentrations once a week. After August, less fertilizer should be given and certainly very little nitrogen, for that will encourage further growth and prevent the existing growth from maturing sufficiently to withstand winter storage, which can cause problems.

Young plants that spend winter in a heated greenhouse will continue to grow, but they should not be fed at this time. Whatever growth they make will be determined by factors such as the amount of light and the temperature.

chapter 6

Taking Cuttings

The simplest and most usual method of increasing a stock of fuchsias is by taking cuttings. This process has the great advantage that a single plant can be used to provide many cuttings, all of which will display the same characteristics as the parent plant. Many amateurs take cuttings, either to increase their existing stock or to replace an old plant or to exchange with fellow growers and, as long as care is taken, the results are almost always good.

There are some general rules that, if always observed, should guarantee success:

- Take only cuttings from plants that are healthy and free from whitefly and bugs.
- Use soil and plant pots that are perfectly clean and disease free. Plant pots should be washed thoroughly in a solution of a chlorine-based domestic cleaning fluid and then rinsed in clean water.
- Use a sharp knife. A blunt blade can cause a ragged, torn edge, which will die back and cause infection.
- Do not allow the cutting to dry out. If it cannot be planted straightaway, keep it in an inflated polythene bag with a few drops of water or wrap the whole cutting in damp newspaper or tissue paper.
- Do not stand a cutting in direct sunlight, which will scorch the tender young leaves. However, good light is necessary, especially when growth begins.
- Keep the soil at the correct temperature to promote the formation of roots. A temperature of 15–20°C is ideal. If you allow the soil to become too warm, you will increase the risk of mildew, which will have to be treated (see Chapter 8).
- Cover the pot with a pane of glass or put it in a plastic bag, taking care that the leaves are not in contact with the plastic.

Rooting mediums

It is perfectly possible to put a cutting in water until roots form. The cutting can then be transferred to a growing medium and grown on in the normal way. This method usually meets with success, although it will take time for the water roots to be replaced by normal ones, which will check the plant's development.

Best results will be obtained if you use a rooting medium of two parts peat to one part sharp sand or of one part peat to one part perlite or vermiculite. Alternatively, peat blocks or a compost specially formulated for cuttings can be used. Do not use garden soil or a proprietary potting compost, both of which contain too high a proportion of nutrients, which will inhibit the formation of roots.

Timing

Fuchsia cuttings can be taken at almost any time of the year, although in practice there are three main periods: in the spring, when the soft growing tip is taken; in the summer, when a semi-ripe, flowering shoot can be taken; and in the autumn, when a woody cutting can be taken. The optimum period is, perhaps, from mid-February to mid-April, when the plant is in full growth, producing many tender shoots that can be rooted in as little as two weeks. Always water a plant well before taking a cutting.

Spring cuttings

The ideal is a cutting 3–6cm long with from two to four pairs of leaves. Such a cutting will root not only from the node in the leaf axil but also from the stalk.

Remove the lowest pair of leaves and use a sharp knife to cut the stalk just below the node of the leaves you have removed. Then put make a small hole in the rooting medium with a thin stick and carefully insert the cutting in the hole, gently pressing it in with two fingers. If you are taking just a few cuttings, you can put several in a small container – a 6–8cm flowerpot, for example – and place it in a plastic bag that is fastened to

A spring cutting

make, in effect, a mini-greenhouse. If you are taking large numbers and of different kinds, use a small tray and cover it with a sheet of glass. After planting, the cuttings must be misted to keep the air moist, which helps them to take root. Make sure that each cutting is properly labelled with the name of the parent plant.

Although soft tip fuchsia cuttings root easily, you can use a hormone rooting powder which, as well as encouraging the formation of plenty of roots, will probably also contain a fungicide of some kind, which can be a useful precaution. The same rooting powders can be used for both soft tip cuttings taken in spring and the semi-ripe and woody cuttings taken in summer and autumn. Use one that is recommended for herbaceous cuttings and that contain concentrations of 0.1 per cent or 0.05 per cent. When the cutting is ready to be set into the compost, mist it lightly, then dip the bottom end of the stalk (at most 1cm) into the rooting powder. Carefully shake off any excess powder that adheres to the plant – it needs only a small amount – make a small hole and put the cutting into it. You need to make a hole because if you place the cutting directly into the growing medium, the powder will be pushed to the top, where it is not needed. You can then gently press the surrounding compost down with two fingers.

Summer cuttings

Cuttings taken later in the year will be somewhat woodier and need some extra preparation. The cuttings should be taken a few millimetres below the node, and the lowest pair of leaves and all flowers and buds should be removed. One pair of leaves, or better still, two or three pairs of leaves should be left together with a growing point. Then proceed as before, although rooting powder is recommended.

Other kinds of cutting

Longer cuttings

It is possible to plant these, but they take longer to root. Once they have done so, however, you will have a larger plant than from a normal soft tip cutting.

Small cuttings

It is possible to use a small cutting, no larger than a growing point, with just one pair of leaves, and you can still make it root, although the initial plant will be very small.

Intermediate cuttings

It is quite easy to take several cuttings from a single, long shoot. The uppermost section becomes the tip cutting. The lower of the next two pairs of leaves is cut off and a cutting is taken from underneath – that is, below the node. These intermediate cuttings mostly take root quite fast, but they do not begin to grow until the axil buds sprout from the lowest pair of leaves.

Lengthwise cuttings

To get more cuttings still, it is possible to split stems of intermediate cuttings lengthwise, so that each small section of stem has one leaf and one axil bud. Here, too, the axil buds must sprout before growth begins. The initial plant obtained in this way will be small.

Several cuttings can be taken from a single shoot (at *a* and *b*) and by cutting the stalk lengthwise (as at *c*)

Autumn cuttings

Although the stems are much woodier, the year after such cuttings have been taken you will have large plants suitable for use in hanging-baskets or for pole tops.

New shoots from pruned plants

If a large plant has been trimmed back in autumn, it will quickly sprout again in a heated greenhouse, especially if the weather is mild. These tender shoots can easily be used as cuttings in November and December, and they will quickly produce large plants in the following year. Look out for botrytis and, if necessary, use a fungicide. The young plants must be kept growing in winter at about 12°C.

Suckers

Rooted suckers can be removed from the main plant without damaging it. If there are a few small roots are on the runner, these will soon develop if they are potted up. Not all fuchsias produce suckers.

Cuttings with three leaves

Almost all cultivars have two leaves per node or joint, but some have three. Cuttings taken from these readily yield a much fuller plant in the same time as a cutting with two leaves if all the axil buds sprout.

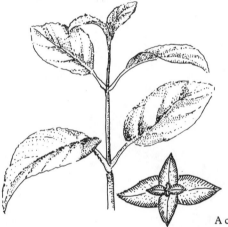

A cutting with two leaves to a node

Looking after your cuttings

Once you have placed the cuttings in the rooting medium, you must make sure that they will not dry out. However, you must also check to see if too much water condenses on the sheet of glass covering a tray of cuttings. If necessary, turn it over and place it at an angle so that water can run off. Plastic bags which have accumulated too much water can be turned inside out so that the dry side is inside.

You should also inspect the cuttings regularly. Dropped leaves and flower stalks must be removed to avoid mildew.

The first small roots will form very quickly, in one or two weeks. When the roots form, the cutting will start to show growing points and the small leaves will look fresher. After a few more days you can test whether small roots have formed by lifting the plant slightly with a twig. If you can see no roots, gently push the cutting back and wait for another week.

Potting

When the roots are about 1cm long, the cutting can be potted on. As when putting a fuchsia plant into another container, take care that you do not damage the roots. As much soil as possible should be left adhering to the root ball. Put some good quality compost in the bottom of a 6–8cm flowerpot and place the root ball, still with its own compost around the roots on top. Carefully fill the pot with more compost, then gently press the soil against the rim with two fingers. Finally, water. If the soil is too compacted, root growth will be inhibited, so do not press down too firmly.

Hardening off

When the potted cutting is growing again, it must be hardened off. That is, it must get used to drier air than that in the propagator or in its plastic bag. After potting on, place the cutting back in the tray and under the sheet of glass, but push the glass a little way to one side, increasing the gap gradually. After about four days the tray should be completely uncovered further, so that after four days it is completely uncovered. You should continue to mist regularly.

In a greenhouse, hardening off takes a little longer. On an overcast day, pot on the cuttings and put them in a shady spot in the greenhouse. Place the pots on a base of sharp sand, which should be kept moist to create a moist climate. Proceed as before, but you must remember to shade the cuttings on very sunny days, or the leaves will be scorched.

Foliar feeding

In spring vegetative growth – that is, growth before flowering – should be as strong as possible. Never add fertilizer to the compost around newly potted cuttings: that would be asking for trouble. Instead, you can fertilize the leaves by misting them with a proprietary foliar feed, dissolved in water. The nutrient will be quickly absorbed and the plant encouraged to put on top growth without causing the root growth to be checked. On the contrary, even the roots will grow more vigorously. Look for a fertilizer specially prepared for this purpose and mix it as recommended by the manufacturer. If some trace elements are present, so much the better. With care, unrooted cuttings can be treated in the same way.

When you use a mister in a greenhouse in spring there is a danger that the plants are not dry by the evening, which makes mildew infection more likely. You should always try to mist spray as early in the day as possible, and on cold, dark days it is better not to spray at all. If you plants are indoors, the danger of mildew is less because the air is not as moist. On sunny days, even when you are not applying a foliar feed, it is advisable to mist with fresh water.

Sources

Jennings, K. and Miller, V., *Growing Fuchsias*
Manthey, G. *Fuchsien*

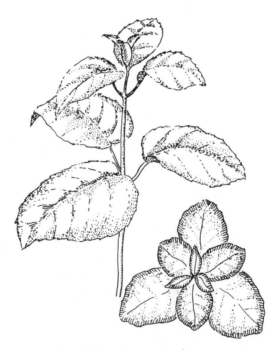

A cutting with three leaves to a node

chapter 7

Shaping

As we have seen, species fuchsias growing in the wild can be bushes or even small trees; some grow as lianas or even epiphytes. Although species fuchsias can look extremely attractive when they are allowed to grow as much as possible as they do in the wild, this is not usually practicable or possible when it comes to cultivars. Most cultivars look and grow best when the natural shape is altered by stopping, nipping out and trimming.

Bushes

In the autumn, when you are preparing the plant for winter, you can prune a bush. Not only will a thorough trimming now give you more room, it will be easier to grow a well-shaped plant in spring. You can, of

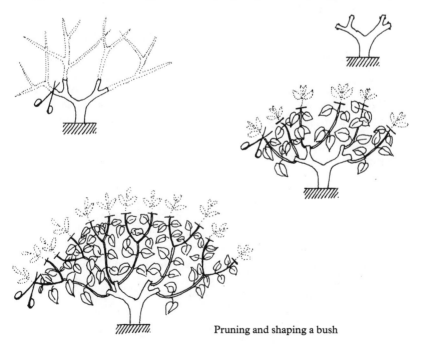

Pruning and shaping a bush

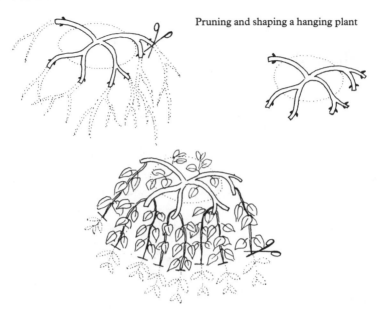

Pruning and shaping a hanging plant

course, prune in spring as well, but without gaining the additional space.

The illustration shows that a plant that is cut back to four stems in spring will, after being stopped twice, produce sixteen new stems. As soon as the plant begins to bud in spring, shaping can begin by stopping and nipping. Whether you are working on an established plant or a new cutting, the principle is the same. After two pairs of leaves, cut out the top of the stem, and repeat the process until the plant is bushy and well shaped.

Take out any stems that grow across the plant and also any stems that spoil the shape you are aiming at. If you can start stopping early in the growing season, strongly growing cultivars can be stopped four times.

Trailers

Plants with a naturally lax or trailing habit are somewhat awkward to keep, because of their shape. You will save yourself trouble if you prune them before winter sets in. Make sure that the centre stems overhang the rim of the pot so that stiff stems form at the edge that will be strong enough to carry the weight of new stems and flowers.

When buds start to appear, stopping and nipping out can begin. When you are dealing with trailing fuchsias, it is advisable to stop after three pairs of leaves (rather than after two pairs, as is the case with a bush). If you want a sturdy plant after one year, put rooted cuttings together in a large pot, again stopping after every three pairs of leaves.

Standard

Some cultivars are better suited to some shapes than to others. To train a plant into a standard you need a strongly growing cultivar such as 'Checkerboard', 'Dollar Princess', 'Mission Bells' or 'Celia Smedley'.

The best time to start is the end of August, when the plants are less likely to form flower buds but will put on strong leaf growth. It is then easier to get a good height in a relatively short time. You will need to make sure that the plant goes on growing in winter, and regular re-potting is essential. If growth is disrupted for any reason, the final results will be disappointing, and this is even more so for the shapes described below.

Start with a normal unstopped cutting and allow the top shoot to grow on. It should be regularly and carefully tied to the same side of a stake. The ties must not be too tight; you should check this from time to time, because as the stem grows thicker there is a tendency for a tie to cut into the stalk, which may so weaken it that it easily breaks later on. Give the tie a single twist between the stem and the stake.

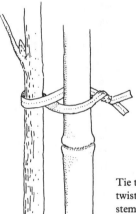

Tie the main stem to a stake, twisting the tie once between the stem and the stake

Leaves should be left on the stem until they fall off. However, if the buds in the lower leaf axils being to sprout, the small shoots should be nipped out. When the stem achieves the required height, the top should be nipped out. The three topmost shoots from leaf axil buds should be stopped to two pairs of leaves. After being stopped twice, the three branches will produce twelve stems (for clarity, the illustration shows only two shoots giving eight stems).

From this point, proceed as with a bush fuchsia. A standard plant is really a bush on a stem, and you should prune it in autumn in the same way.

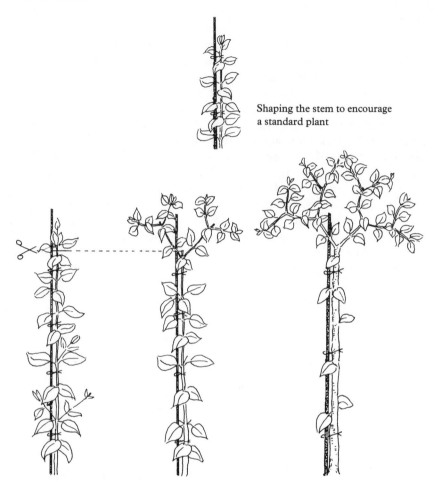

Shaping the stem to encourage a standard plant

Pyramid

This is basically a Christmas tree shape, and it takes several years to train a fuchsia into a tall pyramid shape. Start with a fast-growing plant that readily forms side shoots, which will grow into stiff lateral branches. The idea is that the lowest ones slope downwards while the higher ones are more horizontal. The top stems naturally grow most readily and the lower ones tend to develop less well. To encourage these lower stems to grow more vigorously, the top stems have to be stopped and trimmed.

The main stem should be tied to a stake, and the top should be regularly nipped out. Of the two new shoots that develop, the sturdier is tied

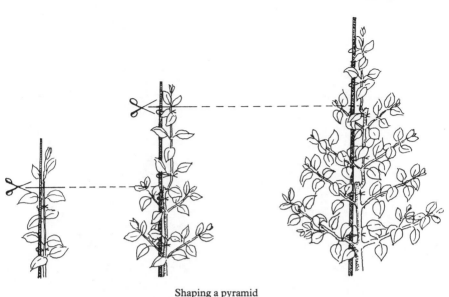

Shaping a pyramid

upwards along the stake and the other removed. By continually nipping out the top shoot to an odd number of leaf pairs, the side shoots will be alternately above each other. If the side shoots develop too close to each other, some must be removed, but you must aim to keep the fuchsia in shape at all times.

While it is being trained, you need to keep the plant growing at all times. If the growth is interrupted before you have achieved the overall shape, the overall results will be disappointing. If necessary, re-pot the plant so that it does not become pot-bound.

Mini-pillar

Beginning with a cultivar that has a good, stiff upright habit and that readily forms side shoots, you can train a vertically growing small tree. You should allow the top to grow on and nip out side shoots to two or three leaf pairs. Turning the pot from time to time will encourage the plant to grow in a uniform shape. You are aiming to have a straight stem with short side shoots of equal length, and any stray shoots must be cut off to maintain the shape. It is difficult to keep the shape growing well for more than a few years, but you can turn the fuchsia into a standard by cutting off the bottom stems completely and allowing the top ones to grow.

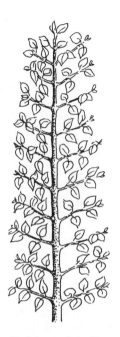
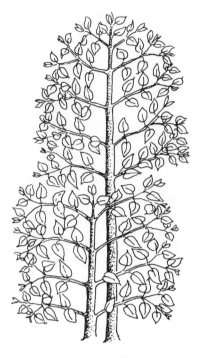

Training a mini-pillar   Training a pillar

Pillar

The pillar is built up in much the same way as the mini-pillar, but the side shoots should be allowed to grow longer, so that the column is wider.

The traditional method starts with a cutting that has been stopped to three pairs of leaves. This makes two new tops of which one is shaped further to form a standard and the other to form a bush.

More recently pillars are grown from two cuttings next to each other in a pot. One is shaped to a standard and the other to a bush to conceal the stem of the standard. This produces a pillar that will achieve a uniform stem length and shape if the pot is regularly turned. The new method is a bit simpler and gives quicker results.

James Lye, the British hybridist and fuchsia grower, was a master at raising pillars, and more than a century ago he succeeded in growing pillars 2 metres tall and more than 1 metre across.

Sources
Manthey, G., *Fuchsien*
Thorne, T. , *Fuchsias for All Purposes*

6 'Pussy Cat'

7 'Le Berger'

8 'Other Fellow'

9 'Violet Bassett-Burr'

10 'Tiffany'

chapter 8

Pests and Diseases

Prevention is, as they say, always better than cure. Worldwide turnover in pesticides and fungicides is now well over £16,000 million a year, leading to a yearly uptake of several 100,000 tonnes of poison by the environment. Many of these chemicals, such as chlorinated carbohydrates, are not bio-degradable or they have noxious side-effects. So, do we have to go along with this?

If we can find out how a pest or mould functions, it is far easier to discover whether a preventive measure will have the desired effect on our plants. Knowing when eggs hatch, for example, will enable us to understand when repeated spraying is likely to be effective. Sensible counter-measures will allow us to prevent outbreaks of pests and diseases by the application of simple remedies. These measures might include changing the microclimate – lowering the relative humidity to prevent mould, for example – catching pests by putting out small flowerpots filled with straw, or interrupting a lifecycle by, for example, keeping *Epilobium* plants infected with rust away from your fuchsias.

If only a few plants are affected by pests or mould, they can generally be treated without having to resort to poisons. Sometimes, however, a plague or infection may threaten to get out of hand – a fierce attack by mealybugs, whitefly or red spider mites, for example – and clearly, if you have a greenhouse of plants infected with black mould you will want to aim the insecticidal spray at the billowing clouds of whitefly that have caused it. You should, however, always try to choose the chemical that is most environmentally friendly and that has the least effect on humans and animals. Also, take care not to poison useful insects such as bees and to keep it away from any water in your garden, or you may harm or even kill your fish.

Even less harmful are biological remedies that involve using the natural enemies of pests. Ladybird beetles can be used against mealybugs; the parasitic *Encarsia formosa* will eliminate whitefly; and even some fungal infections are susceptible to biological control. Unfortunately, many of these natural predators can be let loose only in confined, and usually heated, spaces such as greenhouses. However, kinds that are usable in the open will doubtless be developed.

Insecticides and fungicides (manufacturers prefer to call them 'plant protectors') consist of chemical components, among which are chemicals that are dangerous to both man and animals. Some insecticides are regarded as so toxic that amateur growers are not allowed to use them, while other products that can be used by amateur growers are available only in large and expensive packs, and they usually work over a fairly narrow range, being effective against one or two pests.

All insecticides and fungicides should be used with care, and the manufacturer's instructions should always be followed to the letter.

Fuchsias can also suffer from deficiencies of various kinds. Discoloration or falling leaves are mostly due to a lack of some nutrient or nutrients or to disturbed water take-up. The compost in the container may be wrongly mixed or the wrong fertilizers may have been added (probably too much at once, rather than too little). Watering too much or too little or using water that is too cold can also upset the plant's take-up of water. Yellow leaves may develop if the plant stands in too much shade. The cause of the problem must be established in each case before the appropriate remedy can be adopted.

Fuchsias can also suffer from loss of buds and early flower drop. This is because they are sensitive to ethylene, a characteristic they share with several other pot plants, including hibiscus. Geraniums, on the other hand, are among the least sensitive plants to ethylene.

All plants emit ethylene in very low concentrations. The gas is a plant hormone that plays an important part in growth and development. If the surrounding atmosphere contains too much ethylene, it penetrates into the plant and upsets the hormone balance, leading to loss of buds and flowers. Ethylene is found also in exhaust gases and cigarette smoke; fruit, too, emits comparatively large amounts. If fuchsias are grown in a garden bordering on a busy road, exhaust gases can cause bud and flower loss. Indoors, a bowl of fruit or cigarette smoke can be the culprit.

In a small greenhouse a tightly packed collection of fuchsias produces a lot of ethylene gas, and good ventilation is essential. High sensitivity to ethylene also goes with a tendency to disease, so optimal care is the best way to prevent both disease and deficiency arising in the first place.

We will now consider the various pests and diseases to which fuchsias are prone, describing the life-cycles, some practical countermeasures and suitable chemical or biological remedies.

Whitefly

Hothouse whitefly (*Trialeurodes vaporariorum*) regularly cause trouble. You will probably first notice the small, white insects when you touch the plant. These are not actually flies. They are tiny insects, probably of tropical or subtropical, South and Central American origin, with two pairs of wings. Each whitefly is 1–2mm long, the whole body, especially the wings, covered with white powder, which is exuded by glands at the back. Males are a little smaller than the females, which lay eggs without being fertilized. Fully grown whitefly live for 30–40 days. They can over-winter in heated greenhouses but they cannot usually survive in the open.

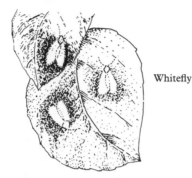

Whitefly

On average, a whitefly lays 25 eggs a day, up to 500 during its life. The eggs are yellow, 0.2–0.25mm long and turn dark grey after a few days. They are laid in tiny circles of 20–40 eggs, especially on the underside of leaves. In a warm greenhouse the larvae emerge within about 10 days. They are flat, 0.3mm long and light green in colour. The nymphs or crawlers move around for a while before settling down to feed. At 21°C the larval stage lasts 3–6 days; the next, pupal stage lasts for 7–11 days and then a fully grown whitefly emerges. From egg to fly takes three weeks at 21°C, and about four weeks at 15°C.

The larvae and flies forage on the underside of leaves. With their piercing and sucking mouth parts they extract plant sap in large amounts, from which they absorb sufficient albumin. Their fluid excrement leaves a sugary coating on the leaves. This sweet, sticky layer, called honey dew, clogs up the leaf pores, which impedes evaporation and absorption of nutrient salts. If the relative humidity in a hothouse is above 90 per cent for some days, sooty mould, *Cladosporium*, will grow on the sticky layer and produce deposits of fungal spores and mycelium. A severe attack can inhibit the plant's ability to photosynthesize by reducing the amount of light that reaches the leaf surface. The sticky leaves become discoloured and drop off, thus stopping the growth of the young stalk.

The speed with which whitefly reproduce is closely linked with the host plant's state of nourishment: the healthier the host, the faster whitefly will reproduce. In a small collection of plants, a few whitefly can be controlled by squashing the insects between your fingers. In larger collections this is not possible.

If your fuchsias are growing indoors, spray them with water – or stand them outside in a shower of rain, which will wash off the grown bugs. A large infestation will probably need chemical treatment. Spray thoroughly with a contact insecticide containing malathion, HCH, pyrethrum or permethrin, or use a systemic insecticide containing dimethoate or heptenophos. You will have to repeat the treatment over a period of about two weeks at four-day intervals because the eggs will not be affected by the spray. Alternatively, use a fumigant containing HCH but, again, you will have to repeat the treatment over a period because the eggs and larvae will be unaffected.

If possible and to reduce the likelihood that the whitefly will become resistant to specific chemicals, alternate the sprays you use.

Available to large, commercial greenhouses, and now becoming increasingly available to amateur growers, is a biological control, *Encarsia formosa*, which is a parasitic, black and yellow wasp that is smaller even than the whitefly. A female *Encarsia* will lay eggs in up to 50 whitefly scales, and the young wasp feeds on the larva inside the scale before emerging to find new scales in which to lay eggs. The greenhouse should be kept at a temperature of 21°C for best results.

Aphids

Of the almost six hundred kinds of aphid (or plant lice) found in northern Europe, the most common and most feared is the peach-potato aphid (*Myzus persicae*), which spreads various virus diseases among plants in orchards, gardens and greenhouse. It is found on an enormous range of plants – from vegetables to ornamental subjects, from antirrhinums to sweet peas and including fuchsias – together with another well-known aphid, the blackfly.

Aphids are barely 2mm long. Some aphids within a colony have wings and others do not, and winged aphids are usually produced at the begin-

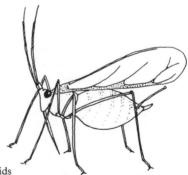

Aphids

ning and end of the summer so that they can migrate to a new host plant. Some aphid species spend their entire lives on a single host species, while others can attack dozens of different plant species. They all have piercing mouth parts with two channels, which they insert into plants. Through one channel the aphid pumps poisonous saliva full of enzymes to loosen plant cells from each other. Through the other it sucks up sap, and a large colony of aphids will greatly reduce a plant's vigour by weakening and distorting young growth. More important, however, is the honey dew excreted by the aphid, which covers leaves and stems of infested plants, encouraging the development of sooty mould, and the fact that viruses from diseased plants are carried in the aphids' saliva and infect healthy specimens.

Aphids hibernate in winter as eggs. The eggs of *Myzus persicae*, for example, overwinter on peach trees or nectarines, although they can overwinter in heated greenhouses or even in houses, while the eggs of the black bean aphid (*Aphis fabae*) overwinter on *Euonymus europaeus* and *Viburnum opulus*.

In early spring the larvae hatch on their winter host. These are all future females. Their presence on the host is revealed by the curled leaves they cause in the shrubs. When in late spring space becomes restricted on the plant, the lice develop wings on which they float from shrub to shrub until they reach their preferred summer site, where they reproduce parthenogenetically. During the summer they tend not to lay eggs but to produce live young. It has been estimated that a single aphid can produce 50–100 offspring, all of which can mature in a week's time given a temperature of 20°C. Towards the end of summer the young aphids develop wings and float to their winter host. Although they are poor fliers, they can be carried for several miles on warm air currents.

Larvae look like the adults but are smaller. They always sit on the lower side of leaves on young shoots, sucking sap and injecting poisonous saliva, causing the leaves to become discoloured and to wilt. Aphids sucking on young shoots will stop growth. As on the honey dew produced by greenhouse whitefly, sooty mildew may grow on the sticky later and interfere with photosynthesis.

Plants in draughty positions in a greenhouse or a room offer a ready landing place for aphids, and in the absence of natural predators they will multiply so fast that they will hardly find enough food. One sign of the presence of aphids on fuchsias are ants crawling along stems and stalks, looking for excreted sugar and 'farming' colonies of aphids.

Among the most effective natural predators are garden birds, insects and spiders. Ladybirds are perhaps the best known insect predator, but the larvae of lacewings and hoverflies also eat huge quantities. It is essential, therefore, not to eliminate these useful insects by the indiscriminate use of insecticides. Two other biological controls are available. *Aphidoletes*, a tiny midge, produces grubs that feed on aphids, and the parasitic wasp *Aphidius matricariae* lays its egg in aphids. Both these will survive outside the greenhouse, although a minimum temperature of about 18°C is necessary.

Another non-chemical solution is to spray an infested plant with a strong jet of warm water: at over 45°C they perish. Spraying or sponging with a horticultural soap solution is effective only if the wash is repeated several times.

There is a range of broad-spectrum insecticides sold by garden centres and florists for combating aphids, and if the infestation is serious you will need to use one containing pirimicarb, which is highly selective. You should also consider applying a winter-wash based on tar oil on dormant wood that may be host to over-wintering aphid eggs. Never use this on plants that still have leaves.

Red spider mite

The greenhouse red spider mite (*Tetranychus urticae*) is very tiny and is often seen as reddish dots on the lower side of leaves. Although small, however, it is a serious and widespread problem, occurring on a range of plants, including buddleias, chrysanthemums and dahlias, and on apple and plum trees. With the aid of a magnifying glass it is possible to identify the mite by counting the legs: it has eight. If you count six legs, it is either another bug altogether or a larval form of this mite. A surer diagnostic sign is silvery webbing on the underside of leaves, which themselves turn bronze or yellow and become brittle.

The red spider mite overwinters in gardens, on woody plants or in crevices in rocks and so on, or in the greenhouse, in compost or in canes. As soon as it gets warmer and leaves appear on trees and plants, each female lays up to a hundred eggs on the underside of the leaves of a suitable host plant. The larvae hatch after three to thirty days. After passing through two nymphal stages, they are fully grown fungal mites. In a heated greenhouse adults may produce eggs throughout the year.

Unfortunately, because they live on the underside of leaves, one usually finds them too late. Look out for a brown mottling on the underside of the leaves or pale yellow spots on the upper surface. Leaves then turn bronze or grey, wither and die. When the pest is well established, the mites swarm over leaves and plants on silvery webbing.

Red spider mite thrives in hot, dry conditions. One way to make infestation difficult is regular spraying with cold water, particularly on the underside of leaves. In exceptionally hot weather, you may need to spray twice a day, and good ventilation is essential. Affected plants should be removed and, ideally, burned.

A natural predator is the mite *Phytoseiulus persimilis*, which is orange and slightly large than the red spider mite. An adult can eat about five adult red spider mites a day or 20–30 immature mites.

Chemical methods are less satisfactory, largely because the mites become resistant to most formulations. An insecticide containing derris may help. The best way of counteracting this mite is, however, to ensure that your fuchsias are kept in a moist, well-ventilated greenhouse.

Vine weevil

The vine weevil (*Otiorrhynchus sulcatus*) is a serious pest of greenhouse and garden plants, and the proliferation of container-grown plants supplied by nurseries seems to have exacerbated the problem. The main damage is done by the larvae, which live in the compost. When the majority of plants were bought as bare-rooted specimens, some, at least, of the larvae rolled out when the plant was moved and stayed at the nursery. Now that most plants are container-grown, the compost in which the larvae are present will simply be transferred to a new site – your garden.

The adult weevils are dark brown, almost black, insects, 10–15mm long. They are mostly nocturnal, and you may suspect their presence only when you notice that irregular holes and notches have been eaten in the lowest leaves of a fuchsia. They feed on leaf pulp, which they extract from the edges towards the central vein.

There are only female vine weevils, and reproduction is parthenogenetic. They are wingless, which limits their spread, but although they crawl sluggishly, they can go far. A typical feature is the snout with two antennae.

In spring and early summer a female vine weevil can lay up to one thousand eggs in the top layer of compost or soil close to a suitable host plant. Sometimes a weevil will start to crawl about as early as February, but in the garden they more often first come out at the end of May. From mid-July to mid-September they lay eggs. Two or three weeks later the larvae hatch out and begin to feed on plant roots, which is when the main damage is done. They feed for about three months before pupating in the soil ready to emerge the following spring, so that, in general, there is one generation a year. In a greenhouse, however, adults can emerge in autumn, and, given the long period over which eggs are laid, there can be eggs, larvae, pupae and adults present at the same time, especially in a greenhouse.

While adult weevils merely gnaw leaves, the larvae cause far greater damage. Vine weevil larvae in a container will quickly consume the plant's roots, and their presence becomes evident when the leaves turn pale and limp; the leaves turn yellow and fall off. If you pull the plant up, you will find it rootless.

Vine weevils have few natural enemies, mainly because the adults stay underground in daytime, like larvae. Some birds pick up a few. Fuchsia-growers who allow chickens to scratch around among their outdoor collection will rarely find larvae.

The adults can be caught in several ways: you could try laying wooden slats between the plants – when you turn them over in the morning you will catch the weevil; put a flower pot full of fine wood shavings or hay upside down among the plants with a pebble under the edge to let the weevils in so that you can catch and kill them in the morning; or, at dusk, put a white cloth around plants you think may be infested and train a torch on them, which causes the weevils to fall off from shock and stay still so that you can kill them.

Larvae are more difficult to catch. When you pot up, shake the soil ball and catch any larvae that fall out. Do not put the old soil from the container on your compost heap, which will simply help the larvae spread to other parts of the garden.

You can limit damage if, before storing for the winter, you put the pruned plants into new pots. If this reveals larvae, put the plant in a bucket of water (not too cold). Rinsing in water will bring out hidden larvae. Pot the plant into a new pot with clean compost and clean the old pot with water to remove the remaining traces of soil, which may be harbouring eggs. Above all, if you are growing species that have fleshy roots – *F. fulgens*, for example – check to see if there are any hidden larvae.

Using a spray or fumigating with HCH will kill the insects before they can lay eggs. Try drenching the compost with an HCH solution to kill the larvae. The only sure way to get rid of these larvae is by using a parasitic nematode (*Heterorhabditis*). Tests in tree nurseries have shown that this environmentally friendly method works better than the more toxic substances an amateur is barred from using. The nematodes work when the soil temperature is above 14°C, and they should be added to the soil in late September or early October.

Froghoppers and leafhoppers

Of the many species of froghopper and leafhopper, three regularly trouble fuchsias – the rose leafhopper (*Typhlocyba rosea*), the common froghopper (*Philaenus spumarius*) and, in the last few years, *Empoasca vitis*. This species was first noticed on fuchsias by the plant disease service in Wageningen in 1983, although it had been known on various other plants before.

Leafhoppers, which belong to the family Cicadellidae, are small, sap-

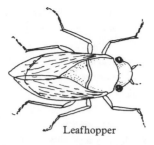
Leafhopper

feeding insects. They move by erratic flight or by jumping, and are found both in the greenhouse and in the garden. Adults, nymphs and cast skins may all be present together. The rose leafhopper causes the leaves to become mottled or spotted white, and even wholly white if the infestation is severe. Premature leaf fall may result. Leafhoppers produce honey dew, encouraging sooty mould, and can transmit viral diseases.

The insects are pale yellow to light green and about 7mm long. Females lay eggs on shoots or the underside of leaves in autumn. The eggs hatch in spring and mature by late summer, when the females lay eggs, which hatch in early autumn, producing adults which lay overwintering eggs.

Froghoppers have long, powerful hind legs, and are rather sturdier than leafhoppers. They, too, are sap-feeding insects. The nymphs, which are pale, feed on stems and leaves, and sometimes roots, under masses of froth, commonly called cuckoo spit. They may be easily dislodged by jets of water.

Attack by *Empoasca vitis* is more serious and the loss of leaves is often so great that the plant pines away and dies. The tips of affected leaves turn brown and later curl up. This sort of damage is reminiscent of burning. No antidote to this is known. A serious attack by *Empoasca* can be forestalled by substances containing malathion or pyrethrum.

Shieldbugs

These are beak insects resembling chafers with an articulated sucking snout and unequal sized front and back wings. The most common bug on fuchsias is the parent bug (*Elasmuchea grisea*), which is most commonly found in birchwoods. Full grown bugs are about 10mm long. They are green and brown, recognizable by the triangular shield behind the head. They are often known as stink bugs, because of the pungent smell produced by some species – when they are disturbed they empty their smelly glands with their hind legs.

Shieldbugs overwinter as eggs deposited by the female under the bark of the plant by means of the ovipositor, in July and August. In April to May the first larvae emerge. When they are adult, the parent bug lays

30–40 eggs on the underside of the leaf, where the female will sit on them for two or three weeks. The green larvae are a little bigger than aphids, from which they differ by their visibly red eyes and their fast walk. If you place a cloth under a shrub with aphids and shieldbug larvae and then tap the branches, the insects will fall onto the cloth. If the green ones stay put they are aphids, if they run off they are bugs.

Shieldbugs and their larvae feed on plant juice sucked from the leaves and shoots, where they stick their sucking snouts into the still unopened leaves and buds. When the leaves and flowers open, they look as if they have been riddled with pinholes surrounded by brown tissue, which dies off. Shoots can be seriously damaged and fail to develop, so that subsidiary buds open and cause misshapen, woody growth at the tips of the stems.

Because of the noxious smell, they have few natural enemies. If you find only a single bug, it is best to try to catch it and to cut out and destroy the growth points carrying larvae. Another method is to spray with a horticultural soap solution, as described for aphids. Only if the infestation is serious should one consider using a chemical remedy, including malathion or pyrethrum.

Mealybugs

Fuchsias may be troubled by both kinds of mealybug – the glasshouse mealybug and root mealybug. These are small insects, up to 4mm long, with roundish bodies covered by white, waxy powder.

Colonies may develop on stems and in leaf axils, and they are common on cacti, where they gather on spines. They cover plant surfaces with honey dew and often, as a result, sooty mould, and they weaken plants. They are difficult to control because they favour inaccessible places on plants and they are protected by the waxy coating. Small infestations may be cured by using a small paintbrush dipped in a solution of malathion. Systemic insecticides, including dimethoate, should be used because non-systemic sprays are of little avail.

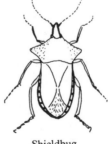

Shieldbug

A biological control is available in the form of the predatory *Crypolaemus*, a black and orange ladybird. In the greenhouse this has proved successful.

Root mealybug (*Rhizoecus* spp.), a common plague of cacti, which are kept in dry soils, develops on roots and on the bases of stems. You will usually spot evidence of an infestation when you are re-potting plants – they leave bluish-white deposits on the root ball. Immerse an infected root ball in a solution of malathion. Prevention involves keeping the compost around the soil moist at all times.

Next, a brief account of pests that do minor harm to fuchsias and for which it is best not to use protective remedies; the methods given will help to limit the damage.

Caterpillars

These rarely attack fuchsia leaves, because they dislike the sharp calcium dioxide crystals on the leaves. Only one species does not mind these crystals and constantly eats fuchsia leaves – the beautiful Scarce Swallowtail butterfly (*Iphiclides podalirius*) – and can quickly denude a fuchsia. They are best transferred to other plants whose leaves they like, such as willow-herb, where the butterfly itself is sometimes seen.

This caterpillar has a small head and a small trunk on the thick grey body. When threatened or disturbed, it retracts its head. Once sated it creeps into the soil where it pupates.

Snails and slugs

On the whole, snails and slugs cause little damage to fuchsias, mostly gnawing only a few leaves, but they do disfigure the leaves with their slimy trails. They rasp the leaf tissue with their toothed tongues, and they are especially found of young shoots, which they eat at night.

Slugs are the more destructive of the two, and snails can easily be picked off by hand. Both like well-mulched soils with a high organic content, moisture, warmth and darkness. Both dry out in sunny, dry conditions. The more favourable their environment, the faster they multiply, by means of eggs laid in the soil.

To keep damage to a minimum, restrict the potential hiding places in soil or pots by regularly removing fallen leaves and flowers. Rather than putting down slug pellets, try to catch them in inverted pots containing damp straw (which will also help catch vine weevils).

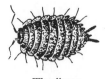

Woodlouse

Woodlice

These regularly occur in a greenhouse, where they are found under fallen leaves, in rotting wood and on other decaying vegetable matter. They avoid light and often crawl into and under flowerpots. At night they can cause some damage to the fleshy parts, especially of young fuchsias, and leaves and stalks are irregularly gnawed near the soil.

To counter this damage, regularly uncover hiding places to catch the creatures. You can catch them in handfuls of damp hay, an old damp rag or half a hollowed potato. Clear away all fallen leaves and other debris which attracts them into the greenhouse in the first place.

Earthworms

These are useful animals which cause damage only to overwintering plants. If an earthworm gets into the container and you do not pot on the plant until February or if, on re-potting, you do not shake them from the earth ball, it can survive only by feeding on healthy roots. In spring will you notice the pining plant and observe that they have lost most of their roots. When re-potting, watch for worms crawling away. Small heaps of casts under a pot show that there is a worm in the pot. Keep the pot wet with tepid water for some time or tap the pot to encourage the worms to come to the surface, when they can be transferred to the garden.

Bumble-bees

These are useful insects, but they have the bad habit of damaging the crowns of several small-flowered species such as 'Mephisto' and 'Rose van der Berg'. In large-flowered fuchsias the bees can crawl into the crown looking for honey. So that they do not fall out, they wedge themselves more or less tightly among the stamens and petals. With a small flower this is impossible: the bee has to hang from the petals, striking the hooks on its forelegs into some of them and damaging them. This causes the petals to turn dark and shrivel. This is unfortunate but does not greatly disfigure the plant.

Moulds and fungi

Moulds and fungi of one kind or another occur in many plant collections. In some cases these are useful; some plants, for example, can exist only in symbiosis with a specific fungus. Other fungi help to dispose of diseased plants or vegetal remains, although sometimes too much so. For recognition, here are the kinds that might occur in a fuchsia collection:

Fuchsia rust

Rust fungi are true parasites that are hard to grow outside living cells. Flower growers particularly fear Japanese rust (*Puccinia horiana*), which affects chrysanthemums, and pelargonium rust (*Puccinia pelargonii-zonalis*), since these two kinds do not change host.

The rust that affects fuchsias, *Pucciniastrum epilobii*, does so change, from godetia to willow-herb with silver spruce as an intermediate stage if needed. The fungus sits on the underside of leaves as orange-brown spots. As the spores become more numerous the leaves shrivel and dry out. The spores develop special feeding structures within the host leaves so that they can drain nutrient from the plant without actually killing it. If the rust reaches an advanced stage, many leaves fall off and the plant can die.

Rust is often introduced through plants brought in or bought as gifts. It spreads readily via the spores. Some fuchsias – 'Fiona', 'Symphony' and 'Lolita', for example – seem more sensitive to infection. Rust overwinters as spores with a thicker wall.

One of the best preventative measures is to plant as few intermediate hosts as possible. New plants should be regularly checked for rust during the first few weeks, and any infected plants are best isolated and nipped back to an uninfected leaf. The affected leaves must be destroyed, preferably by being burned. After handling infected plants, carefully wash your hands and make sure you do not transmit spores on your clothes.

Rust is difficult to fight because it adheres so closely to the plant tissue, although some fungicides are effective. Fungicides containing copper sulphate can be used; spray at intervals of ten to fourteen days. If you neglect a rust infection, the whole soil may become tainted, in which case the whole top layer must be dug up and removed.

Botrytis

Grey mould (*Botrytis cinerea*) is a parasite on weak plants and is one of the most troublesome of all fungal infections as it can affect such a wide variety of plants. In conditions favourable to the mould, healthy plants may become infected, too, especially those that do not grow very fast.

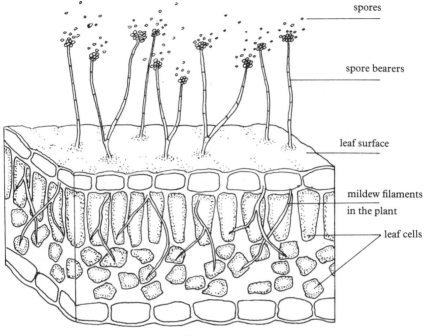

spores

spore bearers

leaf surface

mildew filaments
in the plant

leaf cells

Botrytis

On infected tissue a greyish-brown mould develops. This contains millions of spores, which readily drift off. In fuchsias it occurs also under the bark where it is difficult to fight and it is, in addition, easy to confuse grey mould with root rot (see below).

Grey mould grows in cool and damp conditions and overwinters on dead material or as sclerotia in the soil. High humidity in a greenhouse promotes infection, so that regular ventilation and warmth are needed. Remove all dead leaves and flowers, but take care not to allow the spores to drift off.

If plants in your greenhouse are regularly infected with mould, spray with a fungicide containing benomyl or thiophanate-methyl.

Root rot

This is caused by the moulds *Phytophthora nicotianae* or *Pythium spinosum*. These enter through the roots. *Phytophthora* can spread via water or air (for example by soil splashing up when watered). The plants wilt, and the stalks can turn brown, which streaks the bark at the foot.

A plant that suddenly wilts in very wet compost but the stalks above ground do not show discolouring or mould formation, may have *Pythium*

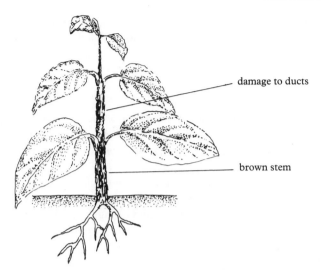

damage to ducts

brown stem

Root rot: effect of the mould *Phytophthora*

mould in the roots. This causes black rot on the bark layer of the roots. The ends of the roots become nothing more than thin, wiry cylinders. The spores spread via the moist tissue.

Remove and destroy all infected plants and thoroughly wash the containers with a horticultural disinfectant. For prevention, ensure optimal

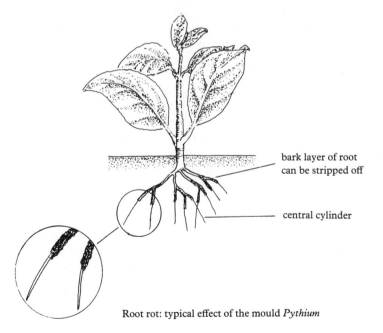

bark layer of root can be stripped off

central cylinder

Root rot: typical effect of the mould *Pythium*

hygienic conditions in the greenhouse. The moulds thrive in high relative humidity; regular ventilation and warmth will help lower its incidence.

Safe Handling

The only rule for the safe handling of all chemical products is to realize that they are all poisonous, even if this is not stated on the packing. The most dangerous may bear a black cross on the packet or the words 'Harmful' or 'Irritant'.

Many such substances can penetrate through the skin, so remember to wear gloves and boots when spraying. The skin should be protected particularly while you are preparing the spray and filling the can or atomizer. Use a funnel to avoid splashing the liquid, and if any liquid gets on to your skin, rinse immediately in clean water.

Prepare the solution in the open. Never leave either the product itself or the solution you have mixed unattended. Do not prepare too much, and do not store excess solutions in misleading containers, such as lemonade bottles. Check that after use the reservoir of the hand atomizer or pressure nozzle is empty, spraying any that is left over in another part of the garden, and do not pour it into a drain or gutter. Thoroughly rinse the reservoir of a hand-atomizers, which seem to be particularly attractive to children.

Do not eat, drink or smoke while using these substances, and do not inhale the spray – you might want to tie a handkerchief over your mouth or wear a mask as an additional precaution. Take care that the spraying mist does not drift into your eyes and that it does not settle on food, drink or animal food. Take care that no garden fruit that may have been contaminated by spray is eaten soon afterwards. If you have an ornamental pond, take care that spray does not drift into the water, where it may kill your goldfish. If you are spraying in a greenhouse, keep the door locked or securely fastened immediately afterwards.

The best time for spraying is at dusk in still weather and on dry plants. If it is sunny, leaves may be burnt by spray, and in the evening there are fewer useful insects on flowers at dusk.

After spraying, clear up everything and wash your hands and arms. Keep all chemicals under lock and key if possible, and certainly well away from children. Make sure they are kept in the original container, so that there can be no doubt about what is being used and so that the manufacturer's instructions are not misplaced. Liquid products must not be allowed to freeze because that usually makes them useless.

chapter 9

Winter Care

If fuchsias are to be enjoyed the following year, they must be suitably stored in autumn for overwintering. Except for a few winter-hardy fuchsias, which are discussed in Chapter 15, fuchsias cannot cope with the kind of winters we experience in northern Europe.

So what is the best way to help them through winter? This will depend on the species and varieties you grow; on how many plants you have; and on how much space is available for them. It also depends on how the plants are grown – whether they are in pots or in large containers, or are planted out in the garden.

First of all, it is important to consider how fuchsias behave. In autumn, as days become shorter and temperatures begin to fall, growth slows down, no new buds are formed and leaves begin to fall off as the plants prepare themselves for winter rest, and this is the time to store them. Depending on weather, this should be done in October. For some weeks before storing, do not water plants in containers, and if the weather is rather wet, move them to a dry place. If you have plants growing in the garden, dig them up and put them into pots. Alternatively, you can deal with them as described below.

All the plants should be cut back now, which reduces the amount of storage space required. Remove thin, non-woody stems and any broken or damaged ones. Use sharp secateurs or a knife to make clean cuts. To prevent rotting, take off any remaining leaves and flowers, which will also remove any insects, such as aphids and whitefly, which may be left on the plants.

Young, non-woody plants are treated differently because they still lack adequate reserves to winter without leaves. Try to keep them growing in a light, moderately warm spot – about 10°C. You should treat cuttings being raised to standard shape in the same way. To overwinter older plants in pots, take the plants out of the containers or dig them up from the garden, and use your secateurs or a sharp knife to cut off the thick roots that are no longer forming hair roots. Check the root balls for the larvae of the vine weevil and for other insect pests.

Remove plants growing in pots by gently tapping the edge of the pot to release the plant and then examine the soil for moulds and insects. If all seems well, put the plant into a clean pot and leave it until next year: the plant does not need food in winter, and the soil must not be too wet or the roots will rot.

Make sure that the name tags are still legible and securely attached, but fastened in such a way that they do not crush any shoots. If new tags are needed, write them with a water-resistant pencil so that you do not have to guess the name later on.

For storing your fuchsias, a frost-free greenhouse kept about 4.5°C is ideal. Triphylla hybrids need a slightly higher temperature and can be put on higher shelves. A warm greenhouse – one in which the temperature is 15°C or higher – is not suitable because the plants would continue growing and require more light than is available in winter.

The compost in the pot should be on the dry side, but not completely dry. The plants need hardly any water, and the danger is often that they get too much rather than too little. The stems and crowns of standard fuchsias can be kept from drying out by occasional misting with water.

To stop the temperature in the greenhouse rising too much on sunny days, remember to ventilate it in good time.

If your greenhouse cannot be heated and you do not have any heated trays, it is better to store the plants out of the pots, a method similar to storing them in a hole in the ground, which is discussed below. If you do not have a greenhouse, a conservatory or an unheated attic room will do, provided the room is light and frost free. Prepare the fuchsias in the same way as for storage in a greenhouse. A cellar, outhouse, garage or barn will do equally well, just as long as it is frost free.

Before allowing them to re-grow in spring, move the plants to a lighter, warmer place for a short period. Always check them regularly throughout the winter months to make sure that they do not dry out completely. If the plants continue growing they are too warm or moist, so lower the temperature and keep the compost drier.

There must always be adequate light. When they are stored in the dark, plants sometimes develop white shoots, because chlorophyll, which gives leaves their green colour, cannot be formed in the absence of light. These shoots can be removed without harming the plant. Another method is to supply extra light by special horticultural lighting; there are bulbs which are specially produced for greenhouses.

All these methods involve you in checking your plants regularly for almost half the year, but your reward will come when the flowers appear in the summer.

Because of the work involved, some gardeners prefer to grow new plants from cuttings taken in late summer, keeping them growing throughout the winter so that they will flower the following year. This technique does not produce huge plants or well-grown standard fuchsias, however, and a heated greenhouse is needed to overwinter the cuttings.

Another way to solve the problem of winter care is to store the plants in a hole. Provided that ground-water levels are low – remember that they can rise appreciably in winter – dig a hole 80–100cm deep – the width and length will depend on the number and size of the plants you have to store. To stop it caving in, dig the edges so that they slope outwards at a slight angle.

The plants are put into the hole without pots. If you have dug up plants from the garden, shake their roots well and cut away any thick roots as described above. Examine the root balls carefully for insects and moulds, and trim the plant as closely as possible. Remove all immature and thin stems and cut off all leaves, flowers and buds. The plants are going to be out of sight for some time, and you cannot be too careful in the precautionary measures you take. Standard fuchsias should be treated in the same way, but keep the shape of the crown.

Triphylla hybrids may survive this treatment, but the problem is that the next year they will flower far too late. It is better to plant them in pots in late summer or early autumn and keep them growing throughout winter, so that they can be brought out with flowers in spring. 'Chang', too, does not winter well this way, flowering with difficulty and rather late. It is better to replant this cultivar. As far as other cultivars are concerned, however, you can confidently let them overwinter in a hole.

After checking the name tags, lay the plants sideways in the hole, up to three layers deep. Standard plants should be laid horizontally with any intervening space filled with smaller plants, although they should all lie as flat as possible. This makes them produce better shoots in spring than if they winter vertically, quite apart from the fact that you need a deeper hole for standing plants. When you have placed three layers carefully in the hole – do not throw the plants down, but treat them gently – it is advisable to add a dusting of fungicidal powder. Then fill the hole almost to the rim with peat, making sure that all the plants are covered. The peat must not be moistened, but should be spread directly from the bale or bag over the plants. A pressed bale is best. In spring, the peat can be put into bags for re-use next time, or it can be used in the garden to improve the soil (it makes the soil more acid). Instead of peat you can use the dry leaves of beech, chestnut or hazel trees, but not oak. The leaves must be dry and free from mildew and pests, and although peat is more expensive, it is certainly safer in this respect.

When the peat is about 15cm from the top of the hole, provide some extra insulation by laying some sheets of hardboard over the hole. Then lay some strong wooden beams across the hole. Railway sleepers are ideal,

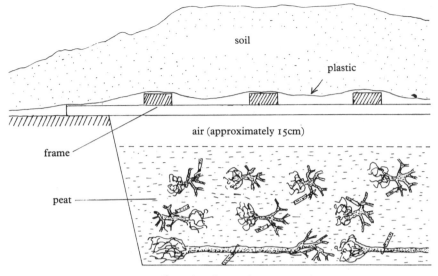

Overwintering cuttings

provided that they have not been newly treated with a tar-based preservative. Lay a stiff sheet of plastic over the top of the sleepers so that it reaches at least 25cm beyond the edges of the hole. Finally, heap the soil you took out of the hole over the sheet, sloping the sides so that rain water runs away rather than downwards. This pile of soil is heavy and becomes even heavier as it rains, which is why the beams must be strong.

Instead of sleepers or beams, you could use a flat tray to cover the hole completely. The top of the tray should be covered with several layers of newspaper, and the strong plastic sheet can be spread over the newspaper and held down with earth around the edges. This method means that you only have to move the soil once.

If ground-water levels are too high for digging a hole in the garden, you can bury plants under cover. An ideal place for this is in a shed or cool greenhouse – under a bench, for example. Dig out a small area (mind the foundations), protect the sides with hardboard, especially if they are near windows, and store the plants as described above. The hole should be dusted with anti-mildew powder and covered with peat. For extra protection use wicker mats or canvas. During frosty weather check regularly that the temperature does not fall too low; in mild weather, ventilate the shed or greenhouse and keep the peat reasonably moist to prevent it from drying out.

In a normal winter you will have no problems. Sometimes, however, winters can be exceptionally cold. If you have no greenhouse, you can use large, deep plastic trays or an old, deep insulated box. The procedure is as described before. The tray or box is first surrounded with sheets of hardboard or with a lid. If the position is neither too cold nor too warm, you need pay no further attention to this 'hole' throughout winter.

Depending on the weather, the fuchsias should be brought out again in early March. Carefully remove the covering and the peat, and the plants will be revealed, just like surprise parcels in a bran tub. You may find that some shoots have developed in the dark, but these will be white ones, because of lack of chlorophyll, and they can be cut off. Sometimes hair roots will have grown, and some plants may look dead. If you scratch the surface of the stem with a fingernail and green shows underneath, the plant is alive.

Examine the fuchsias before you pot them up, removing dead or wrongly growing branches. Take care, however, because fuchsias flower on young twigs: only new shoots will produce flowers. Do not cut off the name tags.

Look for suitably sized, thoroughly clean pots. When you are potting up, you can trim a root further – the few root hairs lost in this way will soon be replaced. Inspect roots for the creamy white larvae of the vine weevil. If necessary the whole root ball can be rinsed in tepid water. If everything looks all right, pot the plant, pushing the compost well down between the roots but not too tightly, and fill the pot to within 2.5cm or so of the rim, which makes watering easier.

If you have many plants, you can take a few days to complete the process, potting a few at a time. As long as they do not dry out, those fuchsias without compost will come to no harm. You can cover them with bags or plastic sheets while you attend to the others.

After potting, put the fuchsias in a light and fairly warm spot, keep them moist but not too wet, and mist regularly until new shoots begin to appear. This treatment is vital for standard plants.

Plants in new compost will not need be treated with fertilizer for the first 4–6 weeks, but plants that have been kept in pots, and those that have

'Kaboutertje'

not been put in new pots before wintering, will need potting into a fresh medium. Check the root ball as described above. If you have plants that have been in the same compost for a year, you must apply fertilizer now because too few nutrients will remain for swift new growth.

Some additional wintering methods fall outside the scope of this book, and it is possible that one of those would be more appropriate for you and your garden than those mentioned here.

If, occasionally, a fuchsia does not survive the winter, remember that a fellow enthusiast will almost certainly be able to provide a cutting, so all will not be lost.

chapter 10

Fuchsias in the Greenhouse

Raising fuchsias is one of the most rewarding of pastimes, but the main problem is the length of the flowering period. We do not live in the tropics but in a temperate climate, with a natural growing season that lasts from mid-May to mid-October. In these five months the plant must develop shoots, grow leaves and buds and also produce flowers. Some artifice on our part is needed to make sure that all this happens smoothly.

A keen amateur grower who has mastered the essentials of growing fuchsias will have bought some plants from a garden centre and found that he can keep them alive through the winter. At first this is easy: it is always possible to find a frost-free corner indoors in which a few fuchsias can be overwintered. However, if you are an enthusiast, you will acquire ever more plants, and there will come the time when all the spare corners are full of bare and ugly plants and your family begins to curse your hobby. At this point, other methods must be found, and you decide to get a greenhouse.

Before taking this step, stop and think. What will you use a greenhouse for? If it is simply going to be for winter storage, you must decide how many fuchsias you are going to keep in the garden, because overwintering them requires space. There are no hard and fast rules. Some gardeners just want to put the plants in plastic flowerpots in the greenhouse, which they can do at a density of approximately twenty-five 18cm containers to a square metre or thirty-six 16cm containers to a square metre. Other gardeners prefer to take the fuchsias from the pots and bury them close together in soil in the greenhouse, although this can cause a few problems in spring. Still others like to stack the containers in the greenhouse, with some under the benches and staging, or on shelves in a lean-to greenhouse.

Because almost any greenhouse will inevitably become too small, buy or build the largest one you can.

Planning permission

It is better consult the local council to see what structures need planning permission and what do not. Regulations vary, and no general advice is possible.

If you rent your home, the owner must agree, and if nothing is stipulated in your rental agreement, the owner of the property will become the owner of any greenhouse you erect. It is far better to put down the details in writing.

Information about what can and cannot be built is available free from your local council, but you will have to pay for planning permission if it is required. If you have to submit plans to get permission, the manufacturer or supplier will often give you these for free. The planning laws take account of the effect any building on your property may have on your neighbours, and such matters as your neighbour's right to light must be respected. In addition, your building must be done in such a way that rain water does not drain onto your neighbour's property.

Buying or building a greenhouse

When you want to keep fuchsias only, the problem is not urgent – you have all summer to decide. However, if you wish to sow annuals, as well as potting a fair number of fuchsia cuttings, it is best to have a greenhouse ready as early as possible in the year, although the possibility of ground frost will delay things until March. For the purposes of this chapter, we shall consider a greenhouse built only to keep fuchsias over winter.

What type of greenhouse?

The main criterion is space. In most gardens this is so limited as to be the only factor determining your choice. If you have ample space, the choice will, obviously, be wider.

Lean-to or free-standing?

A free-standing greenhouse is always preferable, because it provides better levels of light and ventilation. Nevertheless, lean-to greenhouses do have some advantages: lower heating costs, easier installation of gas, electricity and so on, and a more uniform temperature during the day because the wall absorbs heat. Being in a lean-to greenhouse is not a handicap as far as fuchsias are concerned, as long as the sun shines in for part of the day to give slightly more than the minimum light levels needed. You should not, therefore, place a lean-to against a north- or south-facing wall.

A free-standing greenhouse is best, but there is little doubt that a lean-to is better than no greenhouse at all.

Wood or aluminium?

Your choice will depend largely on whether you are going to build it yourself, merely assemble it or employ a builder to do it for you.

Wood is easy to work with; double-glazing can be easily installed; the basic material is easy to obtain; and the finished greenhouse looks nicer. The drawbacks are that a wood frame needs regular maintenance and is less durable.

Aluminium, one the other hand, lasts forever. The problems are that it usually has complicated profiles, and installing the glass and keeping the framework clean is more difficult, especially if it stands near trees that shed leaves or needles.

Although it is not as nice to look at, aluminium is, in most respects, preferable.

Wooden D-I-Y greenhouse

If you decide to design and build a wooden type, first take a look at one that is already built. There are many kinds, ranging from large ones built out of old frames or windows (which is an excellent way of achieving what is needed), to well-designed and handsome glass shelters that are adapted to suit the environment.

A D-I-Y greenhouse can be designed to fit the available space, and designing and building it may satisfy your creative streak, but you must be good with your hands.

First, choose the right wood: it must be rot resistant. One of the most often used woods is red cedar, which is durable and not too heavy. Teak, too, is possible, but it is heavier and more expensive and, of course, is not an environmentally sound choice. A good alternative is treated pine, which is used for stakes and woven fences in the garden. It can be bought in ready-cut lengths from timber merchants. It will be green because it has been impregnated with a preservative, and you can treat it further with a coat of creosote or a more specialized product, of which there are many available from garden centres and D-I-Y stores.

Draw up a detailed plan and buy all the wood at once if you can. You may be able to get some bargains from a dealer in used or broken timber, and you may even be able to get some good pine, but you will have to saw it to length yourself (consult a D-I-Y guide). Use screws and bolts to hold the wooden framework together.

Building an aluminium greenhouse from a kit

Greenhouses are now popular items, and the trade has adjusted accordingly. Several different makes and styles are available, and although they differ in the profile of the aluminium struts and way in which the glass panes are held in place, they are fairly uniform in size and quality.

Building such a greenhouse needs some skill, building knowledge and commonsense, and you will probably need the help of one or two other people. The instructions supplied are usually clear enough for someone with little experience to follow.

Foundations

Whether your greenhouse has a wood or an aluminium framework, good foundations are vital. These are easier to provide on hard, sandy soil than on a soft loam. There are two main possibilities.

First, you could use artificial foundations bought from the supplier. These are often made of metal or concrete. Although shallow, such foundations will be sufficient for the average aluminium greenhouse. You could use ironwood (hornbeam) railway sleepers – oak or pine will not do. Such hard timber is almost impossible to lift, and working is difficult because only steel nails can be hammered in.

Alternatively, you can use concrete, which is preferable. The concrete foundation should be approximately 20–25 cm deep. The trench you will need to dig for this must be wide enough to allow access from both sides, otherwise it will be a messy job.

Secondhand materials

In areas where many greenhouses have been built, dealers will often sell secondhand parts of dismantled ones. The pieces are often still in quite good condition, and you can get all sorts of aluminium parts, including louvre windows, doors, panes, window handles and so forth at very reasonable prices, which will be a great saving. Ask for advice from an assistant about the best way to assemble the pieces you select.

Siting the greenhouse

We have already noted that a lean-to must not be placed against a north- or a south-facing wall, because it will get either too little or too much sun. Use an east- or west-facing wall.

If you are building a free-standing greenhouse your choice is wider. Fuchsias need quite a lot of light but too much sunlight must be avoided.

For many plants, the longitudinal axis of the greenhouse should be east-west, so that the sides face south, but for fuchsias it is better to avoid the sun; a fuchsia greenhouse should, therefore, run lengthways north-south, although this is not crucial, because you can, after all, introduce screens to provide protection against the sun.

It is far more important to site the greenhouse in a way that preserves the existing beauty of the garden. If you are going to be re-arranging your garden, consider the position of the greenhouse right at the beginning, making sure that it is not too conspicuous. Once you are happy with its position, arrange the remainder of the garden around it.

Furniture

Flooring

If plants are to be grown in the ground, all you will need is a central path. However, if you intend to work on staging or benches, the whole floor must be paved. The easiest method is to use concrete paving slabs, measuring 30 × 30cm. Gravel chippings can look attractive, but they have the disadvantage that dirt accumulates between the pebbles, which is not only untidy but also a source of disease, fungus and pests.

Staging

Most staging units for greenhouses are made of aluminium, which is expensive, but they are easy to use and to keep clean. If you are good at D-I-Y, however, there are many suitable and less expensive solutions.

So that you are comfortable while you work, the staging or benches must be adjusted to the correct height. Make sure they are not too low. The trestles on which the shelves stand can be of wood or metal.

Staging can be solid or slatted. Solid units are used if the plants are irrigated from below the pot (capillary watering), which is an excellent system if some fuchsias are to be kept in the greenhouse in summer, too. Large plastic trays from a garden centre are useful too. Synthetic resin sheets can be used, too, but they must have a wooden underlay. You will need to spread an absorbent layer of capillary matting or sand over such a surface.

Slatted staging lets through light and heat but it has the drawback that you must regularly check that the compost in the pots is moist, because it will dry out more quickly.

The shelving can be made of wooden planks or laths fixed to the frame at intervals. Alternatively, you can use strong, plasticized metal mesh, which is readily available and less expensive.

Heated propagating trays

Amateur growers will want to produce fair numbers of cuttings from their cultivars, whether to experiment or to grow large and beautiful plants for the summer, and some gardeners will want to keep plants for more than three years.

To propagate plants you will need a heated propagating tray. Seeds can be germinated in it and you will be able to root many cuttings. These trays can be bought at garden centres or from greenhouse suppliers.

The trays are rather small and may soon become inadequate for your needs, so another approach is to get an under-soil heating cable, preferably with thermostat. You will need about 90w per square metre, which means about 7.5 metres of cable. You can use either a rod thermostat or a type fixed to the end of the cable. The cable must lie in a layer of clean sand about 5cm deep. On top of the sand you should spread a 5cm layer of the growing medium. This is an excellent system.

Lighting in the greenhouse

Energy from light is vital for any plant to grow. Blue radiation is absorbed by the leaves and used to make chlorophyll. The plant senses where the source of the blue light is and turns towards it to get the maximum energy.

Chlorophyll is needed to make carbohydrates out of carbon dioxide from the air and water from the soil. The energy for this, too, comes from light. The transformation of carbon dioxide and water into nutrients is promoted by all visible light. If radiation is relatively weak, energy absorption is concentrated on some definite ranges. Red light is then very effective: it makes the plants shoot out of the ground, but leaf growth is limited. Blue radiation, too, is involved in the production of nutrients, but less so than in leaf formation. If there is too little light, therefore, plants cannot develop fully.

Various ways of providing light in the greenhouse are available. A normal light bulb can be useful while you are working in the greenhouse, but it will be less suitable for promoting growth. You will get better results if you use a special lighting colour (daylight or warm white) tubes. These must be placed about 50cm above the plants. Good quality lighting is also provided by a low-energy bulb, giving 700 lux at a daily cost of about 3 pence. You should reckon to have about 80w lighting per square metre. In most greenhouses, it is better to use a tube of, for example, 40w or 60w, 120cm or 154cm long, respectively. Low-energy 36w and 58w bulbs are also available. Sodium and mercury vapour lights are more powerful and provide 2,600 lux over about 20 square metres.

Whatever kind of bulb you use, the lights must be on for 12–14 hours each day whenever natural light is poor. An automatic switch is easy to add.

Heating your greenhouse

The oldest system, burning solid fuel (wood or coal) and the newest, using solar energy, are not discussed here.

The temperature level in the greenhouse will determine what you can grow, and what the heating cost will be. Four levels are usually considered:

● Tropical greenhouse: this requires a constantly high, almost tropical, temperature of the kind in which you might grow orchids. Providing this kind of heat is a costly business. One way of limiting cost is to instal a heating boiler in the greenhouse, thus eliminating conduction losses.

● Warm greenhouse: a temperature of about 10–12°C will allow many plants to continue to grow through the winter. Sustaining this temperature throughout winter is not cheap but is not prohibitively expensive.

● Cool greenhouse: frost-free greenhouses, in which the temperature is never lower than about 5°C, are most often used for many fuchsias. After February or March, depending on the available space, natural sunlight may produce temperatures greater than 10°C. A separate propagating tray works particularly well in this setting.

● Cold greenhouse: when there is no artificial heating, the temperature depends on that outside. Such a greenhouse is not suitable for overwintering fuchsias apart from winter-hardy ones.

Choosing a fuel

An oil stove is a good source of heat but, for various reasons, it is the least often used. Among the drawbacks are the constant need to provide adequate oil or paraffin; the associated maintenance and cleaning, and occasional water vapour and carbon dioxide fumes. These burners are actually very economical to use and offer the most efficient way of using what is now an expensive fuel. There are various models on the market, and they have been much improved of late.

Gas offers good, safe heating. Various systems are available, and the laying of pipes by experts, which is essential, is not too expensive. In many gas fires and cookers, the waste gases are drawn off by a pipe, which can sometimes be lengthened to extract some additional heat. A good gas stove or fire (preferably secondhand) with a thermocouple and adjustable thermostat temperature can be easily regulated and the cost of the device is not too great.

Other systems do not draw off waste gases. These produce some water and carbon dioxide. Some have four hoses to spread warm air over the floor. You must always make sure that there is sufficient oxygen in the greenhouse, perhaps by using a hose from outside to the heat source.

Providing heat by a system of pipes containing warm water was used long before more modern systems were known. The source heats water that is carried in the pipes, the warm water rises to the highest point of the circuit and then, under gravity, returns. If water circulation is sluggish, a pump can be installed to help. If you have solid fuel (wood or coal) this system is hardly feasible, but if you use oil it is an effective and widely used system. The hot-water pipe system provides the following heat when there is a difference of about 45°C between the temperature of the pipe and the air: pipes with diameters of 50mm, 60mm or 70mm give about 30w, 40w or 60w respectively. Before you dismiss hot water systems as outmoded, remember that they remain the most common form of central heating. It is an efficient and widely used method.

A boiler in the greenhouse with a system of pipes is a very economical way of heating, since the heat radiating from the boiler is used as well.

It can be fairly easy to connect pipes or radiators in a greenhouse that is very close to the house or into a lean-to and to link the greenhouse system with the domestic system. The temperature can be regulated by means of one or more thermostats. There is, however, the problem that the house thermostat is usually lowered at night. It is, therefore, best to have an extra thermostat and a three-way valve to ensure that the greenhouse is safely and effectively heated.

A further safety measure in the greenhouse is to install an electric heating system with a thermostat that switches on when the set minimum temperature is reached.

The most widely used heating system is provided by electricity, which is the most uniform heat distributor, especially when it is controlled by a thermostat. A very reliable and watertight heat source is the ribbed pipe cylinder.

Calculating the heat in the greenhouse

The heat required will be expressed in watts and kilowatts, for any system. Glass readily transmits sunlight and heat, which means that heat can easily escape, too. Other materials such as wood, brick and concrete, also transmit heat. The losses are as follows (in watts per square metre):

Glass – 3.5mm: 7.90
Wood – 2.5cm: 2.85
Brickwork – 11cm: 3.60; 22cm: 2.65; 27cm: 1.70
Concrete – 10cm: 4.25; 15cm: 3.45

By precisely calculating the quantities of each material that you have used in building the greenhouse, it is possible to work out the total heat loss and to find the optimum size of heat source to give the desired temperature.

As an example, let us look at a greenhouse 3 metres long, 2.4 metres wide and 1.8 metres high from the ground, with a roof side 1.3 metres wide. The glass surface (in square metres) consists of:

two sides	$2 \times 1.8 \times 3 = 10.8$
two gables	$2 \times 1.8 \times 2.4 = 8.64$
two roof sides	$2 \times 3 \times 1.3 = 7.8$
two gable tops	$= 1.2$

Which gives a total of 28.44 square metres. The heat loss for each square metre of glass 3.5mm thick is 7.9w, so that the total loss is $7.9 \times 28.44 = 225$w (to the nearest whole number) for each degree Celsius temperature difference. For 10°C this is 2250w = 2.25kw. The calculation must take into account not only the temperature required within the greenhouse, but also how cold and windy it is outside. Sometimes there are long periods of very low temperatures. It is, therefore, best to select a heat source somewhat larger than would be suggested by the above calculation.

Insulating the greenhouse with hessian or canvas and draughtproofing all the joins will enable you to limit heat loss to less than 3w per square metre (as against 7.9w for glass). Remember that when the greenhouse is completely insulated, you will need to provide a proper oxygen supply, especially for heaters using gas or oil.

Energy prices have changed a lot in recent years, which makes an accurate calculation of the costs almost impossible. Whatever the fuel – gas, electricity or oil – it makes economic sense to insulate the greenhouse, either partly or completely, in winter.

Insulation

Whatever is put between the outside air and the inside of the greenhouse contributes to the insulation. The material you use must, however, let through light, and so we are limited to plastics and glass. Double-glazing is the best form of insulation, and the greater the insulating gap, the better the results. For an amateur gardener, double-glazing can be installed only in a wooden greenhouse. To make it attractive, double-walled synthetic plates of various thickness can be bought. They are based on acrylic or polycarbon and are highly effective, easy to saw and strong. They let through 80–90 per cent of light but are subject to shrinkage and expansion and are rather expensive. If finances are limited, hessian is a good alternative. It lets through less light, but that hardly matters with fuchsias. In a greenhouse they must in any case be screened from the sun, a canvas-or hessian-insulated greenhouse saves some 40 per cent on heating. The most usual method is to insulate the side walls on the outside, fastening the material with silicon clips that can easily be glued to the panes with silicon mastic (the clips can be bought in garden centres).

The roof is covered with hessian from the inside, and the clips can be wedged in the aluminium posts. Along the top edge, the hessian should be sealed with tape to prevent dripping water from causing algae to form. An incidental advantage is that in summer it is quite easy to remove the hessian, clean it and store it for the next winter.

The simplest method to insulate is to use bubble-polythene. This is fixed in the same way as hessian and is cheap and effective.

Some suggestions and useful hints

If you are installing gas and electricity in your greenhouse, always use a professional. He can recommend the best type of pipes and the safest or most impermeable materials that should be used. He may also suggest that you need a separate electric installation.

Lighting for your plants can be switched on and off by hand, or by a time switch that functions automatically when it is overcast. Suppose you wanted to have the lights on between 6 a.m. and 8 p.m. if the natural daylight was inadequate. The switch could be set to go on at 6 a.m. and off at 8 p.m., and also set to go off automatically whenever there was sufficient daylight. Having two switches in series like this avoids wasting energy.

Using a normal thermostat, a battery and some low-current cable, it would be possible to rig up an alarm signal to indicate, for example, that the temperature was too low. There are various makes and models of high- or low-temperature alarms.

A reserve heating device that switches on when the temperature falls too low may also serve also as a safety measure, if the correct make is selected. A thermostat can switch on a ventilator when the temperature is too high, to expel the hot air. You could also arrange one or more roof lights to open or shut automatically. A 'baby phone', linked to the house by low-current cable and a battery supply, can also be useful.

If you are very good with your hands you can rig up various devices

11 'Carmel Blue'

12 'Come Dancing'

13 'Bicentennial'

14 'Monstera'

15 'Torch'

that will enable you to control the light level in the greenhouse without having to leave your house and to read off the greenhouse temperature on an analogue or digital indicator.

A hygrometer should be standard gear for any greenhouse. Mildew must have no chance of become established in winter, so the air must be kept fairly dry. When the plants are ready to resume growth, humidity must rise considerably. Relative humidity should be between 60 and 70 per cent.

Finally, it is vital to have a minimum-maximum thermometer, showing the lowest and highest temperature in a day.

Pests and diseases

Ideally, all pests should be kept out of a greenhouse by means of preventive measures. An essential procedure is to give the greenhouse a thorough cleaning with water and a dose of horticultural cleaner in spring and autumn. Preventive spraying with a protective compound is also to be recommended.

Controlling the humidity is a matter of judgment. If the air is too moist, grey mould (*Botrytis cinerea*) will be encouraged to spread, but fuchsias dislike a climate that is too dry. The atmosphere in the greenhouse should be moist but not saturated. A ventilator is therefore vital.

'Chickadee'

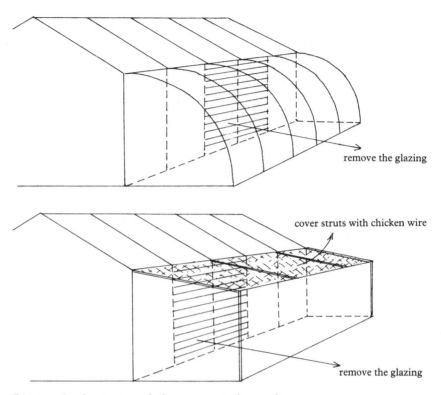

remove the glazing

cover struts with chicken wire

remove the glazing

Diagrams showing structure of a frame annexe to the greenhouse.
If possible, use curved plastic tubes as framework (top diagram); if posts
and slats are used (lower diagram), the plastic sheeting will need
chicken wire as a support

Cold frames

Fuchsias must be started into growth as early as possible in the year. If
flowers are to last as long as possible, the plants must be taken out early in
March, re-potted if necessary and put into a well-lit, warm spot. They
cannot be left outdoors before about mid-May, because frosts may occur,
although if you live in a coastal area, the last frosts will be about two weeks
earlier.

To provide the correct level of light, fresh air and a suitable temperature you can use plastic tubes or posts and slats to make a frame over
which you can stretch a medium to thick translucent plastic sheet. This
will, in effect, be a frame annexe to the greenhouse. If it is practicable,
remove some glass panes from the greenhouse wall against which the
frame will stand so that the heat in the greenhouse will warm the frame as

well. The plastic tubes should be curved. If you use posts and slats, the roof will need to be supported on a framework of chicken-wire so that the plastic sheet does not sag when it rains.

You can now buy a walk-in tunnel made wholly of heavy-duty plastic, which can be set up in the garden whenever you need it; it can serve as an alternative greenhouse for which no planning permission is needed.

Roof greenhouses

A greenhouse can be built on the roof of a garage or as a shed annexe. Local authority planning approval is not enough: the roof must be safe to bear your weight as you walk about. This is quite a complicated structure, and it lies outside the scope of this book. However, if you have the appropriate site, it is a good solution and well worth considering.

Sources

Beckett, Kenneth A. , *Plants Under Glass*
Bruin, E. de, *Een kas in eigen tuin*
Graafland, Christiaan, *Alles over broeikassen*
Hayden, Nickey, *Bezig zijn met kweken in kas en back*
Robinson, G. W. , *The Cool Greenhouse*

chapter 11

Grafting

Grafting fuchsias is done on a rootstock, in much the same way as has long been done with trees, especially apples and pears. In the Netherlands, for example, at a time when plants were grown only from seedlings, apple rootstocks were brought from the experimental fruit-growing station at East Malling in Britain. Today, growers all over Europe use virus-free stock for fruit growing. The stock may have a great or only little influence on the plant's growth, flowering, fertility, time of ripening, colour, size, keeping qualities and so on. For fruit growers the most important factors are early production, better fruit colour and low-growing trees.

The use of rootstocks has also completely transformed the growing of roses. At one time only *Rosa canina* was known; then there was *Rosa rubiginosa*. The rootstock was taken from the woody stems of selected forms of the dog rose.

The rootstock for rowans (*Sorbus* spp.) used always to be hawthorn or *Sorbus aucuparia*, the ordinary rowan or mountain ash. However, the roots anchored badly. The situation has greatly improved since *Sorbus intermedia* (Swedish whitebeam) has been used as rootstock. The change has resulted in trees that produce far more berries.

Throughout the world, vines and many citrus fruits are grown on rootstock. In the national plant nursery at the Hague crossings with *Prunus incisa* (Fuji cherry) were made, from which a dwarf rootstock for cherries was obtained, but all the records were lost during the Second World War, and picking cherries without ladders became just another dream, but happily a dwarfing rootstock is now available again.

Walnuts (*Juglans regia*) were always grown from seeds, and they still are. In practice only about one in two hundred such trees was healthy and regularly productive. To preserve the good qualities of certain clones, they are grafted onto rootstock, and there are now special kinds with properties such as winter hardiness (to $-40°C$), very high fertility, apomixis (asexual reproduction, no pollen), equal flowering of male and female flowers, good health and so on – indeed, there are clones that need props when fruit is plentiful to prevent the branches from breaking under their weight. There can be drawbacks too, however, for it has been known

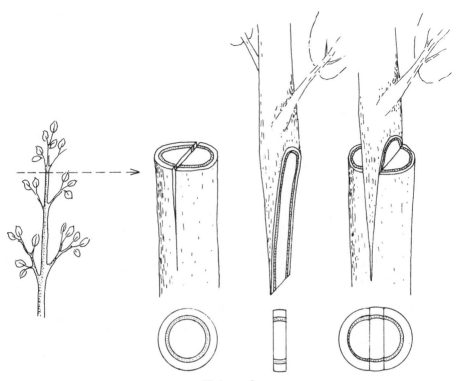

Wedge graft

for elms to be blown down in a storm because they were standing on the wrong type of stock.

Now let us turn to grafting fuchsias. The rootstock must be able to enhance the growth of the scion (the grafted piece), which is always a weak grower. We must, therefore, start with a vigorous, sturdy plant that can be easily and quickly raised and that will grow along with the scion. The bark must not be too soft, because it may suffer damage. The stock must last for many years, reaching, say, 10–14cm in circumference. Among the suitable cultivars are 'Monsieur Thibaut', 'Corallina', 'Mrs Popple', 'Checkerboard', 'Cardinal' and the like. They grow fast and are soon able to support scions. In addition, they are stiff enough to go on standing straight without being propped. On these we can graft cultivars that will not produce such vigorous stock without much effort, such as 'Auntie Jinks', 'Baby Chang', 'Cascade', 'Cecile', 'Harry Gray', 'Nellie Nuttall', 'Postiljon', 'Pussy Cat', 'Vobeglo', 'Elfriede Ott', 'Leverkusen', 'Trumpeter', 'Humbolt Holiday', 'Pop Whitlock' and some species.

These cultivars can be grafted onto stock 1.1m high or higher if you

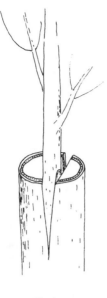

Detail of a wedge graft where the scion is smaller in circumference than the rootstock

wish. Shorter stock can be used, but it hardly makes sense to use it, unless significantly stronger and better growth is wanted. Certainly, strongly growing rootstock has a good effect on the growth of weakly growing scions.

It is by no means impossible, indeed, it is very likely, that certain combinations are incompatible. This will show itself in yellow leaves, bad growth, dying shoot tips and, ultimately, by the graft as a whole breaking off. If this happens, the combination must be abandoned.

Although further research is awaited, the best time for grafting seems to be in March or April. Use strong secateurs to cut off the selected rootstock about 5cm above the area chosen for the graft. Trim back all branches to between two and four leaves, and give the plant little or no water. Do not cut off all the branches from the stock; you need to keep a few sap-drawing branches on the plant. Grafting can take place between eight and ten days later.

Wedge grafting

The best and simplest method is wedge grafting. The method takes well on the stock and is unlikely to break off.

Having chosen the cultivar to be grafted, set aside a few plants in winter. Keep them free from botrytis, and place them in a light position. Do not cut them back at all and give them little water. This will produce a good stock. Make sure that the plants have good buds that will produce strong shoots.

Never use grafting wood from plants that have been overwintered. Good stock must be grown on, but even more important is raising good grafting wood.

To graft, cut off the rootstock 3–4cm below where it was cut before, and make a split in the centre to a depth of no more than 4–5cm. Into it carefully slip the graft, which you will previously have cut to a wedge shape. Use a grafting hook to bend open the split a little so that you can more easily insert the graft without damaging the scion. The cambium layers of each plant stem must be in contact. Do not make the grafts too long; 8–10cm long at the most, and the shorter the better, provided that there are well-developed axil buds on it. Wind plastic tape around the cleft (the type used in growing fruit trees) and fasten it in place. If the top edge of the stock remains open, cover it with grafting wax but do not wholly close it, or the top edge and cleft will dry out and the scion will not take. Take care that the wax is not too hot, otherwise the stock and scion will be burnt. If you have to shorten the scion, either from the top or the side or even both, the cuts must be covered with wax. The wax must be fluid but not too hot, and it can be softened over a spirit burner. Do not use paint or other products for covering wounds on trees, because these may contain substances that will prove fatal to the tender graft.

Next, put a small polythene bag over the scion and tie it below the graft. This prevents the scion and its leaves from drying out. Place it out of direct sunlight, otherwise the temperature in the bag will become too high, and use a syringe to put a few drops of water into the bag – do this only once – to stop it drying out.

At the point where the grafting wood is taken off, spray regularly against botrytis. Do not cut off all the twigs from the stock and keep a few sap-drawing stems on. These can be removed after two months, when the crown is growing well. Do this gradually. Between ten and fourteen days after grafting, loosen the bags and remove them completely after a few days.

To acquire skill and experience in grafting fuchsias, practise on 'Dominyana', which is a good rootstock, and you can sometimes graft two or three scions onto a single plant, or work with shorter stock such as bush fuchsias. My own record is thirty scions on one bush of 'First Success'.

Summer grafts on soft wood succeed too – I have had 100 per cent success. Use wedge grafts and cover each one with a small plastic bag – do not spray water inside. Remove the bags after about eight days.

Grafting on pear or cherry trees is also carried out in autumn. The aim is to make sure that the cambium takes and that the scion will not send out shoots. You can try autumn grafting with fuchsias too. I have only tried it once, on a single plant after a failure with another graft. There must not be too much growth on the stock. You can pot it on between eight and fourteen days before grafting, which slows down growth for a while.

Test grafts will show which stock is best. At first, keep to only one cultivar – some suitable cultivars are noted above and my own favourite is 'Pussy Cat' – otherwise you will not be able to compare your results. You should make notes later on about any differences in growth, time of flowering, colour, compatibility and so on. You can then start working with other cultivars.

'String of Pearls'

It is likely that using a rootstock of a cultivar that flowers in winter – 'First Success', for example – will produce earlier flowering plants, while one that naturally flowers later, such as 'Fanfare', will produce later flowering fuchsias.

What effect can the rootstock have on colour? The many combinations give much scope, and you must experiment to see what happens. There are so many potential combinations that one person alone cannot do it all. It would take a team working exclusively on the project, and even so it would take several years.

Is grafting essential? Fuchsia cuttings grow readily and keep the characteristics of the parent plant, but this does not tell us what we want to know, which is how the rootstock can affect a plant. Neither process need be merely experimental. Some cultivars produce much more handsome standard shapes when they have been grown as grafts, and this fact alone may lead enthusiasts for that form to experiment. Throughout history, improvements and novelties have often been developed by amateur growers.

Source

Garner, R. J., *The Grafter's Handbook*

chapter 12

Improving Fuchsias

Since Man evolved from being a hunter-gatherer to being a farmer, which involve cultivating all his produce, we have found it necessary to 'alter' wild plants and animals in various ways so that the cultivated forms give better yields than their wild ancestors. If we did not, the Earth could not sustain the 5,000 million people now on it.

The first step is to select stronger or more suitable forms that occur in nature. Now that we know this greater suitability or 'fitness' is due to heredity and we have learnt to manipulate it, we can make forms more attractive to us by 'improving' them.

As far as decorative plants such as fuchsias are concerned, the improvement is largely a matter of bringing about different looks and greater beauty, although this does not necessarily exclude greater usefulness, especially in new cultivars. There are many handsome, large-flowered, orange fuchsias, but how many of them will remain in flower for a whole season under normal circumstances? How resistant to rust are they?

Beauty is an awkward concept, involving as it does questions of subjective taste and fashion. Is size important? You may like a new seedling, but someone else may find it disappointing, and another grower at a different time may have different points of reference and hold a different opinion.

Growing novelties can be a risky business, but an unusual plant can bring success. You might think that every possible combination already exists, but what about a double fuchsia with a pure white calyx, the tube of *F. procumbens* and the yellow petals of *F. splendens* in the shape of 'Ting-a-Ling'? Or consider the colour of the fairly small petals of *F. excorticata*. Some improvers achieved this colour in free-flowering cultivars, and 'Highland Pipes' is one of the most obvious successes.

There is scope for new combinations, especially with the genetic material currently available. Only a very few of the known species fuchsias are used for improving, and there remains much unknown material in the wild, which will be discovered sooner or later.

Improvement comes about either through the mutation of existing material or by the crossing or hybridization of different plants to produce new cultivars.

Mutations

Mutations can occur in nature, and they can lead, for example, to multi-coloured leaves, which contain less chlorophyll and therefore grow less strongly, so that in the wild they cannot compete with the green varieties and eventually die out. However, human nature tends to like what deviates from nature, and so have preserved 'Golden Marinka', 'Princess Pat' and others.

To obtain mutations we can simply let nature take its course, but this takes a long time, because it is a rare event. We can get there faster if we use artificial means. However, the methods are outside the scope of the average amateur grower. For example, in the past radiation has led to good results with such plants as streptocarpus (Cape primrose), saintpaulia (African violet) and chrysanthemum.

Another form of mutation, achieved by doubling the number of chromosomes (the carriers of genetic information), has produced giant forms. It is artificially done by treating the germinating seed with colchicine, a strong poison derived from autumn crocus (*Colchicum autumnale*). This retards cell growth while the nucleus grows on as normal. Because the chromosomes are in the nucleus, their number per cell is doubled. The intervention has to be made as early as possible in the growth process in case normal (diploid) cells, formed earlier, grow alongside the mutated (tetraploid) ones and displace the latter, causing a normal diploid plant to develop. Laughing gas (nitrous oxide), which is best known as an anaesthetic, can lead to similar results.

As far as I know, these methods are now used for improving fuchsias, but the process has not been crucial in terms of the development of fuchsias, because those species that were important in producing today's cultivars, *F. magellanica* and *F. triphylla*, do have double numbers of chromosomes. We now have cultivars with eighty-eight chromosomes and possibly more.

Hybrids

This is not the place for a detailed study of Mendelian genetics. However, some knowledge of it is necessary for proper hybridization. Simplifying the subject to some extent, we can say that fuchsias have many hereditary characteristics, which can be widely combined by various crosses. The number that can thus arise is practically limitless. More than 6,000 are known, a mere fraction of what is possible.

Growing a new hybrid is quite simple: some pollen from one plant is placed on the pistil of another, the seed is harvested and the new plant grown on. This is always a worthwhile process, for the chances of getting something that already exists are minimal, although crossing two species (primary crossing) always gives the same result, and if a cross exists already, there is nothing new. The chances of getting something new by crossing a naturally occurring variety with existing cultivars to extend or improve the existing range is similarly slight. It has been done for a long time.

It is better to work towards a given goal. This requires no greater effort and offers a much greater chance of success.

Suppose you want a so far unknown combination of white calyx and yellow corolla. Both exist, the latter in *F. splendens*, the former in 'Ting-a-Ling', for example. If you cross these two, the first generation (F1) may have some white-yellow members. If so, white and yellow are genetically dominant. Because the combination does not yet exist, it is more likely that yellow and white are dominated by other properties visible in F1. If that is the case, white and yellow are called recessive. Pollinating flowers of F1 with their own pollen can make these recessive features visible, in a second generation, F2. Why, then, is there no hybrid with a white calyx and yellow corolla? The problem is that the offspring from *F. splendens* and 'Ting-a-Ling' are sterile (do not propagate), which is one of the improver's many problems.

In principle, however, it remains possible to produce a combination of all properties, provided that the forms can be crossed.

The question now arises whether one should grow one's own new cultivars. The average amateur fuchsia grower will not be waiting with bated breath for your new crossings. There are so many, often very similar, fuchsias available, that it takes an expert to tell them apart. Adding to this plethora of cultivars is merely a nuisance. You would have to produce something completely new or better.

Experience shows that only about 1 per cent of all seed is worth keeping. Unless you are prepared to destroy ninety-nine out of every one hundred plants on which you have spent a year or more, they will only be in the way. If you are foolish enough to give cuttings of them to others, there will be yet another set of unrecognized, nameless fuchsias. Even worse, if you do name it first, you will cause much confusion; and if you do not, others may.

Suppose you have destroyed the ninety-nine unwanted plants and brought the survivor to be tested for novelty, and, luckily for you, it was accepted. Your name will figure on the official list of new cultivars. However, the fuchsia-growing public is much more critical than any official body. Fuchsia buyers want something usable, and in time, four out of every five new raisings disappear. In total, 500 plants must be grown to produce one useful new cultivar. Improving that one plant will mean that you spend less time on the rest of your garden. An amateur would surely prefer a garden of well-tended, healthy plants.

If, despite this, you decide to go ahead, you may be a born improver and the rest of this chapter is for you. But think before you start: here as elsewhere, creating something new involves more perspiration than inspiration. You have been warned.

Growing from seed

The simplest method is to buy a packet of fuchsia seed and to sow them as instructed. Seed mostly comes from nurseries in warmer climates where plants stand outside summer and winter. To ensure a good yield you must choose prolific cultivars. The question is whether in our colder climate they are likely to grow successfully.

Another way is to collect ripe berries in autumn and use seed from these. If you are careful and selective in your collecting and choose only handsome plants, your chances of success will increase. Good cultivars, such as 'La Campanella', arose in this way.

If the paternal plant is chosen just as astutely, good results are even more likely. That is why we mentioned improving by specific crosses from known parents. An incidental advantage when improving later generations is that we know more about the genetic characteristics that are present, even if they are recessive.

As to your selection, it would be nice if it were insight based on knowledge, but little is as yet known about the genetics of fuchsias. For the time being at least, elusive factors such as grower's luck and inspiration remain vital. Hence the charm of improving. However, earlier improvers working in the Netherlands have tended to neglect much work that would increase our knowledge (and this topic is addressed in more detail in the next chapter).

Pollinating

To pollinate your fuchsias you need small tweezers to transfer the pollen and some self-adhesive labels stating where the pollen came from (attach these around the stalk just above the ovary). You will also need some small strips of aluminium foil, measuring about 1 × 2cm, which are used to cover the pollinated pistils to prevent further, unwanted pollination. The strips are bent round a small stick to form sheaths with a closed end and these are slipped over the pollinated pistils and closed tight with tweezers (do not injure the pistils). By using sticks of different diameters, the sheaths can be made to fit different pistils.

The most important factors, however, are the parent plants. Suppose you take pollen from the cultivar 'Golden Glow' (the paternal plant) and transfer it to the pistil of 'La Campanella' (the maternal plant), which will

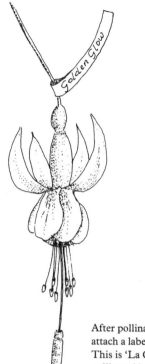

After pollinating,
attach a label to the plant.
This is 'La Campanella',
pollinated by 'Golden Glow'

produce the seed. This cross is described as 'La Campanella' × 'Golden Glow' (the female plant is always named first). Your label need not state the name of the female plant, which is always the plant whose berries containing seed are collected.

We could also try the cross 'Golden Glow' × 'La Campanella', but unfortunately 'Golden Glow' gives no seeds because the fruit drops off prematurely. As a maternal plant, therefore, 'Golden Glow' is useless. Some cultivars are no use at all, either for producing seeds or usable pollen. Such a plant is sterile – 'Marinka' is one such.

'Golden Glow' is sterile only as to seed. 'La Campanella' provides both pollen and seeds and is thus doubly fertile. Only experience will show what plants are fertile and sterile: there are no firm rules.

Use tweezers to take a stamen from a mature flower of 'Golden Glow' and rub the open top against the pistil of a newly opened flower of 'La Campanella'. For this a flower bud that is just in the process is squeezed open to make sure that it has not already been pollinated. After pollinating cover the pistil as described above and fasten the label in place.

Obtaining seed

Some of the flowers pollinated in this way will produce seed. The fruit is ripe when it becomes soft and, in many fuchsias, turns from green to a reddish colour. They generally fall off of their own accord, but when this happens they may get lost and you will no longer know for certain from which plant they came. It is, therefore, better to harvest them just before they fall off.

The next step is to separate the seeds from the flesh. If you have good eyesight or a hand-held magnifying glass and if you like fiddly work, cut the berry open, pick out seeds with a pin and place them on blottingpaper. Another method is to squash the berry in a small dish, or better still pass the contents of the berry through a plastic tea strainer with a little water. Good seed, about the size of a pin-head, and pale brown and spherical, will sink to the bottom. The rest can be drained off and poured away.

Because harvesting seed hardly ever coincides with the best time for sowing, the seed must be dried and kept in a paper bag at room temperature. Remember to write the names of the parent cultivars on the bag.

Fuchsia fruit ripens best in autumn, so that is when most seed is collected. If they are sown at once, they have the hardest season ahead of them. The worst problem they have to overcome is lack of light in winter, which is the commonest cause of failure for seedlings. Provided it is collected in time, ripe fuchsia seed can, fortunately, be kept for at least six months without loss of germinating power. Unripe seeds will germinate only if they are sown directly from the fruit.

Sowing and raising

By the end of January days begin to lengthen noticeably, and your fuchsias in the greenhouse will start to send out shoots. This is the ideal time for sowing. The young plants will have enough light and by the time they begin to take up space, your main fuchsia collection will be standing in the open, leaving enough space inside the greenhouse.

With a bit of luck, plants sown in January will be in bloom in August, so that much selecting can be done in the same year. Only a small proportion of the seedlings need be kept throughout winter, which is a clear advantage.

Fuchsia seed needs little attention. The soil in which it is sown must be light, moisture-retentive and not too heavily manured. Any peat-based compost sold for seedlings or cuttings will do. Because the number of seeds obtained from each cross is small, it is best to use small sowing trays. If you put large numbers of different seedlings in a large tray you will run the risk of mixing up the crosses.

Various kind of small trays of the kind used for food packaging and that are 1–4cm deep, are quite adequate. Fill them half-full with compost and moisten well. Sow the seed uniformly over the surface, making sure they are not too close together. Make sure a label stating the parents is attached to the tray and cover with plastic film. Fuchsia seed must not be covered with compost because it germinates in light.

The moist air between the plastic film and the compost provides an ideal micro-climate for the initial development of the seedlings. Unfortunately fungal infections that will harm the plants thrive in roughly the same conditions. It is therefore vital to work with material that is as clean as possible. The small trays and other aids that are not factory clean must first be well rinsed in water containing a small amount of bleach. In addition, you can spray the surface of the compost with a weak fungicidal compound.

Put the trays in a light spot but out of direct sun, at a temperature of about 15°C. Germination is usually fairly fast, and after a week the first trace of green will become visible. Keep the film in position until the plants are almost touching the plastic.

When it comes to dividing them, views differ. My own advice is to wait until the plants are a bit stronger and have at least three pairs of leaves. Other growers like to separate them as soon as the plastic film is removed. Use small pots to start with and soil that is not too rich, you can always add fertilizer later on.

By early May the plants should have reached the size of a cutting and are ready to be re-potted. The new pots, which should be at least 8cm, can be filled with normal container compost and the plants can henceforth be treated like growing cuttings. There is a difference, though: to decide whether a seedling is worth keeping we must see flowers. Plants that are not stopped will give fewer flowers but will bloom earlier, which is important. Therefore, do not stop them.

Selecting

The hardest task is selecting the most valuable plants. Remember that no single grower can judge his own seedlings correctly and that the improver's most important tool is the refuse bin. The adage 'when in doubt throw it out' should guide your selection.

You will depend on your own insight and the more impartial judgment of others for we are all prejudiced in favour of our own handiwork. Most seedlings will be untidy in shape and reddish-white or reddish-peach in colour, and there are far too many of these already.

The few that remain will cause problems. Every plant that you decide to keep will require much work, which will probably be pointless, as you

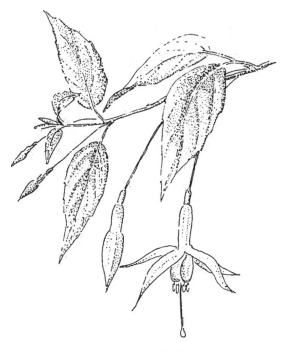

'Trailing King'

will find to your cost and embarrassment. If you believe that a given plant belongs to the élite, it is vital to take as many cuttings as you can as quickly as possible. This enhances the chances of survival and provides material on which to test for existing characteristics and new features. Once experts agree that you have grown something good, you will have to think about naming and registration.

Registration of new cultivars

In the Netherlands the practice is to register cultivars as soon as a certificate of approval has been issued by the selection commission of the Royal Horticultural and Botanical Society. For this, five specimens of the same new item must be presented at one of the commission's monthly meetings. The plants may be of different shapes but they must all be in good condition and adequately in bloom. A certificate will be given only if the commission thinks that the plant is an improvement or an addition to the range. Such an opinion is not lightly given. In unclear cases you will probably be given the benefit of the doubt. As regards naming, you have considerable freedom. However, cultivars must not be given Latin names, which are reserved for scientific names of species.

For practical reasons, names must not be too long, must contain no titles nor praise the quality of the plant. If you transgress these guidelines, the commission will soon correct you.

Improving Fuchsias in the Netherlands

The first fuchsia book to be published in the Netherlands, in 1882, was by H. Witte, a horticulturist from Leyden, and in it the author quotes an amateur gardener from Amsterdam. This gentleman gave a very workable description of the sowing of fuchsias, and in a letter dated 17 September 1878 he says of his improvement work that he felt more attracted to this since recently acquiring a brochure entitled *L'Histoire et Culture du Fuchsia* by Porcher, which showed him that all new cultivars obtained by crossing since 1837 had been produced and brought into the trade by British, German, Austrian, French and Belgian growers, while not a single Dutch grower was named. However, this account is not entirely correct. *Tuinbouwflora van Nederland* (1855) names a Dutch-grown fuchsia 'Robusta', Tengbergen. Presumably it had disappeared by 1878 and it cannot, therefore, be regarded as a first Dutch success. The efforts of the grower from Amsterdam seem to have remained fruitless too, and so things remained for almost another century. This is odd, since Dutch growers were no less adept at developing new cultivars than their colleagues in neighbouring countries. Was the failure perhaps because there was no material advantage for Dutch growers in developing new fuchsias?

The earliest Dutch cultivar, named in a list of 1970, is 'Garrechien' by de Groot (1967). It was not successful and may well have disappeared, but it paved the way for future cultivars. In 1968 we find, among others, 'Greet Altena' by Steevens from Groenekan, said to be a cross of 'Chang' × 'Marinka', which is very unlikely, for 'Marinka' is sterile. We also have 'Suzanna', a seedling from 'Dollar Princess' by van der Grijp, and 'Multa' by van Suchtelen. In 1969 appeared 'Rika' by van der Post, and in 1970 van Wiering introduced six seedlings, of which 'Kwintet' is first rate.

A start had been made, and there was more to follow. Johann de Groot, a professional grower, was the first to work in a systematic way. He grew a series of valuable new cultivars by crossing *F. regia* with tested cultivars. The formula was a success, even if the reddish-peach colour of *F. regia* predominated in most hybrids, which tends to make most of those fuchsias named after heavenly bodies look too much alike. The early

1970s saw many new introductions by Steevens, but at that time there was no bar to the inflated claims that could be made, and much is clearly due to growers trying to outdo each other. A few very good ones have survived, among them 'Nicolaas Aalhuizen', named after the president of the Dutch Circle of Fuchsia Lovers.

In the mid-1970s people saw the value of establishing a selection commission. Cultivars already in existence were entered on the list, but new ones had to obtain a certificate first. A milestone in the history of Dutch improvement came on 25 August 1979, when an improvement project group was set up jointly by some ten amateurs. Two of their objects have been of lasting importance: first, the completely open exchange of information to achieve the joint aims in the group (this was vital, given the secrecy endemic among most improvers); second, the unchecked growth in the creation of cultivars was to be prevented.

At its first meeting, the group decided that data on all seedlings were to be set down in a specific format, so that computers could be used to help to discover more about the fuchsia's genetics. Results were not slow in appearing. Above all Waldenmaier, a grower from Schaijk, made possible new insights into the genetic properties of plants with more than two sets of chromosomes, which is the case with most fuchsias. This lies beyond Mendelian genetics. Hitherto almost nothing was known about inherited genes in these polyploids. The knowledge gained made it possible to carry out focused research – for example, for a double-flowered, orange fuchsia. More recently research is being carried out to determine what genes are carried on a given chromosome. The use of knowledge about such couplings is that from the visible properties of a given cultivar we can infer the presence of the invisible (recessive) ones.

Unlike professional growers, amateur growers cannot work with great numbers of seedlings, and their chances of growing a plant with specific characteristics are, therefore, small. The group sought to overcome this handicap through collaboration in various projects. Results from recent years show certain trends: 'La Campanella' was much used as a parent, with variable progeny. Compare 'Nutshell', 'Le Berger', 'Contramine', 'Troika', 'François Villon' and 'First Kiss'. The strangest offspring, 'Berba's Trio', has flowers with differently coloured petals on one plant.

The use of 'Speciosa', a hybrid of *F. splendens* and *F. fulgens*, gave in one sowing 'Machu Picchu', 'Oranje Boven' and 'Je Maintiendrai', still rare orange flowers in a garden. Even more striking were 'Greenpeace', 'Walz Meermin' and 'Vincent van Gogh', with a light pink corolla and a light absinthe green calyx, which was a new feature. The yellow corolla of 'Space Shuttle' was also rather unusual, but this hybrid of 'Speciosa' and *F. splendens* is not true in colour in sunlight.

Another important line arose from the use of New Zealand species, with cultivars that faded to peach-red not only in the corolla but also in the calyx. 'Highland Pipes' and 'Rina Felix' are the first cultivars to be so-coloured that have obtained certificates from the commission, but others will no doubt follow.

There were gaps in the classic range: fuchsias with a flat and bowl-shaped corolla did not exist in all colours. 'Loeky', 'Baronesse van Dedem' and 'L'Ingenue' are good additions to the list, especially because they are very free-flowering cultivars.

Then there are those with small flowers. Mrs Reiman raised a whole series of Encliandra hybrids, whose names all being with the word 'Radings'. Slightly larger, and clearly with *F. magellanica* ancestry, are 'Suikerbossie', 'Tsjiep', 'Minirose' and 'Galadriel'. Nor should we forget 'First Success' (*F. splendens* × *F. paniculata*), which bears inflorescences of light pink flowers early in the year, a delightful herald of spring.

Finally a few comments. The outstanding charm of Dutch fuchsias is in their adjustment to the north European climate, for they can cope better with wind and weather than the large US double-flowered cultivars. The good results achieved in the Netherlands are due to its being the only country with a binding selection process for new cultivars. Although the commission cannot guarantee that every chosen cultivar will be first rate, it does prevent a flood of mediocrities. Although Dutch hybridizers were late to begin improving fuchsias, they soon caught up.

chapter 14

Fuchsias in the Garden and in Containers

The Dutch fondness for fuchsias is well known. The maritime climate greatly favours the cultivation of these plants, which have been adjusted to thrive in the humid air. They are a common sight in gardens throughout the country, appearing in as wide a range of form and with as rich flowers in many different colours, shapes and sizes as almost any other type of garden plant. The fuchsia is widely regarded as by far the most suitable decorative plant for use in gardens and on patios, on terraces, balconies or in loggias.

Growing and flowering habit are the main factors to be considered in determining how each individual fuchsia is used. We may use a species or a naturally occurring variety; or a cultivar; a shrub with erect or pendent branches; a vigorously upright plant shaped like a tree or pyramid; a hanging plant, or a creeper; a strongly branched, horizontal shrub, or a climber. In addition, the plants may be half or fully winter-hardy, or they may require special winter care.

We know that many amateur fuchsia growers are also great collectors, a fact that is evidenced by the membership of the Dutch Circle of Fuchsia Lovers and its activities. On visits to gardens the members see dozens of ways in which fuchsias can be used in the open. Some gardeners arrange their plants like stamps in an album, forgetting to create harmonious patterns with the rest of the environment. Any available space in a tree garden, a small area at the front or the back garden are used as exhibition space. These enthusiasts do not consider the decorative element in garden design. They are quite happy with their garden layouts and are, indeed, often the fuchsia growers who keep the total range in order and even manage to extend it.

Other growers, those who are imaginative and have green fingers manage to achieve a happy combination of their fuchsias and the environment. Some have only modest collections of fuchsias; others are keen collectors; but both have an eye for combining fuchsias with other plants to create a harmonious whole. Among these gardeners there are some who like to blend their fuchsias with other flowers, while others treat the rest of the garden as a background for their fuchsias.

Ideas for gardens, therefore, differ, but so do the possibilities. Available space, scope for wintering, climatic conditions, time and money are all important factors. It is impossible to give any simple, definitive rules. However, we can outline a few hints that may be worth considering.

Although the fuchsia came from the tropics (from Central and South America, New Zealand and Tahiti), they do not need high temperatures. In their original habitat, they grow at great heights in a variable climate with a considerable difference between day and night temperatures. In the wild they grow in wooded ravines, which can be quite cool, or in high mountains, where the temperature can range from $-3°C$ to $18°C$. Typical of those areas is a high rainfall and high air humidity, and forest soil that is rich in humus and permeable to water. That, in short, describes the original habitat.

F. magellanica had to adapt itself to the conditions in the Magellan mountains, with its less moderate climate, so that cultivars from that group are generally more winter hardy. Incidentally, like humans, plants can adapt to different circumstances, which is certainly true for many of the cultivars.

When we use fuchsias outside we must observe the following basic ecological guidelines, although there are always exceptions that prove the rule. Fuchsias dislike constant high temperatures; they prefer filtered sunlight (with the exception of Triphylla hybrids); they need ample light and air; they prefer some protection, especially against cold, rough and strong winds. They appreciate moisture from rain or spraying to promote high air humidity and to prevent excessive evaporation from leaf surfaces. They must have permeable soil that is rich in humus, with a pH between 5 and 7. Apart from winter-hardy fuchsias, they cannot withstand frost.

Winter hardiness is a fairly relative characteristic. Some fuchsias thrive in the Netherlands throughout the year and need some extra care only if the weather is extreme. In any case, in autumn it is well to protect the base of the plant by heaping up soil and applying a good layer of compost, leaves or straw to ensure safe overwintering. The fuchsia's ability to survive winter outdoors greatly depends on its location, the protection available, the humidity of the soil, the degree of frost and wind and, perhaps, a the presence of a layer of snow and so on.

F. magellanica, which is used for shrubs in permanent borders or as hedge, is winter hardy. Fuchsia hedges are more commonly seen in areas in Britain than in the Netherlands. *F. magellanica* var. *riccartonii* is a variety used both for shrubs and hedges. The part above ground often freezes off, but by summer the roots produce new shoots and branches at least 1 metre long.

Fuchsia hedges go well with forsythia and lilac, providing a hedge that can be in bloom from early spring to late autumn. Hedges are not only enclosures for gardens but also a means of marking off spaces within gardens – for example, to break up a long, narrow garden and so enhance the visual impression created by the garden.

If you are going to use groups of plants, always start with an odd number. Varieties such as *F. magellanica* var. *variegata* and *F. magellanica* var. *gracilis tricolor,* with their variegated leaves, can be combined with other green, ground-cover subjects to provide a most attractive grouping. Here we must mention *F. procumbens* and *F. hemsleyana.* Although they are less winter hardy, if they are given a good cover of garden peat, leaves and plastic sheeting, they can survive for many years. The same is also true of several more shrub-like cultivars such as 'Achievement', 'Beacon', 'Chillerton Beauty', 'Alice Hoffmann', 'Saturnus', 'Tom Thumb', 'Vielliebchen' and many others. Set out in a border of, for example, early-flowering heathers, they give life and colour in summer against the darker background of the heathers. This is a good combination, because the dense green of the heather protects the fuchsia roots in winter. The fuchsias should be cut back in spring, when the heather starts to flower.

In rock and alpine gardens, too, low-growing varieties can give good effects – for example, *F. microphylla, F. pumila* and *F. procumbens.* You could also use *F. regia* var. *typica* and the cultivar 'Corallina', which do well against a small border wall, too. If they lack extra cover in winter, you had better take them inside.

When you use annual or summer fuchsias, plant them out in the garden about mid-May. You can stretch this rule a bit, but if they are much earlier, put the plants in a protected place and watch weather forecasts for night frost. If the plants come from a protected place – a greenhouse, barn or from under a plastic screen – harden them off for several days in a spot that is protected not only against wind, but also against the often bright spring sun, which can burn tender, small leaves. At night they can be brought inside or given additional protection by means of plastic sheets. In mid-May, take them outside permanently, where they can be enjoyed for many months.

The time to take your fuchsias inside in autumn is less fixed, but is roughly the second half of October. They may still be in bloom, but a sharp frost can destroy in a single night plants of great splendour, because the wood freezes. This is much more likely to happen when sap is still freely rising than later in winter when the plant is at rest. However, even from a frozen tree it is still possible to produce a half stem or a bush in spring.

We mentioned earlier the fact that conditions differ for different growers. The most unfortunate are those who live in the midst of a dense conurbation and at best have only a balcony, loggia or small courtyard.

Yet even in a tiny walled courtyard an enthusiast can raise fuchsias, using posts to hoist them against the walls and bringing them down for watering. They can be combined with climbers and other flowers such as clematis, hortensias, begonias and pelargoniums.

Balconies, loggias and courtyards are often are the only direct contact some town-dwellers have with nature. In modern residential blocks, a balcony needs overhanging green and flowers to break the rectangular pattern. Against a side wall of the balcony one can put climbers in a pot, perhaps hanging against the wall a length of plastic-covered wire mesh against which stems can be trained. The balcony corner and ledge need to be adorned with trays. They must be securely fixed and filled with low-growing and trailing plants, mixed perhaps with busy lizzie and lobelia. There is also a corner for a shrub in a round container, an erect 'Swing-time' in the centre and coloured hanging subjects around it.

On a large balcony there may be room for a second container with a low tree such as willow or a *F. cordifolia*, with periwinkle and similar plants as ground-cover. In this way it is possible to have nature close by even in the depths of winter.

Garden owners are more fortunate. Fuchsias can be used in a garden in many ways, and opinions differ about which is the most satisfactory. Overleaf are two possible garden layouts.

In the first, the starting point is the way in which fuchsias have been integrated throughout the entire garden and successfully combined with other plants and flowers. In the second, fuchsias are concentrated into specific areas, and the rest of the garden is filled to provide a background to the fuchsias and to provide the perfect setting for them.

In the first layout, the beds are planted mostly with plants from single families in narrow, deep plots, with the back of the borders planted to match. What might be called the 'pipe-rack effect' is intensified by long, narrow borders and a long lawn. Such borders give little scope for planting attractive standard trees or pyramids and shrubs. Hanging-baskets can be included only in awkward places.

In such a garden it is essential to create an impression of width, in which the wealth of flowering fuchsias between other flowers and ever-greens will stand out more clearly. Width can be suggested by designing lines that run as little as possible into depth and into small rectangles. That is why the footpath through the almost square terrace runs in a zigzag. Rectangles have been noticeably widened by the run of the border between the terraces and the one in front of the greenhouse. This effect is further enhanced by raising the borders by 15–25cm. The raised borders prevent a direct view of the stone of the sun terrace from the house. You can see the whole garden planted with heather, low conifers and low-growing fuchsias and so on, green and flowering from front to back.

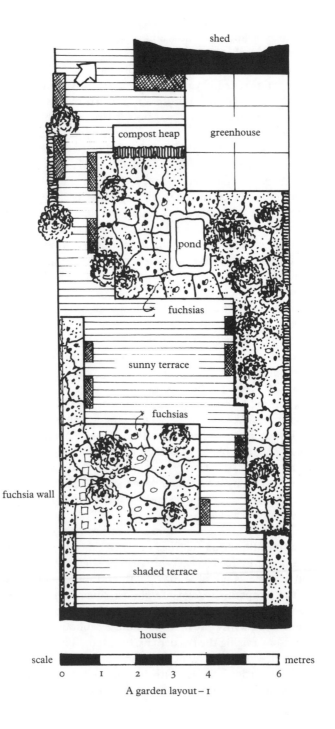

shed

greenhouse

compost heap

pond

fuchsias

sunny terrace

fuchsias

fuchsia wall

shaded terrace

house

scale
0   1   2   3   4   6   metres

A garden layout – 1

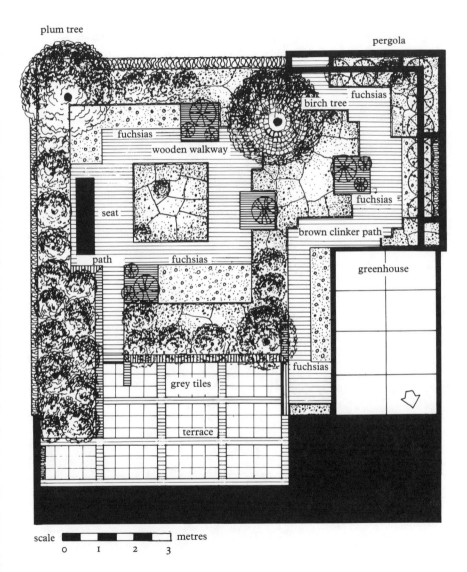

plum tree

pergola

fuchsias

birch tree

fuchsias

wooden walkway

fuchsias

seat

brown clinker path

path

fuchsias

greenhouse

grey tiles

fuchsias

terrace

scale metres

0   1   2   3

A garden layout – 2

The apparent width is heightened by marking the boundary of the plot for 8 metres by a wall of flowering fuchsias. The boundary consists of reed mats supported on a wooden frame, from which thirteen wooden trays have been hung in a varying pattern. This makes it possible to use alternating standard, pyramid and shrub fuchsias, and also hanging subjects. At the back of the garden are placed the taller elements, such as conifers, a mountain ash and a crab-apple tree. On the other boundaries a *Spiraea × arguta* and thornless bramble have been set to provide a green background. The greenhouse border is set with fuchsias, shrubs at the front and standard trees behind, which creates an impression of depth. The fuchsia collection is about two hundred strong.

The second example, an almost square garden, was at first arranged as a large lawn surrounded by borders that were essentially empty in winter. The revised plan started from spreading the fuchsia collection, approximately 150 plants, over the whole garden, so that it is visually full the whole year round. There is no lawn, but a good terrace, stressing the above average width of the garden and using natural materials for the hard surface together with other garden elements. It provides much scope for admiring fuchsias.

'Papoose'

The layout was worked on a the basis of a module of 30cm. There is a sun terrace behind the house, made of common concrete tiles with stripes of old brick, closed off by a low retaining wall of the same bricks. Two walkways, also in old brick, run from the terrace and linked up at the back around a birch 10 metres high in a basin of basalt pebbles.

Behind the garage is a greenhouse and beyond that is a corner pergola, surrounded by protective wooden slats, in which hanging fuchsias can be displayed.

No uniform rules can be given for using fuchsias in the open. It is primarily a personal decision and the garden design must be allowed to evolve artistically. It is, however, always instructive to visit working gardens, and many amateur growers are pleased and ready to open their gardens to visitors.

chapter 15

Hardy Fuchsias

Some fuchsias are winter hardy, and they are always in great demand from garden centres and nurseries, whose catalogues often separately list a whole range of them. The first Dutch-grown collection of these fuchsias to be exhibited appeared at the regional show at Bredevoort in 1983. This created much interest, especially because, where there are no available facilities to overwinter plants, leaving them outside in winter seems a good solution. However, it can be a disappointing practice. In this chapter we shall describe winter hardiness and give some advice on how to treat the plants correctly.

What is a winter-hardy fuchsia'?

John O. Wright once said that 'no fuchsia is completely hardy but most can survive most winters'. This axiom is true, not only for parts of Britain, but also for the Netherlands. We know that if they have well-developed roots, many fuchsias can survive a Dutch winter.

The fact that one species or cultivar will survive and another not is a matter of the cell properties of the fuchsias concerned, which lies beyond the scope of this chapter.

Fuchsias that winter in the open tend to die off above the ground and to put out new shoots from the roots in spring. There are three groups:

- those that do not survive outside in frost, among them most large-flowered cultivars, more tender cultivars, Triphylla hybrids and some species originating from frost-free regions;
- those that do survive outside but are so sluggish in spring that it is almost autumn before they bloom again;
- those that do survive outside and put out strong shoots in spring, flowering in July, as normal.

The fuchsias in this last group are the genuinely winter-hardy plants.

Background

In the chapter on fuchsias species, we saw that they first came from South and Central America, New Zealand and Tahiti, almost all tropical or subtropical areas. However, fuchsias are not simply tropical or subtropical plants, for most species grow in mountains at heights of 2,000–4,000 metres, in humus-rich soil, with high humidity and light broken by tall trees. Nights and winters can be quite cold at such heights. The habitat of species fuchsias explains why, in general, they like cool and humid weather but not bright sunlight.

One of the species that contributed much to the rise of the new fuchsias in the early years of cultivation in the first half of the nineteenth century was *F. magellanica*, which is probably the best known species. It is originally from Chile and occurs down to the tip of South America, where the climate is temperate but winters can be cold.

Winter hardiness in our fuchsias comes mainly from that species, and many winter-hardy fuchsias still resemble this ancestor or its varieties; a collection of them will include many strongly growing shrubs with peach-red, single flowers. Many such cultivars still closely resemble their forebear.

These cultivars often derive from the early hybridization experiments and so are quite old. One of the best known raisers was the French grower Victor Lemoine (1823–1911) of Nancy. He brought some four hundred new cultivars to the market, many of which still are still in the catalogue. He probably used *F. magellanica* for some crosses, since many of them have peach-red, single flowers and are winter hardy. Of Lemoine's winter-hardy cultivars, the following can still be found: 'Abbé Farges' (1901), 'Brutus' (1897), 'Bouquet' (1893), 'Caledonia' (1899), 'Carmen' (1893), 'Dollar Princess' (1912), 'Drame' (1880), 'Dr Foster' (1899), 'Graf Witte' (1899), 'Gustave Doré' (1880), 'Heron' (1891), 'Enfant Prodigue' (1887), 'Monsieur Thibaut' (1898), 'Phenomenal' (1869), 'Phyrne' (1905), 'Royal Purple' (1896) and 'Voltaire' (1897).

The British grower, W. G. Wood, who died in 1955, specialized in the development of new winter-hardy fuchsias and the testing of existing kinds for winter hardiness. His aim was to produce plants with larger flowers and with more variegated colouring. Among his cultivars are: 'Admiration' (1940), 'Cupid' (1946), 'Dorothy' (1946), 'Eleanor Rawlins' (1954), 'Joan Cooper' (1954), 'Margaret' (1937), 'Margaret Brown' (1949), 'Mrs W. P. Wood' (1949), 'Margery Blake' (1950), 'Peggy King' and 'W. P. Wood' (1954).

Another British grower, James Travis (1904-80), produced some well known winter-hardy cultivars, too, including 'Hawkshead' (1962), 'Susan Travis' (1958), 'The Tarns' (1962) and 'Silverdale' (1962). Also from Britain was Clifford Gadsby (1920–78), who has enhanced the range of winter-hardy fuchsias and has grown many well-known cultivars. He had no greenhouse when he began hybridizing and therefore mainly concentrated on plants that are winter hardy. Among some of his better known raisings are 'Blue Bush' (1973), 'Cliff's Hardy' (1971), 'Flashlight' (1968), 'Margaret Roe' (1968), 'Plenty' (1974) and 'Trudy' (1969).

The Dutch grower J. de Groot of Heerde has grown several excellent winter hardies by crossing various cultivars with *F. regia* var. *typica*, of which he had imported seed in 1963. This species, with single, peach-red flowers, is winter hardy and so are many of its offspring. De Groot always left his raisings to winter outdoors. Well known among them are: 'Andromeda' (1972), 'Isis' (1973), 'Komeet' (1970), 'Mercurius' (1971) and 'Saturnus' (1970). They are good cultivars, all with single, peach-red flowers.

No doubt future growers will extend the range of winter-hardy cultivars.

Growing winter-hardy fuchsias

Success in cultivating winter-hardy fuchsias largely depends on preparing the plants and then caring for them.

The soil

The growing medium must be rich in humus, with plenty of nutrients and water. Good growth requires a deep root structure. The soil must, therefore, first be well dug over and humus-rich matter – well-rotted farm manure, garden peat or compost – included. Some dried cow manure or another slow-release fertilizer, such as dried blood and bone meal, may be added, too. If the soil is heavy, some sand should be added to make it more permeable.

Fuchsias are not too sensitive to soil acidity, but grow best in moderately acid to neutral soil (pH 5–7), so that not too much lime-rich material should be added.

Position

Fuchsias do not in general like the strong sun, but they can cope with some if they stand in firm ground with a good root system. The flowers, especially those with paler colours, may fade somewhat, while some cultivars develop red leaves when they are grown in the fierce sun. However, do not plant fuchsias in deep shade, because, like all plants, they do need light in order to grow.

16 'Winston Churchill'

17 'Speciosa'

18 'Fenna'

19 'Machu Picchu'

20 'Menna'

A position where they may be exposed to rough winds is not ideal because fuchsias readily lose water through transpiration. Strong winds, too, are undesirable, though this depends on the type of plant: compact ones are not greatly troubled by it.

In general, winter-hardy fuchsias are robust and strong growers and less sensitive than other kinds.

When to plant

You should plant out your fuchsias as soon as possible after the danger of night frost is over, say, mid-May. However, because it is important that it can develop strong roots, it must not be too late either, so that the best time is between mid-May and early June.

Before planting, the fuchsias must be hardened off for a while, especially if they come from a heated greenhouse.

How to plant

When the soil has been prepared, dig a shallow trench about 10cm deep with a level bottom, and put the fuchsia in with its earth ball. Do not fill the trench, which will fill of its own accord during the course of summer.

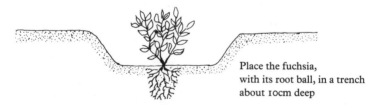

Place the fuchsia, with its root ball, in a trench about 10cm deep

The trench has several advantages: watering, which must continue regularly for some time, will be easier; and extra buds will be formed below ground and will produce shoots.

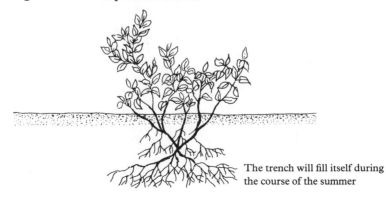

The trench will fill itself during the course of the summer

Care

At first, water regularly, certainly if there is not enough rain. Once the plant starts growing strongly, extra fertilizer may be added, preferably in soluble form for immediate effectiveness. In the first stages, extra nitrogen must be given to promote growth. In the course of summer relatively more phosphorus should be given to stimulate flowering, and as autumn approaches potassium becomes important for better wintering. Too much nitrogen at this stage is harmful, because it leads to drooping leaves and weak stalks that quickly freeze.

Autumn

By the time autumn approaches the plant will have grown and developed a good root system. Towards the time when the first night frosts are expected, heap a mound of soil around the base of the plant soil, as you might with a rose, to a height of about 10cm. Young plants should get some extra protection from leaves or peat.

Do not cut back the fuchsia in autumn; this has the effect of allowing the branches to give some extra protection to the parts of the plant that are below ground, and in winter the protecting pile of soil will not be blown away as quickly. Moreover, leaving the branches on the plant avoids the problem of rotting.

Because it is uncertain whether the plant will survive (particularly the first winter), it is well to take some cuttings to overwinter in the greenhouse.

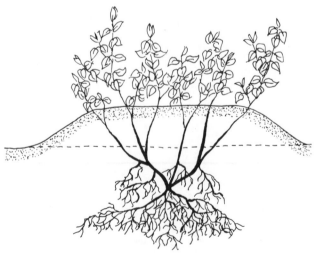

Prepare for winter by covering the stems with soil to a depth of about 10cm

Next spring

Early in April, new shoots will begin to appear, but you should still beware of night frosts and rough, east winds. Unless the winter has been mild, the plants will usually have died off to ground level. This, at least, often happens to *F. magellanica* var. *molinae* (*alba*), which may be regarded as the most winter hardy of all fuchsias. If it is clear that the plant is dead above ground, cut the stems back. Even if the stems them-selves are not frozen, take this opportunity to cut back awkwardly grow-ing stems to give the plant a better shape. The soil or compost heaped up at the base of the plant must be carefully dug away again and some more fertilizer added. Thus treated, the plants will be fully in flower again in July, and should continue to flourish for many years.

Fuchsias as decorative hedges

Anyone who has been to the south of England, Wales, Ireland or the Scottish west coast in summer will have seen the profusely flowering fuchsia hedges and large shrubs that are so typical of the landscape. In these areas the old wood rarely freezes completely because the effect of the Gulf Stream ensures that winters are generally mild.

Such hedges also grow in several areas in the Netherlands, but they are more likely to freeze off towards the ground, although this applies less to areas near coasts and along the dams of large rivers. In the hedges we mostly find the species *F. magellanica* and its varieties, which are the most suitable for them. When it comes to varieties of *F. magellanica*, it is not always possible or easy to know whether we have true varieties or cul-tivars closely resembling the original form. Some fuchsias are regarded as both cultivars and as varieties of the species, although most reference books frown on this practice.

The following naturally occurring varieties of *F. magellanica* can be found: var. *americana elegans* (also sometimes known as the cultivar 'Americana Elegans'); var. *conica* (growing to 50cm); var. *corallina* (better known as the cultivar 'Corallina', which grows horizontally and is thus not suitable for hedges); var. *discolor*; var. *globosa* (a strong grower); var. *gracilis* (growing to 80–100cm and very suitable for hedges); var. *longipedunculata* (growing to 80–100cm and suitable for hedges); var. *magellanica* (growing to 100–150cm and suitable for hedges); var. *molinae* (var. *alba*; growing to 100–150cm and very suitable for hedges, although it should not be fertilized too much); var. *pumila* (growing to 30cm and also, wrongly, known as 'Pumila'); var. *riccartonii* (growing to 150–200cm, very suitable for hedges and also known as the cultivar 'Riccarto-nii'); var. *thompsonii* (growing to 60–80cm, suitable for hedges and also known as the cultivar 'Thompsonii'); var. *variegata* (growing to 50–60cm, suitable for hedges and with variegated leaves).

To grow a hedge using one or more of these varieties, proceed as indicated above. The plants should be set 45–50cm apart, depending on how tall the shrub will grow. In general, they reach full height in the second summer, when the roots will have fully developed.

Few shrubs in a garden can flower so constantly from July to October.

Fuchsias in the rock garden

Some winter-hardy fuchsias – those that form small, compact shrubs – are suitable for inclusion in rock gardens. Treat them as you would other winter-hardy subjects. Some suitable fuchsias are: 'Carmen', 'Dunrobin Bedder', 'Alice Hoffmann', 'Lady Thumb', 'Pumila', 'Son of Thumb', 'Tom Thumb', 'Trase', 'Venus Victrix' and 'W. P. Wood'.

Winter-hardy fuchsias

Only those fuchsias that are known to be winter hardy in the Netherlands are included in the following list.

Species

F. magellanica and its varieties
F. procumbens
F. regia

Cultivars

'Abbé Farges' (Lemoine, France, 1901)
'Achievement' (Melville, UK, 1886)
'Admiration' (W. P. Wood, UK, 1940)
'Alice Hoffmann' (Klese, Germany, 1901)
'Americana Elegans' (raiser and date unknown, but UK pre-1934)
'Andromeda' (De Groot, Netherlands, (?)1972)
'Army Nurse' (Hodges, USA, 1947)
'Avalanche' (Henderson, UK, 1869)
'Beacon' (W. Bull, UK, 1871)
'Berliner Kind' (Eggbrecht, Germany, 1882)
'Blue Bush' (Gadsby, UK, 1970 or 1973)
'Blue Gown' (Milne, UK, date unknown)
'Bouquet' (Lemoine, France, 1893)
'Brilliant' (W. Bull, UK, 1865)

'Brutus' (W. Bull, UK, 1901)

'Caledonia' (Lemoine, France, 1899)

'Cardinal Farges' (Rawlins, UK, 1958

'Carmen' (Lemoine, France, 1893)

'Charming' (Lye, UK, 1895)

'Chillerton Beauty' (Bass, UK, 1847)

'Cliff's Hardy' (Gadsby, UK, 1966)

'Clifton Charm' (Handley, UK, 1981)

'Constance' (Berkeley Hort. Nursery, USA, 1935)

'Corallina' (Pince, UK, 1843)

'Cupid' (W. P. Wood, UK, 1946)

'Display' (Smith, UK, 1881)

'Dollar Princess' (Lemoine, France, 1912)

'Dorothy' (W. P. Wood, UK, 1949)

'Drame' (Lemoine, France, 1880)

'Dr Foster' (Lemoine, France, 1899)

'Dunrobin Bedder'/'Dobbie's Bedder' (D. Melville, UK, 1890)

'Eleanor Rawlins' (W. P. Wood, UK, 1954)

'Elfin Glade' (Colville, UK, 1963)

'Empress of Prussia' (Hoppe, UK, 1868)

'Enfant Prodigue'/'L'Enfant Prodigue'/'Prodigy'
  (Lemoine, France, 1887)

'Ethel Wilson' (J. W. Wilson, UK, 1967)

'Eva Boerg' (Yorke, UK, 1943)

'Flash' (Hazard & Hazard, USA, (?)1930)

'Flashlight' (Gadsby, UK, 1968)

'Florence Turner' (Turner, UK, 1955)

'Frau Hilde Rademacher' (Rademacher, Germany, 1901)

'Genii' (Reiter, USA, 1951)

'Golondrina' (Niederholzer, USA, 1941)

'Graf Witte' (Lemoine, France, 1899)

'Gruss aus dem Bodethal' (Sattler & Bethge, Germany, 1893)

'Gustave Doré' (Lemoine, France, 1880)

'Hawkshead' (J. Travis, UK, 1962)

'Henriette Ernst' (Ernst, Germany, 1841)

'Heritage' (Lemoine, France, 1902)

'Heron' (Lemoine, France, 1891)

'Howlett's Hardy' (Howlett, UK, 1952)

'Isis' (De Groot, Netherlands, 1973)

'Joan Cooper' (Wood, UK, 1954)

'Justin's Pride' (G. Jones, UK, 1974)

'Komeet' (De Groot, Netherlands, 1970)

'Lady Boothby' (Raffill, UK, 1939)

'Lady Thumb' (Rose, UK, 1966)
'Laleham Lass' (Dyos, UK, 1978)
'Lena' (Bunney, UK, 1862)
'Lottie Hobby' (Edwards, UK, 1839)
'Madame Cornelissen' (Cornelissen, Belgium, 1860)
'Margaret' (W. P. Wood, UK, 1937 or 1943)
'Margaret Brown' (W. P. Wood, UK, 1949)
'Margaret Roe' (Gadsby, UK, 1968)
'Margery Blake' (W. P. Wood, UK, 1950)
'Mephisto' (Reiter, USA, 1941)
'Mercurius' (De Groot, Netherlands, 1971)
'Mission Bells' (Walker & Jones, USA, 1948)
'Monsieur Thibaut' (Lemoine, France, 1898)
'Mrs Popple' (Elliott, UK, 1899)
'Mrs W. P. Wood' (W. P. Wood, UK, 1949)
'Neue Welt' (Mahnke, Germany 1912)
'Nicola Jane' (Dawson, UK, 1959)
'Oetnang' (raiser and date unknown, Austria)
'Papoose' (Reedstrom, USA, 1960)
'Pee Wee Rose' (Niederholzer, USA, 1939)
'Peggy King' (W. P. Wood, UK, 1954)
'Phenomenal' (Lemoine, France, 1869)
'Phryne' (Lemoine, France, 1905)
'Phyllis' (Brown, UK, 1938)
'Pixie' (Russell, UK, 1960)
'Plenty' (Gadsby, UK, 1974)
'President' (Standish, UK, 1841)
'Prince of Orange' (Banks, UK, 1872)
'Prosperity' (Gadsby, UK, 1970)
'Pumila' (Young, UK, 1821)
'Riccartonii'/*F. magellanica* var. *riccartonii* (Young, UK, 1938)
'Rose of Castile' (Banks, UK, 1855)
'Rose of Castile' improved (Banks, UK, 1869)
'Royal Purple' (Lemoine, France, 1896)
'Rufus' (Nelson, USA, 1952)
'Saturnus' (De Groot, Netherlands, 1970)
'Scarcity' (Lye, UK, 1869)
'Schneekoppen' (Twrdy, Germany, 1866)
'Schneewittchen' (Klein, Germany, 1878)
'Sealand Prince' (Walker-Bees, UK, 1967)
'Sharpitor' ((National Trust, UK, *c.*1974)
'Silverdale' (J. Travis, UK, 1962)
'Snowcap' (Henderson, UK, date unknown)

'Son of Thumb' (Gubler, UK, 1978)
'Susan Travis' (J. Travis, UK, 1958)
'Tennessee Waltz' (Walker & Jones, USA, 1951)
'The Tarns' (J. Travis, UK, 1973)
'Thompsonii' (Thompson, UK, 1837 or 1840)
'Tom Thumb' (Baudinat, France, 1850)
'Trase' (J. Dawson, UK, 1959)
'Tresco' (Tresco Abbey Gardens, UK, date unknown)
'Trudy' (Gadsby, UK, 1969)
'Venus Victrix' (Gulliver, UK, 1840)
'Vielliebchen' (Wolf, Germany, 1911)
'Voltaire' (Lemoine, France, 1897)
'White Pixie' (Merrist Wood, UK, 1968)
'Winifred' (Chatfield, UK, 1973)
'W. P. Wood' (W. P. Wood, UK, 1954)

Sources

Boullemier, L. B., *The Checklist of Species, Hybrids and Cultivars of the Genus Fuchsia* (revised edition)
Ewart, Ron, *Fuchsia Lexicon* (revised edition)
Manthey, G., *Fuchsien*,
Proudley, B. and V., *Fuchsias in Colour*
Thorne, T., *Fuchsias for All Purposes*
Wilson, S. J., *Fuchsias*
Wood, W. P., *A Fuchsia Survey*
Wright, J. O., Hardy Fuchsias

chapter 16

Triphylla Hybrids

The average Triphylla hybrid has dark, olive-green leaves, which are reddish on the underside, and long, slender brick red flowers. Some forty Triphylla hybrids are known, ranging from erect shrubs to trailing plants, suitable for hanging-baskets.

The first known parent is *F. triphylla*, which was discovered by Charles Plumier in Haiti in 1689–97 and which is, in fact, the plant on which the entire genus was founded. It was described by Plumier as *Fuchsia triphylla flore coccinea* (that is, three-leaved and scarlet) in his *Plantarum Americanarum Genera*, which was published in Paris in 1703. Plumier's name remained current until 1753, when Linnaeus, in *Species Plantarum*, described it simply as *Fuchsia triphylla*.

The plant was not introduced to Britain until 1882, and it spread from there to the mainland of Europe. The first cross is believed to have been made in 1855 by the British grower C. Turner, who called the resulting plant 'Thalia' (*F. triphylla* × unknown). This 'Thalia' seems to have disappeared from the catalogues.

Interest in hybridizing with *F. triphylla* increased, and many crosses were made with *F. boliviana* (now regarded as synonymous with *F. corymbiflora*). The first to appear came in 1895, when the French grower Victor Lemoine (1823–1911) produced a plant named 'Triphylla Hybrida' (*F. triphylla* × *F. boliviana*), which has a vermilion flower.

In 1897 the first German hybrid appeared. This was 'Andenken an Heinrich Henkel' (syn. 'Heinrich Henkel'), which was raised by F. Rehnelt and was probably *F. triphylla* × 'Edelstein'. It grows as a lax bush, and flowers freely with the long tube typical of Triphylla hybrids. Another cultivar to appear in the nineteenth century was 'Mary', which was raised by Carl Bonstedt in 1894. This cross, *F. triphylla* × *F. boliviana*, grows as a freely flowering bush, although it is not an easy plant to cultivate. In 1902 Bonstedt produced what some regard as one of the best of the Triphylla hybrids, 'Leverkusen' (*F. triphylla* × 'Andenken an Heinrich Henkel'). The tube is shorter than that of its parents and the flowers are cherry red.

In 1903 Rehnelt raised 'Grossherzogin Adelheid' (*F. boliviana* × *F. tri-*

phylla) and 'Otto Nordenskjold' (*F. triphylla* × unknown), both of which
seem to have disappeared, while in 1904 Bonstedt enjoyed great success
with 'Göttingen', a lovely cultivar with vermilion flowers that, unfortunately, is not easy to grow.

In 1905 Bonstedt produced four new cultivars. One of the best known
is 'Koralle' (syn. 'Coralle') (*F. triphylla* × *F. fulgens*), which has an
upright, vigorous habit and bears coral red flowers. 'Thalia' (which
should not be confused with Turner's earlier introduction) is a strongly
growing bush with the leaves of 'Gartenmeister Bonstedt' and the flowers
of 'Koralle', but with a slightly smaller tube. 'Gartenmeister Bonstedt',
which has dark green leaves and orange to brick red flowers, forms a freely
flowering, upright bush. 'Traudchen Bonstedt', which has salmon pink
flowers and bronze leaves, also has an upright habit.

An old German periodical suggests that in 1904 Bonstedt also produced 'Fraulein Bonstedt' and 'Otto Furst' and, in 1907, 'Clio', 'Eros'
and 'Perle', but these seem to have vanished, as probably have the other
German cultivars 'Gartendirektor Hample', 'Garteninspektor Monke-
meyer' and 'Obergartener Koch' (all possibly Sauer, 1911–12).

One cultivar that is still widely available is 'Bornemann's Beste', which
was probably raised by Bonstedt and introduced *c.*1926. This is an erect
and vigorous plant with pink-red flowers. It needs regular nipping out.
This cultivar is in fact very similar in appearance to a fuchsia that was
known as 'George Bornemann', with which it may be synonymous. All
the cultivars raised by Bonstedt were introduced to the market by his
friend George Bornemann, a professional nurseryman from Blankenburg
in Germany.

In 1946 the American grower Victor Reiter raised 'Trumpeter' ('Gartenmeister Bonstedt' × 'Mrs Victor Reiter'), which has light red flowers
and is suitable for a small hanging-basket. In 1948 Reiter raised another
hanging-basket subject, 'Mantilla' ('Mrs Victor Reiter' × *F. triphylla*),
which has extraordinarily long tubes, up to 5cm long. John Wright
believes that the *F. triphylla* used was a natural hybrid with *F. pringsheimii*, which would account for the unusual colour and flower shape.
Another of Reiter's cultivars is 'Rocket' ('Gartenmeister Bonstedt' × 'Mrs Victor Reiter'), which appeared in 1942 but is not widely
available in Europe.

'Tickled Pink' was raised by P. F. Reedstrom in America in 1957, and
'Bernard Rawlins', which has a long white tube, flushed with pink, was
produced by the British grower Thorne in 1959. Neither is widely grown.

More widely available is 'Billy Green', which was raised by Bernard
Rawlins and introduced in 1966. Although the parentage is unknown, it is
thought to include *F. triphylla*, 'Andenken an Heinrich Henkel' and
'Leverkusen'. The salmon pink flowers are produced in the leaf axils and

the plant needs regular nipping out to keep it in shape. It also needs good light. In the right conditions, however, it makes a handsome plant and is essential in any collection of cultivars.

The first Dutch Triphylla hybrid appeared in 1968. This was 'Tourtonne' ('Leverkusen' × 'Water Nymph'), and it was bred by F. van Suchtelen. It is an erect shrub that requires regular nipping out; it is not frost hardy.

In 1974 the British growers Baker-Dunnett brought out four new cultivars. 'Baker's Tri' has geranium red flowers; it is a slow, rather weak grower but a good subject for a hanging-basket. 'Harry Dunnett' is a self-branching, bushy cultivar with rather unusual, slightly curved tubes pink-red. 'Timlin Brened', which has pretty, flamingo pink tubes, is a freely flowering, self-branching shrub. The most vigorous of the four, however, is 'Stella Ann', which has poppy red flowers, freely borne on an erect, self-branching shrub, which can be trained as a standard.

The German grower Karl Nutzinger became well known for his Triphylla hybrids. In 1976 he raised 'Elfriede Ott' ('Koralle' × *F. splendens*), which is a spectacular plant, vigorous and free flowering, although not among the easiest to grow because it is needs more warmth than other Triphylla hybrids and because it needs to be nipped out frequently. The flowers are salmon pink. Another of Nutzinger's great successes is 'Erika Koth' ('Koralle' × *F. boliviana*), which also appeared in 1976. This forms an erect shrub that bears rose-orange flowers. Unfortunately, it is very tender. 'Präsident Walter Morio' ('Koralle' × *F. fulgens* var. *rubra grandiflora*) was named by Nutzinger to honour the president of the German Dahlia, Fuchsia and Gladioli Society. It is a tender plant with a rather slack habit with long branches, but if it is regularly pinched out it forms good bush with plenty of rose-orange flowers. 'Lilo Vogt' ('Koralle' × *F. boliviana*) is a good hanging-basket subject, with small pink flowers, but it, too, is tender and the flowers will open only in warm weather. It should never be over-watered. It is, in fact, a challenging fuchsia to grow successfully, even for enthusiasts. 'Schönbrunner Schuljubiläum' ('Koralle' × *F. fulgens* var. *rubra grandiflora*) bears bright red flowers late in the year, but it must be pinched out regularly.

In Britain in 1967 J. O. Wright produced 'Whiteknight's Ruby' (*F. triphylla* × *F. procumbens*). The small purple flowers are borne on a bushy, erect shrub. In 1980 Wright introduced a small version of 'Whiteknight's Ruby': this was 'Whiteknight's Cheeky' ('Whiteknight's Ruby' × *F. procumbens*), an unusual cultivar, which has small, dark purple flowers borne in erect, terminal racemes. Also in Britain, but in 1977, A. Harris raised 'Vivien Harris ('Rufus' × 'Leverkusen'), which has turkey-red flowers. It is an attractive bush fuchsia, which requires frequent nipping out and which can be grown as a standard.

The Dutch grower, C. Felix, produced an unusual Triphylla type fuchsia in 1978. This is 'Pussy Cat' ('Leverkusen' × 'Checkerboard'), which has pink-orange, freely borne flowers, which appear late in the year. There is abundant foliage and the stem sections are short, so the plant is prone to mildew; hence it should not be grown in areas where there is a lot of rain. Waldenmaier, another Dutch grower, introduced 'Walz Toorts' ('Leverkusen' × unknown) in 1981. This fine cultivar has an upright, free-flowering habit, with long-lasting, pink-red flowers.

The cultivar 'Axel of Denmark', a Danish raising of unknown parentage, has red flowers borne in profuse clusters and an upright habit. It needs frequent nipping out. Another Triphylla type is 'Taudens Heil', which is a cultivar from California, probably imported from Germany, but of otherwise unknown origin and possibly with a corrupted name. It is an upward growing shrub with salmon red flowers.

In 1983 Mrs Reiman brought out 'Challenge', a cultivar with cream-coloured flowers. It is a seedling of *F. triphylla*, and although it is rather hard to grow the unusual colour makes it worth the effort.

J. O. Wright introduced 'Lechlade Fire-Eater' (*F. triphylla* × *F. denticulata*) in 1984. This has a long, crimson tube and rose-crimson sepals, tipped with green. The bronze-green, red-veined leaves have slightly serrated edges. It is tender and suitable for greenhouse cultivation.

'Menna', a seedling of 'Leverkusen', which it greatly resembles, was introduced by the German grower Bögermann in 1984. It bears large rose-red flowers and will grow as a bush or a standard. 'Coral Drops', which is not widely available, is a Triphylla hybrid of unknown origin. It has blooms rather like 'Andenken an Heinrich Henkel' but has rather more lax growth.

Growing Triphylla hybrids

In general, Triphylla hybrids are not difficult to grow. Cuttings should be taken in spring, when the plants are not in flower. The flowers are borne in clusters at the top of shoots and, if you wait until summer, when the plants are full of buds, you will be able to take a top cutting very easily. If you prefer to wait until August or September, you will do best with cutting taken from side shoots. Although the cuttings need only be small, you must have at least 2.25 sq cm of leaf area. When the cuttings have developed good roots, they can be put into medium-sized pots – weak growers into 6.5cm pots and more vigorous growers into 8cm pots.

Autumn cuttings need careful attention in winter. They should be kept in a greenhouse where the temperature will not fall below 8°C, although 10°C would be preferable. Keep them reasonably moist. The soil in the pots must not be allowed to become too cold or to dry out.

If you have plants overwintering in the greenhouse, you can take cuttings as early in January so that you have a new plant every year and will not risk losing a cultivar. Triphylla hybrids do not always overwinter well, and a good plan is to keep one-year-old plants in the greenhouse and an older one in a cold frame.

In mid-May Triphylla hybrids can be put outside, with your other fuchsias. They will stand full sun, but make sure that the containers are large enough. If the temperature is over 25°C you will have to water them once a day, soaking the soil thoroughly. If you notice the leaves or stems begin to droop again within 24 hours, the pot needs to be one size larger. You will soon learn from experience what size pot is suitable for each plant.

The hybrids flower profusely and will remain in bloom until they are pruned. Groups of Triphylla hybrids in the same colour can look especially effective, and you will be able to achieve some striking effects if you can arrange them so that shades and colours flow into each other.

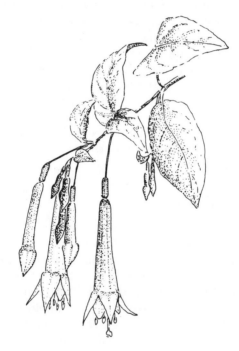

'Bornemann's Beste'

chapter *17*

Growing Fuchsias
for Exhibition

Producing well-shaped, profusely flowering plants for exhibition purposes requires considerable extra work.

The first important task it to choose, well in advance, free-flowering, well-growing fuchsias.

Hanging-baskets and pots

These are grown in a greenhouse at about 12°C. In the autumn preceding the show you should take cuttings from the chosen cultivars – those that naturally grow with shoots that climb and trail such as 'Troika', 'Elfriede Ott', 'Trailing King', 'Trailing Queen' and 'Pink Marshmallow'. The advantages of using a new cutting is that it takes up less space in the greenhouse during the winter, it grows more strongly, and it eventually flowers better.

After about four weeks the cuttings will have developed good roots and can be transferred to 6cm pots. Use compost that is not too well-fertilized. When the pot is well filled with roots, transfer the plant to a larger pot, with fertilized soil. To get handsome, bushy plants, you must start pinching out as soon as two pairs of leaves have fully grown. This is especially important for trailing plants if you are to get more profuse blooming later on.

Be careful with watering. From time to time spray the plants with a foliar feed in solution. If the fuchsias have been potted into a 10cm pot, wait until the pot is full of roots before transferring the plant again. You can tell when the plants are ready to be re-potted when the hair roots have developed a white layer of felt against the inside of the pot, and you can check if this stage has been reached by carefully tapping the plant loose from the pot. Only when the roots are at this stage should the plant be put into its final pot or hanging-basket, which should be about 26cm across.

To make sure the basket is well filled, put one plant in the centre and six round it. You must always use an odd number of plants. Transferring the plants to a larger pot stimulates growth, and it is now even more important to pinch out the growing shoots regularly. Water the pot as necessary.

Watch out for greenhouse whitefly, aphids and other pests and take suitable action in good time (see Chapter 8).

Weather permitting, put the plants outside for hardening off, first in a wind-free, sheltered spot out of direct sun, and bring them in at night. After about ten days they will be hardened and, if no further frost is expected, the pot or hanging-basket can be left hanging in place until it is time to take it to the show.

If you want to hang a pot that is not already fitted with hoops, fit a ring of smooth, galvanized, 6mm gauge iron wire neatly around the pot, just below the lip of the rim. Solder three evenly spaced hooks to the wire and to these attach three chains, which should be fixed at the top to a non-rusting eye.

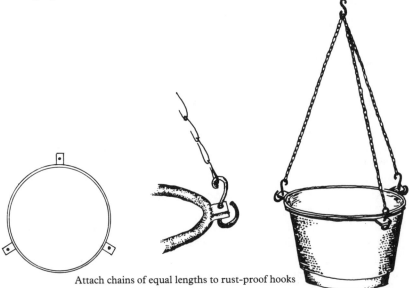

Attach chains of equal lengths to rust-proof hooks

If you want your fuchsias at different heights, use longer or shorter chains. Having all the containers and hanging-baskets at the same height is rather unattractive.

Depending on the cultivar you are growing, stop pinching out the shoot about eight weeks before the show. The length of time between the last stopping of the growing shoots and full blooming depends on light and weather, but also on the characteristics of the individual cultivar. For example:

Six week: 'Abbé Farges', 'Dorothea Flower',
Seven weeks: 'Mrs Lovell Swisher', 'Mrs W. Rundle'
Eight weeks: 'La Campanella', 'Marinka', 'Tom Thumb'

Nine weeks: 'Bon Accorde', 'Lakeside', 'Upward Look'
Ten weeks: 'Thalia'

Discontinuing the process of pinching out about a week earlier means that the flowers are at the height of blooming when you arrive at the show. This is fine for a two-day show, but if it lasts ten days it is better continue to pinch out for a further week.

Fuchsias have to reach their peak in a short time, so it is important to fertilize them for about two weeks, the first time with a high nitrogen product, for growth, and thereafter with a mixture of high phosphorus and potassium content to encourage flowering (see Chapter 5).

If you do all this, your trailing fuchsia, which must be properly labelled, will be ready for the show, profusely flowering and in perfect condition.

Bushes and shrubs

Fuchsias that are several years old make better show plants than one-year-old plants because they have better root systems and more nutrient is stored in the wood.

In a greenhouse, bushes and shrubs that have been pruned in autumn must be brought back into growth at the end of February. You will need to trim the plants a little to get them into shape. If you have overwintered plants by burying them, pot them up. The pots of plants that have over-wintered in their pots must have the old soil cleared away, and the pots be refilled with new compost. You need water only moderately, for at this stage there is no transpiration (evaporation from the leaves) and no water take-up (because there are few root hairs).

Once shoots appear, you can begin to give more water and apply a foliar feed, as you have done with your trailing fuchsias.

You must keep your fuchsias growing. Whenever two pairs of leaves are formed you should pinch out the growing tip. Flower buds should also be removed. You should pinch out the shoots about four times in all, the last time about eight weeks before the show.

The plants should be put outside in mid-May. Bushes and shrub fuchsias will already be getting fuller, and standard fuchsias will be acquiring a good crown. Remember that the plants are still tender and must not yet be placed in full sun, and they also need protection from wind.

Water regularly, even if it has rained. Check daily that the soil is moist enough. A sturdy crown will act as an umbrella in rain, so that the water does not get to the compost around the base. Continue to add a fertilizer.

Tie up new shoots on shrub fuchsias regularly and make sure that the plants keep a good shape. If the pot becomes too small, transfer the plant to a larger one, but do not pot on after July. Make sure that a large plant is not in too small a pot and that a small plant is not in too large a pot. Check that the supporting stake is clean and not rotted; if it shows any signs of damage, replace it. The stake must not be taller than the plant. The plants should be tied on as invisibly as possible; green garden twine is best. You should take care that it is not pulled too tight, because as the stem grows it will thicken and will be damaged by the wire cutting into it, which may allow viruses and diseases to infect the plant.

Another method of growing for shows is to prevent the plant from flowering the year before the show. Take cuttings in early spring and set them into separate 7cm pots so that they develop roots. This happens in

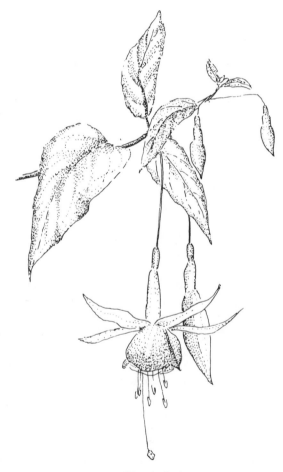

'Temptation'

about a fortnight. The plants should be put into larger pots, and constantly pinching out the shoots prevents the formation of buds or flowers so that all the plant's strength goes into growing. At the end of October, the fuchsias are put into 10cm pots and coaxed along during winter at 5–10°C. When the days lengthen again at the end of January, transfer them to new, fertilized compost, then proceed as with other methods for shrubs and stems.

Checklist for showing fuchsias

If you follow these guidelines you should be sure of success:

- One week beforehand, check for rust, greenhouse whitefly, aphids and other pests; spray if necessary and repeat after three days. The plants must be absolutely free from disease and pests. Your neighbours at the show will not be pleased if you infect their plants.
- The pots must be clean and all the same colour. Make sure there are no rusty chains on hanging pots.
- Check supporting stakes: they must be clean (no signs of rot!), nor protrude above the plant (sloppy and dangerous).
- Tie the plants on as invisibly as you can with green twine, but make sure it is not too tight.
- Remove dead flowers, berries, unattractive buds and damaged and faded leaves.
- Putting a new layer of soil over the top of the pot indicates care.
- Make sure that the labels are clean, give the correct name of the plant and of the exhibitor. Use a water-resistant pen and fix them securely with, for example, a loop label.
- Before transporting them, water the plants well, even dunking if need be.
- For transporting your fuchsias, it is best to use a closed, high-sided vehicle, such as a flower car, a horse box or a caravan. These are high enough to accommodate stems. Place hangers on the floor and above all do not hang them. The branches are put into paper crushed between them; take off the chains to prevent damage.

A whole season of hard work can be lost if fuchsias are transported the wrong way. Proper transport is as vital as growth and flowering.

When, at last, the fuchsias are on show, more beautiful than ever, it's time to remember the old proverb: 'The eye of the master makes the horse grow.'

Using Fuchsias in Nosegays and Corsages

Fuchsias are not really suitable as cut flowers, although if you cut a stem in the autumn it may remain fresh for a few days, as long as you provide some support for it. They can, however, be used in corsages and nosegays, but they do require some special attention.

The most important factor for success is to use fresh, undamaged blooms that are still open. You will also need some foliage. Fuchsia leaves can be used, but better are sprays of leaves from plants such as aucuba and euonymus. You can also incorporate sprigs of heather as well as seedpods or berries, which contrast well with fuchsias. Use your imagination to find different colours and textures that will complement each other.

When they are used in miniature arrangements fuchsia flowers and leaves need to be prepared individually. You will need a sharp knife, a reel of fine gauge florist's wire or pre-cut stub wires, cotton wool, wire cutters, scissors and narrow florist's tape. Each flower and leaf is supported in a wire framework with a tiny amount of damp cotton wool.

Carefully insert a length of wire through the calyx of a flower, bend the two ends down and twist them around each other, so that a tiny piece of damp cotton wool is held in the wire. Do not use too much cotton wool or you will make a rather unattractive lump. You can lengthen the wire stem at this stage by twisting another stub wire or length of wire around the original wire, then you should cover the wire by neatly winding a length of florist's tape over and around it.

Individual leaves can be wired by taking a fine wire around the spine of the leaf between half and one-third of the way up and twisting the ends around the leaf stalk. Again, a tiny piece damp cotton wool should be held by the wires and the whole wrapped in florist's tape.

When you have prepared the individual flowers and leaves, begin to build them up into corsages and nosegays. If you want a simple corsage twist a leaf and flower together, then add more leaves and flowers until you have built up a dainty bunch. Remember to trim off any ends of wire that protrude from the bottom and cover all bare wires with florist's tape. If you wish you can, when you are adding the final covering of tape, add a brooch pin at the back.

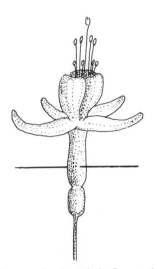

Insert a wire through the flower tube

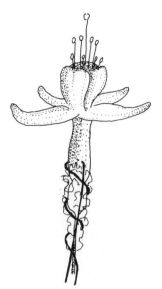

Twist the ends of the wire together
around a small piece of cotton wool

Bind the wire with florist's tape

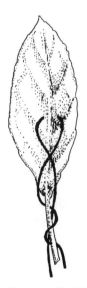

Use fine-gauge florist's wire
on individual leaves

Build up a corsage by wiring together
single blooms and leaves, remembering to cover
the ends of the wire with florist's tape

Nosegays are made in much the same way, although you can add sprays
of other plant material, wiring seedpods and heather stems to give added
length if you wish. Again, trim all the ends of the wire to neaten them, and
cover all the stems with more florist's tape or wind around a length of
florist's ribbon in a matching or contrasting colour.

Drying fuchsias

On the whole fuchsias are not good subjects for drying because they
change colour during the process.

Individual flowers can be pressed, however, for use in pressed flower
arrangements. Use good quality blotting paper and a small flower press.
Lay the flowers on tissue paper between the blotting paper and check
progress after a few days. Fuchsias retain a lot of moisture and you will
probably find that you need to change the blotting paper before the
flowers are completely dry, so that they do not become mildewed. Laying
them between tissue paper means that you can change the blotting paper
without having to disturb the flowers themselves too much. The forms
and varieties of *F. magellanica* seem to keep their colour best.

A drying agent such as silica gel (which you can obtain from chemists,
photographic suppliers or dried flower shops), borax, fine sand or even

washing powder can be used, but results are not always satisfactory. Use the most perfect flowers you can find and lay them on a bed of the crystals in an airtight container. Carefully add more crystals, making sure that the flowers are completely filled and covered with the crystals. Place the lid on the container and leave it in a warm, dry place for anything from few days to two weeks. Check to see if the petals are drying after a few days, but do not remove them until they are completely dry. Then very carefully remove them from the container and gently brush the petals with a paintbrush to remove every trace of crystal.

chapter 19

Photographing Fuchsias

In recent years cameras have become largely automatic and easier to use, and photography is now within everyone's reach. In the old days, you had to have a good understanding of all the processes involved in taking a decent photograph; today it is quite different. Anyone can put in a spool of film and use a camera. If the aperture is properly adjusted, you have to be behaving rather stupidly for something still to go wrong. In addition, modern developing services will print your negatives perfectly. All you need do is to choose the subject and angle, and take the shot. That is all you have to do, and each time you pick up your camera you will find that the possibilities are endless.

Many amateur photographers have begun to find that everyday subjects no longer challenge their capabilities, and they now prefer to specialize. One possible specialty is flowers, especially fuchsias. There are several possible approaches:

- Taking a group of plants. This gives a overall view of the plants, but it is often difficult to make out any detail. This rather basic plant photography can be undertaken just as well with an ordinary fixed focus camera as with the more versatile single lens reflex camera.

- Taking a single plant. Here the detail will become clearer. Again, this can be done with a fixed focus camera, but better results will be obtained using an SLR.

- Taking part of a plant so that you have a good close up view of the flower in full bloom, its buds and overall shape.

- Taking a single flower. This clearly shows the colour of stamens, pistil and petals.

For photographing part of a plant or a single flower a single lens reflex camera is by far the better option, allowing accurate composition in the viewfinder and precise focussing on the main elements of the picture subject.

You can buy a wealth of auxiliary devices if you are interested in taking close-ups. Perhaps most important is the mountable lens, which is like

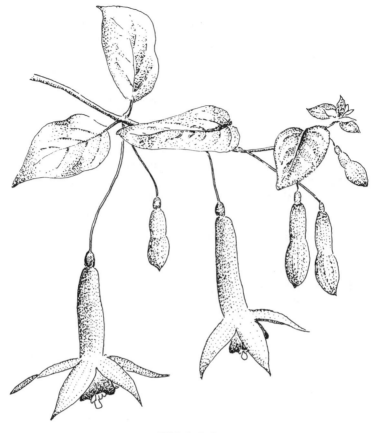

'Elfriede Ott'

putting a pair of spectacles on the camera, so greatly does it improve focus at small distances. Setting the aperture (11–16–22) will help achieve this.

Such a lens can be mounted on an SLR camera, and in some cases on a fixed focus one as well. A better solution, however, is to use more intermediate lenses. Make sure you buy good ones that transfer all automatic functions. A disadvantage is that too fine an aperture setting is needed for perfect focus for close-ups.

The best way to take close-ups is to use a macro-lens, by which the chosen flower can always be brought into sharp focus. For good results, use a tripod and cable release, and choose the shortest exposure possible (1/125–1/250 or 1/500 sec) to avoid any fuzziness caused by movement. The greatest depth of focus is obtained by the smallest diaphragm settings (11, 16 or 22).

The best colour reproduction and scope for enlargement are achieved with a slow film (25 or 50 ASA). The following tips may be useful: take your time in choosing the right composition; make sure that the plant is undamaged, remove brown leaves and flowers with spots (caused for example by rain); never take shots in full sunlight, because this gives too much contrast; work early in the morning when the fuchsias look best, or late afternoon; try to avoid including reflective surfaces in the composition; place the camera so that no other plants can be seen in the corners; and make sure that parts of pots remain invisible. If the background is much lighter than the subject to be taken, you can adjust the aperture by using a light meter or, if your camera is automatic and has one, using the exposure override facility provided . Many owners of small cameras with automatic focusing are a bit vague about the override button: when should they use + 1 and when −1? The following may help:

− 2: very dark subject in grey light
− 1: dark areas predominate
no correction: normal contrast
+ 1: light areas predominate
+ 2: the picture is *contre jour* or there is a lot of blue light

These guidelines, combined with your enthusiasm, should enable you to take some beautiful photographs of fuchsias.

If you are on the point of buying a camera or have just bought one, stick to one type of colour print or transparency film in the beginning, and have it developed by the same service, because this is the best way of getting to know and evaluating the equipment and the film.

chapter 20

Fuchsia Species

The word 'species' is the scientific term for plants found in the wild, and it is Latin for 'sort'. Fuchsia species are shrubs or small trees, sometimes lianas or epiphytes growing on rocks or tree trunks without roots in the soil. Most fuchsias have small to medium-sized flowers, mostly red or orange but with some light violet or almost white flowers. Sometimes whole bunches flower together. They are thus fairly conspicuous and have for long been taken from the woods and planted in gardens. Fuchsias from South and Central America are pollinated mostly by humming-birds, which catch small insects in the flowers and suck honey. They hover almost motionless in front of the flower. Once pollinated, the plant forms edible, red or dark violet berries, sometimes as large as small plums. In Europe it is bumble bees and large nocturnal butterflies (such as swallowtails, with long sucking tubes) that pollinate the plants.

Their natural habitats are far apart, and the different species have not-able differences, yet they share some qualities that attract amateur growers. For a start, they flower as small cuttings; they are not sensitive to the type of soil in which they are grown, provided they are adequately fertilized; and a well-kept fuchsia garden can be in full bloom from early July until frost sets in.

Interest in growing species fuchsias has increased among growers in recent years, and after concentrating on the many cultivars that are now available, these original forms are a welcome change. Looking after these plants, although they are exotic by origin, is hardly more difficult than caring for 'ordinary' fuchsias. Indeed, they are much less prone to many infections, and they show amazing re-growth after injury. Growth can be a problem, of course, since these forms have not been carefully selected for producing good shapes to grow in protected environments. They have to struggle for existence in the wild, among many competitors, and most of them therefore need a large pot and a spacious site to develop fully. There are a few problem plants among wild fuchsias, including *F. jimene-zii*, *F. magdalenae* and *F. triphylla*. Given the conditions in the various countries of origin, it is amazing that there are so few species. When we consider the open spots in forested mountain sides, with the full morning light and, when the sun becomes too strong, protection against too much heat and the danger of drying off provided by a thick curtain of mist, our problem is how to meet such demands, not to mention the different mountain soil. Species must be tolerant to grow in a garden in a pot with a largely peat-based compost.

Overwintering in temperate climates such as that found in northern Europe is, of course, quite different from what the plants are used to, so that most of them die in that period. A well-lit place at the top of a well-ventilated greenhouse is best. If this fails, it is always possible to take new cuttings.

The genus *Fuchsia* is divided into nine sections or groups.

Key to Identifying Sections
Start at 1a and 1b. Having chosen, look further under the number or section given at the right-hand side and proceed down the list until you have pinpointed the correct section. Then proceed to the relevant section on the following pages.

1a Petals absent or reduced to scales, leaves usually one per bud.   **2**
1b Petals as long as sepals or longer, leaves crosswise or in rings.   **3**

2a Flower tube wide open (at most 1.5cm long), sepals turned back, loose.
New Zealand and Tahiti   **Section 4, Skinnera**
2b Flower tube funnel or tube shaped, mostly longer than 2cm. Sepals spread out or upright, more or less joined at base.
South America   **Section 5, Hemsleyella**

3a Leaf with thickened stalk at base, growing to a permanent thorn, sepals turned back, small flower.
Chile   **Section 3, Kierschlegeria**
3b Leaf base impermanent or growing into thorn.   **4**

4a Flowers upright at end of branches.
Mexico to Panama   **5**
4b Flowers mostly hanging, not branched as in 4a.   **6**

5a Stamens upright.   **Section 6, Schufia**
5b Stamens before petals short, bent back in tube.
Panama and Cost Rica   **Section 6a, Jimenezia**

6a Flowers sometimes partly without stamens, small and modest, short stamens and those before petals bent back in the tube. Berry with few seeds.
Mexico to Panama   **Section 7, Encliandra**

6b Flowers complete (with stamens and pistils in each), mostly conspicuous; stamens mainly longer than petals, multi-seed berry.
South America and West Indies   7

7a Flower tube many times longer than petals, stamens hanging out far below corolla.
East Brazil to Patagonia and Chile   **Section 1, Quelusia**
7b Flower tube many times longer than petals, stamens not much longer than corolla.
Andes, central Argentina to Mexico and West Indies   8

8a Normal fuchsia leaf.   **Section 2, Fuchsia**
8b Heart-shaped leaf.   **Section 2a, Ellobium**

The different sections are described separately on the following pages. We shall indicate how many species belong to each section, by means of a key and some of the more commonly seen species will be named. In determining a species you need a preparation pin (a stiff steel pin with a glass head will do just as well), a small ruler and a magnifying glass that will enlarge by about ten times.

In many species we must look at the inside of the tube to examine the nectary and to see whether small hairs grow in the tube and, if so, how high. The species grown here for years all came to Europe as seed, from berries gathered in America along the roadside and in or near villages. Very likely there were hybrids among them. In recent years, many well-identified fuchsia cuttings have been imported from America.

For sections 1, 4 and 5 we have followed Philip A. Munz, 'A revision of the genus Fuchsia' (*Proceedings of the California Academy of Sciences*, 1943). For section 3, in addition to van Munz, *Annals of the Missouri Botanical Garden*, vol. 69, 1982 (article by Arsett and Rundel). For sections 2, 2a, 6 and 6a the research by Berry and by Breedlove, Berry and Raven in the same publication. Section 7, Encliandra, is described after Breedlove in *University of California Publications in Botany*, vol. 53, 1969.

Section 1, Quelusia (Vand.) D. C.

Fuchsias in this section have complete flowers with a tube not longer than the petals. Flowers are fairly small but as in ordinary cultivated fuchsias. Leaves are set crosswise. Six species are known: *F. bracelinae*, *F. campos-portoi*, *F. coccinea*, *F. hybrida* cult., *F. magellanica* and *F. regia*. Of these, only *F. bracelinae* was not grown in the Netherlands in 1984.

Key for Section 1, Quelusia (Vand.) D. C.

1a Flower tube short (3–6mm); young branches, hairy to felted.   **2**
1b Flower tube longer (8–20mm); young branches almost or quite bare.   **5**

2a Leaves 4–10cm long, 2–4cm wide, edges whole.
Brazil (Rio de Janeiro, Minas Gerais)   **F. regia** var. **alpestris**
2b Leaves 1.5–5cm long, 3–20mm wide, mostly dentate.   **3**

3a Young branches thinly haired; leaves leathery.
Brazil (Itatiaya)   **F. campos-portoi**
3b Young branches downy to hairy; leaves mostly wider than 6mm; herb-like.   **4**

4a Wholly herb-like with non-lignified branches 20–50cm high, leaf stalks 1–2mm long; stems densely and roughly haired.
Brazil (Erito Santo)   **F. bracelinae**
4b Well-developed shrub, 1–3 metres high, leaf stalks 2–4cm long, stalks hairy to downy.
Brazil (Minas Gerais)   **F. coccinea**

5a Leaves smooth-edged 4–10cm long, 2–4cm wide; sepals connected for 2–15mm.
Southeast Brazil   **F. regia**
5b Leaves saw-toothed 1–5cm long, 2–4cm wide; sepals mostly separate.   **6**

6a Leaf stalks 3–10mm long; flower tube 8–10mm long; sepals 15–25mm long, 3–4mm wide.
Southeast Chile and southeast Argentina   **F. magellanica**
6b Leaf stalks 10–25mm long; flower tube 10–20mm long or more; sepals 25–30mm long, 8–11mm wide.
Gardens, wild in, e.g., Colombia and Venezuela   **F. hybrida**

Section 2, Fuchsia, Berry (Eufuchsia Munz)

This section is identified by long small flowers, mostly red or orange, a long tube (sometimes much longer than calyx and petals) as, for example, in Triphylla hybrids. Some have flowers in axils, others in clusters at the end of stalks. All come from the misty and cloudy zone of the tropical Andes. In our gardens, conditions are indeed quite different. There are 61 known species, a good half of which are in cultivation.

Key for Section 2, Fuchsia, Berry

1a Flowers in leaf axils of leaves, which differ little or not at all from normal leaves, not in bunches at the top of the branches or of the small side branches.   **2**
1b Flowers close together, at top of stalks, in bunches or on short diverging side branches.   **41**

2a Flower tube 3–32mm long.   **3**
2b Flower tube 33–80mm long.   **13**

3a Flower tube 3–6mm long, shorter than the ovary.   **F. verrucosa**
3b Flower tube 10–32mm long, longer than the ovary.   **4**

4a Flower tube (inversely conical), truncated funnel, 9–16mm wide at top edge, sepals 18–25mm long.
Hispaniola   **F. pringsheimii**
4b Flower tube cylindrical to almost funnel-shaped, 2–9mm wide at top edge, sepals 6–17mm long.
South America   **5**

5a Well diverging branches, short tertiary side branches; leaf 15–35 (45)mm long, 7–15mm wide, four to six side veins on each side of the main vein.
Central to south Peru   **F. decussata**
5b Branches less clearly divergent, slack, short tertiary branching almost absent; leaf mostly longer than 40mm, more than 15mm wide; six to fifteen side veins on each side of main vein.   **6**

6a Leaves crosswise, very rarely three per bud; surface clearly wrinkled; stalks, leaf and flowers with rigid diverging hair, two to six flowers per branch.   **F. scabriuscula**
6b Leaves not quite crosswise, sometimes three or four leaves per bud. Leaf not clearly wrinkled, hair not rigidly divergent, sometimes absent; flowers mostly eight or more per branch.   **7**

7a Young branches and leaf bare or with fine hair; leaves sometimes with velvet hair on the underside of the central vein.   **8**
b Young branches and leaves with grey or rust-brown hairs.   **9**

8a Leaf strongly herb-like, elliptical to broadly oblong, edge smooth or lightly dentate, leaf stalk 5–25mm long; flowers bright orange or red. Peru and Bolivia   **F. sanctae-rosae**
8b Leaves thin, elliptic oval-shaped, edge with gland hair on the teeth, leaf stalk (15) 25–50mm long, flower tube and sepals pale whitish pink, petals darker red to purple.
Colombia and Ecuador   **F. pallescens**

9a Flower stalks 3–10mm long, ovary and berry thin cylinder to funnel-shaped; berry 13–25mm long; dense young branches with grey hair.   **10**
9b Flower stalks (6) 8–32mm long; ovary elliptical, berry oval to almost round 9–18mm long; young branches without thin hair.   **11**

10a Leaf finely veined or wrinkled, flower tube almost funnel-shaped, 3.5–7mm wide at top edge; sepals 10–13mm long, petals red, berry narrower at top 13–17mm long, 5–7mm thick.
Ecuador   **F. sylvatica**
10b Leaf not wrinkled, mostly with deeper set side veins; flower tube cylindrical 3–6mm wide at top edge; sepals 6–10mm long; petals dark purple; berry not narrower at top, 15–25mm long, 5–10mm thick.
Colombia and Venezuela   **F. nigricans**

11a Leaf edges slightly dentate; stalks with thin to dense non-red hair; ovary clearly square; petals oval-elliptical to round, (2) 3–8mm wide.
Ecuador   **F. loxensis**
11b Leaf edge dentate or saw-toothed; stalks mostly upright, lightly covered with white to reddish hair; ovary long and thin or slightly angular; petals narrow to elliptical 2–3mm wide.
Peru   **12**

12a The lowest leaves in rings of four; much larger than the higher leaves, not bluish in colour; they have eight to fourteen veins on both sides of the main vein; flowers at top of branches accompanied by smaller leaves; flower pink to red, flower tube 4–6mm at the top edge.
Peru (Amazonas)   **F. fontinalis**
12b Lowest leaves mostly three per bud and not much lager than higher ones, often bluish; six to ten side veins on each side of the main vein; flowers between normal leaves, not just at top of stalk; flower red to blue-violet, flower tube mostly 6–9mm wide at top edge.
Peru (San Martin to Junin)   **F. ferreyrae**

13a Leaves quite or almost stalkless, petals 0.5–3mm long.   **14**
13b Leaves not or almost stalkless, petals longer than 3mm.   **16**

14a Leaf 10-50mm wide, edge dentate or saw-toothed, not rolled up; branches bare or with downy hair.
Bolivia   **F. cochabambana**
14b Leaf 2–6mm wide, edge not cut, sometimes rolled up; branches with rust-coloured hair.
Ecuador and Peru   **15**

15a Leaf oval, elliptical 8–12mm long, 3.5mm wide; flower stalk 9–15mm long.
North Peru   **F. concertifolia**
15b Very narrow, linear leaf 20–70mm long, 2–3mm wide; flower stalk 16–20mm long.
South Ecuador   **F. steyermarkii**

16a Petals wide, less than twice as long, top round or bluntly pointed.   **17**
16b Narrow petals, more than twice as long, top sharp to blunt point.   **28**

17a Sepals strongly bent back shortly after blooming; petals upright.
Central Ecuador   **F. ampliata**
17b Sepals more or less turned up to diverging, not clearly bent back after blooming; petals spread out to diverging.   **18**

18a Leaves crosswise, usually narrow oval.
South Peru   **F. vargasiana**
18b Leaves not always crosswise, rings of three or four occur; leaf not usually oval.   **19**

19a Side veins mostly three to eight on both sides of main vein.   **20**
19b Side veins mostly eight to twenty-two on each side of main vein.**24**

20a Petals mostly longer than sepals; rhomboid or broadly elliptical, base narrower or claw-shaped; leaf shiny on top, usually glowing when dry and more or less convex, with glands on the dentate edge.
South Colombia to central Ecuador   **F. corollata**
20b Petals shorter or almost as long as sepals, not rhomboid or with a narrowed claw-shaped base; dry leaf usually not glowing and convex at top.   **21**

21a Petals elliptic-oval usually shorter than sepals 5–6 (9)mm wide; ovary more or less triangular, 5–6mm long; leaf edge usually with obvious glands on teeth; flower tube pink-cherry red to lavender-purple, mostly more or less swollen in the middle; petals usually rather darker than sepals.
South Colombia   **F. caucana**

21b Petals round to broadly elliptic-oval, little shorter than sepals (6) 7–13mm wide; ovary clearly square and 6–9mm long on average; leaf edge smooth to saw-toothed with gland at top of teeth; flower tube orange to deep red, mostly not clearly swollen in the middle; petals and sepals roughly the same in colour.   **22**

22a Leaves crosswise or three per bud, the edge with glands on the teeth; flower stalk 10–15mm long.
South Ecuador   **F. harlingii**
22b Leaves in rings of three to five, edge smooth to dentate; flower stalk 5–55mm long.   **23**

23a Flower stalk quite often with small knots; flower tube somewhat warty, 4–6mm at base and 10–12mm at edge, inside dense downy hair for $\frac{1}{4}$–$\frac{1}{2}$ from base, sepals thick and spongy about 1.5mm thick when fresh; petals dull purple; berry 16–18mm long, 8–11mm thick.
South Peru to Bolivia   **F. austromontana**
23b Flower stalk smooth 5–25 (40)mm long; flower tube smooth 3–4mm wide at base, 6–10mm at edge, hairy inside for most of its length; sepals solid, less than 1mm thick (fresh), not purple on drying; berry 11–15mm long, 7–9mm thick.
South Colombia and Ecuador   **F. vulcanica**

24a Flower tube 5–8cm long, mostly more or less curved; sepals 7–8mm wide at base; leaves mostly crosswise 6–27cm long.
Ecuador and Colombia   **F. macrostigma**
24b Flower tube 3.5–6cm long, straight; sepals 3.5–7mm wide at base; flowers mostly in rosettes of three or four, 2–18cm long.   **25**

25a Young branches and leaves bare or with slightly rising hair; honey gland a flat ribbon 3–6mm high, along inside of flower tube below edge.
Northeast Colombia   **F. magdalenae**
25b Young branches with marked downy hair; honey gland ring-shaped downy 1–3mm high and for the largest part of the base of the flower tube.
South Colombia and Bolivia   **26**

26a Petals 8–11mm long, 5.5–8mm wide, clearly smaller than sepals; flower tube 5.5–8mm wide at edge; branches and leaves with grey hair, strands lying flat to diverging, leaf 6–18cm long. 2.2–7cm wide.
Peru   **F. ayavacensis**
26b Petals 12–17mm long, 8–13mm wide at edge, almost as long as sepals; flower tube 8–12mm wide at edge; branches and leaf almost bare to densely haired, hairs mostly standing; leaf 2.5–8 (10)cm long, 1.4cm wide.   **27**

21 'Tristesse'

22 'Fanfare'

23 'Fiery Spider'

24 'Grasmere'

25 'Bergnimf'

26 'Falling Stars'

27 'Trailing King'

28 'Swanley Yellow'

29 'The Doctor'

30 'Oranje Boven'

31 'Oranje van Os'

32 'Orange Flare'

33 'Orange Crush'

34 'Daisy Bell'

35 'Lord Lonsdale'

36 'Mia van der Zee'

37 'Valerie'

38 'Amélie Aubin'

39 'Water Nymph'

40 'Impudence'

41 'Loeky'

42 'Belle de Spa'

43 'Willie Tamerus'

44 'Diana Wills'

45 'Frosted Flame'

46 'Eusebia'

47 'Abbé Farges'

48 'Foxtrot'

49 'Jack King'

50 'Stad Elburg'

51 'Bernadette'

52 'Rose Bradwardine'

53 'Multa'

54 'Tsjiep'

55 'Rika'

56 'Berba'

57 'Celia Smedley'

58 'Cross Check'

59 'Checkerboard'

60 'Checkerboard'

61 'Margaret'

62 'Whiteknight's Ruby'

63 'Cambridge Louie'

64 'Pink Bon Accorde'

65 'Marie Punselie'

66 'San Leandro'

67 'Tourtonne'

68 'Whirlaway'

69 'Blue Ribbon'

70 'Pink Marshmallow'

71 'Annabel'

72 'White Spider'

73 'Sleigh Bells'

74 'Aquarius'

75 'Walz Floreat'

76 *F. magellanica*   77 'Constance'

78 *F. magellanica* var. *gracilis tricolor*

79 'Archie Owen'

80 'Pink Galore'

81 'Blanche Regina'

82 'Elfriede Ott'

83 'Göttingen'

84 'Mantilla'

85 'Andenken an Heinrich Henkel'

86 *F. triphylla*

87 'Gartenmeister Bonstedt'

88 'Coralle'/'Koralle'

89 'Achievement'

90 'Pumila'

91 'Regal'

92 'Boerhaave'

93 'Lady Boothby'

94 'Dollar Princess'

95 'Vobeglo'

96 'Kwintet'

97 'Little Beauty'

98 'Jan Bremer'

99 'Arcadia'

100 'Tangerine'

101 'Mandarin'

102 'Baby Chang'

103 'Texas Longhorn'   104 'Postiljon'

105 'Galadriel'

106 'Tennessee Waltz'

107 'Party Frock'

108 'Heather Hobbs'

109 'Peppermint Stick'

110 'Tuonela'

111 'Estelle Marie'

112 'Blue Pearl'

113 'Troika'

114 'Preston Guild'

115 'Baroque Pearl'

116 'Belle de Lisse'

117 'Sugar Blues'

118 'Powder Puff'

119 'Blush o' Dawn'

120 'Moonraker'

121 'Cloverdale Pearl'

122 'Radings Michelle'

123 'Vincent van Gogh'

124 'Alison Ewart'

125 'Caroline'

27a Leaf mostly bare on topside; flower tube 4–6mm wide at base, more or less knotty, wall about 1.5cm thick when fresh, flower tube with dense velvety hair inside subdivided 1/4–1/3; petals purplish when drying; berry 16–18mm long when ripe.
South Peru to Bolivia   **F. austromontana**
27b Leaf with downy hair on top; flower tube 3–4mm wide at base, smooth, not as thick-walled (less than 1mm when fresh), most of tube with inside hair; petals do not dry purplish; berry 11–15mm long.
Ecuador   **F. vulcanica**

28a Leaf edge whole, sometimes curled; small teeth with honey glands visible only with magnifying glass.   **29**
28b Leaf edge dentate or saw-toothed, glands at top of teeth clearly visible.   **31**

29a Petals 9–11mm long, smooth and not turned back.
South Ecuador   **F. scherffiana**
29b Petals 15–22mm long, wrinkled and turned back when fresh.   **30**

30a Leaves (mostly three per bud) between seven and twelve side veins on each side of main vein; tops of sepals linked in bud.
Colombia and Venezuela   **F. venusta**
30b Thirteen to fifteen side veins on each side of main vein; leaves mostly four per bud, tops of sepals mostly free and divergent in bud.
North Peru   **F. rivularis**

31a Leaves always crosswise, mostly narrow oval.
North Peru   **F. vargasiana**
31b Leaves not always crosswise, rings of three to four occur, not oval.   **32**

32a Petals as long as sepals.   **33**
32b Petals rather shorter than sepals.   **38**

33a Leaf stalk 3–9mm long.   **34**
33b Leaf stalk 10–40mm long.   **36**

34a Three to eight side veins on each side of main vein.
Colombia and Ecuador   **F. corollata**
34b Nine to fifteen side veins on each side of main vein.
North Peru   **35**

35a Three or more often four leaves per bud; thirteen to fifteen side veins on each side of main vein; leaf edge whole to dentate; branches smooth.
Peru   **F. rivularis**

35b Leaves crosswise or in threes; nine to thirteen side veins on each side of main vein; leaf edge dentate, branches with warts.
Peru   **F. llewelynii**

36a Flower tube with small ribs, coarse hair, 3.5–5.5mm wide at base, 1–2mm thick, solidly sponge-like when fresh, dull orange, flower stalk 5–13mm long.
South Colombia   **F. canescens**
36b Flower tube smooth, bare to hairy (erect hair), 2.5–4mm wide at base, less than 1mm thick and not solidly sponge-like when fresh, bright red to pink; flower stalk 12–40mm long.   **37**

37a Petals elliptical to rhomboid (5) 6–10mm wide; solid leaf 2–7cm long, 0.7–3cm wide, fairly bubbly and drying shiny at top edge. Leaf stalks 3–12 (22)mm long.
Southwest Colombia and Ecuador   **F. corollata**
37b Petals elliptical, long to somewhat oval, 4–8mm wide; thin leaf 3.5–12cm long; 1.5–5cm wide, dull and not bubbly when dry; leaf stalk 10–48mm long.
Venezuela and northeast Colombia   **F. gehrigeri**

38a Flower tube cylindrical (3) 4–8mm wide at base, solid wall 1–1.5mm thick when fresh; ovary 10-13mm long, stamens 4–6mm long.
Peru and Bolivia   **F. denticulata**
38b Flower tube funnel-shaped 2–4 (6)mm wide at base, wall less thick and solid, less than 1mm thick when fresh; ovary 5–8mm long; stamens 2–4mm long.
Colombia and Ecuador   **39**

39a Young branches angular, thick camel-coloured hair; leaves mostly four per bud; flower tube 5–6 (8)mm wide at edge; sepals 3–4mm wide at base.
Colombia and Ecuador (border area)   **F. cinerea**
39b Young stems triangular, not densely haired; leaves mostly three per bud; flower tube (4) 6–12mm wide at edge; sepals 5–9mm wide at base.   **40**

40a Petals elliptical-oval, 9–11 (14)mm long, blunt to wedge-shaped at top, bare, purplish, mostly darker than sepals; sepals 5–6mm wide at base.
South Colombia   **F. caucana**
40b Petals lanceolate to oval-lanceolate (8) 12–20mm long, mostly with clear point and downy to velvety hair on the back, red and not much darker than sepals; sepals mostly 6–9mm wide at base.
Central Colombia and Venezuela   **F. petiolaris**

41a Flower tube 12–23mm long.   **42**
41b Flower tube 24–130mm long.   **58**

42a Leaf horizontal or almost, stalk 0.5–5mm long; side veins
18–25mm on each side of main vein.
Ecuador   **F. sessilifolia**
42b Leaf standing, stalk over 5mm; five to eighteen side veins on each
side of the main vein.   **43**

43a Leaves wholly or mostly crosswise.   **44**
b Leaves in rings of three or four.   **49**

44a Three to eight side veins on each side of the main vein; flower tube
light cream to pink, petals much darker than sepals.
Ecuador and south Colombia   **F. pallescens**
44b Nine or more side veins on each side of main vein; flower tube red
to orange, not light coloured or whitish, petals not much darker than
flower tube or sepals.   **45**

45a Branches and leaves densely haired; leaf mostly oval.   **46**
45b Branches and leaves not densely haired, bare to downy or with
erect hair; leaf mostly elliptical, not oval.   **47**

46a Flowers in dense bunch at end, 1.5–7cm long, flower stalks
18–30mm long; sepals 7–9mm long.
South Peru   **F. tincta**
46b Flowers in axils in bunches or plumes 5–10cm long, stalks
10–20mm long; sepals 10–13mm long.
Central Peru   **F. ovalis**

47a Flowers bunched at ends or on short side branches, leaves in
bunch not very different or smaller.
Peru   **F. macrophylla**
47b Flowers bunched at ends, much reduced, almost horizontal leaves,
linear to lanceolate small bracts.
Colombia and Ecuador   **48**

48a Bunches mostly lengthened, 5–16cm long, mostly unbranched,
bracts permanent; flower stalk 3–7 (12)mm long, mostly not diverging;
sepals 6–8mm long; twelve to seventeen side veins on each side of main
vein.
Ecuador   **F. orientalis**
48b Bunches mostly short, 1–4 (10) cm long, stipules mostly
deciduous; flower stalks divergent 8–25mm long; sepals 8–11mm long;
nine to thirteen side veins on each side of main vein.
Colombia   **F. putumayensis**

49a Flower stalks 2–10mm long. **50**

49b Flower stalks 10–40mm long. **54**

50a Leaves mostly in rings of four; flowers in dense plumes at end branches; berries almost spherical 6–10mm long. **51**

50b Leaves mostly in rings of three; flowers in bunches, few bunches per plant; berries long to cylindrical 13–25mm long. **52**

51a Leaves in rings of more than four, edge slightly dentate; stalks grey to roughly haired; flower tube 13–20 (24)mm long, 1.5–3mm wide at base.
Colombia **F. hartwegii**

51b Leaves in rings of less than four, edge dentate to saw-toothed; branches grey to densely haired; flower tube 15–28mm long, 3–4mm wide at base.
North Peru **F. fontinalis**

52a Stalks, leaves and flowers with dense rough hair; ovary 5–6mm long; small bracts, narrow, lancet-shaped.
North Peru **F. pilosa**

52b Stalks, leaves and flowers grey or thinly haired, never hirsute or rough; ovary (6) 7–11mm long; small bracts oval to elliptical.
Venezuela to Ecuador **53**

53a Leaves mostly of net-shaped design, wrinkled; flower tube almost funnel-shaped, 3.5–7mm wide at top; sepals 10–13mm long; petals red; berries narrow at top, 17mm long, 5–7mm thick.
Ecuador **F. sylvatica**

53b Leaves not of net-shaped design or wrinkled; flower tube cylindrical, 3–6mm wide at top; sepals 6–10mm long; petals dark purple; berries almost unpointed at top 15–25mm long, 5–10mm thick.
Colombia and Venezuela **F. nigricans**

54a Leaves and small thin branches bare or finely downy, sometimes distinct hairs on the middle vein on underside of leaf. **55**

54b Leaves and thin branches grey, roughly or densely haired. **56**

55a Flowers red, in end bunches or on short side branches; leaves 5–9cm wide; fourteen to nineteen side veins on each side of main vein.
Central Peru **F. macrophylla**

55b Flowers orange-red, mostly not in end bunches or on short side branches; leaves 1–4cm wide, six to fifteen side veins on either side of main vein.
South Peru to Bolivia **F. sanctae-rosae**

56a Leaves broad elliptical to oval; flowers in end bunches or plumes.
Central Peru   **F. ovalis**
56b Leaves lanceolate to elliptical, not oval; flowers in end bunches or
plumes.   **57**

57a Leaves four or more per ring; leaf edge slightly dentate; branches
grey to roughly haired; flower tube 13–20 (24)mm long, 1.5–3mm wide
at base.
Colombia   **F. hartwegii**
57b Leaves four or fewer per ring; leaf edge clearly dentate or saw-
toothed; stalks grey to densely haired; flower tube 15–28mm long,
3–4mm wide at base.
North Peru   **F. fontinalis**

58a Leaves wholly or almost pendent, leaf stalk 0.5–3mm long.   **59**
58b Leaves not pendent; leaf stalk longer than 3mm.   **62**

59a Leaves 8–12mm long, 3–5mm wide; hairy branches.
North Peru   **F. concertifolia**
59b Leaves 30–120mm long, 10–50mm wide; branches bare to slightly
hairy.   **60**

60a Four or five side veins on each side of main vein.
Central Peru   **F. coriacifolia**
60b Eight to twenty-six side veins on each side of main vein.   **61**

61a Leaves 10–24cm long, 4–8cm wide, smooth edge.
Ecuador and north Peru   **F. glaberrima**
61b Leaves 3–6cm long, 1–5cm wide, edge dentate or saw-toothed.
Bolivia   **F. cochabambana**

62a Leaves wholly or mostly crosswise.   **63**
62b Leaves mostly in rings of three or more.   **81**

63a Flower tube 9–13cm long; flowers in wrappings of hollow, pendent
bracts.
Central Peru   **F. ceracea**
63b Flower tube shorter than 9cm; flowers not in hollow pendent
bracts.   **64**

64a Flowers in end bunches or on short side branches.   **65**
64b Flowers in end bunches or plumes; not only on the axis or on a
short side branches.   **66**

65a Flower tube 19–25mm long; sepals 8–9mm long, with green top;
berry almost spherical 10–13mm long, 8–9mm thick.
Peru   **F. macrophylla**

65b Flower tube 32–45mm long; sepals 10–13mm long red; berry elliptical, 15–17mm long, 7–10mm thick.
Peru   **F. macropetala**

66a Flowering axis long, 10–60cm.   **67**
66b Flowering axis short, 0.5–10cm.   **70**

67a Fifteen to twenty-two side veins on each side of main vein. **68**
67b Eight to fourteen side veins on each side of main vein.   **69**

68a Leaf stalk 4–10mm long; sepals diverging after bloom opens.
Peru   **F. abrupta**
68b Leaf stalk 20–70mm long; sepals strongly reflexed after bloom opens.
Bolivia   **F. boliviana**

69a Leaves mostly narrow 2.5–10 (13) cm long, 1–5cm wide; flower tube mostly swollen at centre and somewhat drawn together at edge; petals 6–9mm long.
Hispaniola   **F. triphylla**
69b Leaves slightly hairy, 7–18cm long, 2–8cm wide; flower tube narrow and funnel-shaped, slightly swollen at centre or drawn together at edge; petals 11–20mm long.
North Peru   **F. wurdackii**

70a Mostly three to seven side veins on either side of main vein; flower tube and sepals pale pink, petals purple.
Ecuador   **F. pallescens**
70b Seven to twenty-two side veins on each side of main vein; flower tube and sepals not pale pink, petals not purple.   **71**

71a Stalks and leaves bare, downy or velvety.   **72**
71b Stalks and leaves roughly haired (hairy, felted or erect hair). **79**

72a Flower tube 40–70mm long.   **73**
72b Flower tube 32–40mm long.   **74**

73a Leaves shiny, bare on upper side; eight to twelve side veins on each side of main vein; stalks almost bare.
Colombia   **F. cuatrecasasii**
73b Leaves not shiny, mostly roughly haired or felted on upper side; thirteen to seventeen side veins on each side of main vein; stalks mostly with downy hair.
Central Peru   **F. corymbiflora**

74a Four inflorescences 5–15cm long almost erect to pendnet; leaves rarely to slightly haired.
Hispaniola   **F. triphylla**
74b Two to five inflorescences about 10cm long, divergent to pendent, not erect; leaves bare to downy.
South America   75

75a Leaves lanceolate, 10–24cm long, 4-8cm wide, underside often with purplish red; leaf stalk thick, 3–8mm long; ovary 7–9mm long; stipules thick and persistent.
Ecuador and north Peru   **F. glaberrima**
75b Leaves mostly elliptical, 4–17cm long, 2–10cm wide, mostly no purple on underside; leaf stalks not thick, 4–30mm long; ovary 2.5–7mm long; stipules not thick or persistent.   76

76a Petals 4–6mm wide; ovary 4–7mm long; flower tube (28) 35–40mm long.
South Colombia   **F. cuatrecasasii**
76b Petals 2.5–4mm wide; ovary 2.5–4mm long; flower tube 23–35 (40)mm long.
North Peru to south Colombia   77

77a Leaves elliptical to inverse oval, 2–10mm wide, mostly crosswise; sepals lanceolate, 3–5mm wide.   78
77b Leaves narrow elliptical to narrow lanceolate, 1–4cm wide, rings of 3–4 mostly present; sepals narrow lanceolate, 2.5–4mm wide.
South Ecuador   **F. lehmannii**

78a Third order twigs with fine downy hair; nine to thirteen side veins on each side of main vein, leaf stalks 6–115mm long; flower tube 15–27mm long.
South Colombia to central Ecuador   **F. putumayensis**
78b Small twigs mostly thin; twelve to fifteen, rarely eight, side veins on each side of main vein; leaf stalks 6–30mm long; flower tube 23–40mm long.
South Ecuador and north Peru   **F. andrei**

79a Ovary narrow cylindrical 10–11mm long; berry narrow cylindrical funnel-shaped, often more or less bent or with a much narrower top, 25–32mm long; twelve to eighteen side veins on each side of main vein.
South Peru   **F. vargasiana**
79b Ovary oblong 5–10mm long; berry oblong to spherical, 12–20mm long, not bent or with narrow top; seven to fourteen side veins on each side of main vein.   **80**

80a Flowering axis 4–18cm long, leaf stalk 9–11 (25)mm long; leaf edge somewhat dentate; stipules marked, 3–5mm long.
North Peru **F. wurdackii**
80b Flowering axis 1.5–5cm long; leaf stalks 15–40mm long; petals 6–10mm long; leaf edge dentate or saw-toothed; stipules 2–3mm long.
Bolivia **F. furfuracea**

81a Flowers wrapped in thin, hollow stipules. **82**
81b Flowers not so wrapped. **83**

82a Flower tube 4–5cm long; petals 9–13mm long.
Peru **F. simplicicaulis**
82b Flower tube 9–13cm long; petals 5–7mm long.
Peru **F. ceracea**

83a Flower tube 23–30mm. **84**
83b Flower tube 30–76mm. **87**

84a Leaf stalk (15) 25–50mm long, five to seven (occasionally nine) side veins on each side of main vein; flower tube and sepals light pink cream, petals much darker and purple.
Ecuador **F. pallescens**
84b Flower stalk 4–20 (25)mm long; four to seventeen side veins on each side of main vein; flower tube and sepals not pale pink cream, petals not purple or much darker than sepals. **85**

85a Young stalks and leaves mostly hairy; leaf edge clearly with honey glands on teeth or points; flower tube widest, 4–6mm, at top.
North Peru **F. fontinalis**
85b Young branches and leaves bare or sparsely haired; leaf edge smooth to finely dentate; flower tube mostly widest below edge, 6–11mm at edge. **86**

86a Flowers close together in short, divergent to hanging bunches, 0.5–3cm long; petals narrow, oblong, lanceolate, 2.5–4mm wide.
South Ecuador **F. lehmannii**
86b Flowers mostly not close together, bunches almost erect to bent, 44–15cm long; petals elliptic-oval 4–6mm wide.
Hispaniola **F. triphylla**

87a Leaves wholly or mostly in rings of four or more. **88**
87b Leaves wholly or mostly in rings of three. **93**

88a Leaf stalks 12–35mm long. **89**
88b Leaf stalks 3–10 (15)mm long. **91**

89a Sepals 14–18mm long, 6–9mm wide at foot, thick, spongy and sometimes warty when fresh, petals spade-shaped 14–19mm long, 4–7mm wide.
South Colombia   **F. canescens**
89b Sepals 11–14mm long, 3–6mm wide at foot, not thick, spongy or warty when fresh;petals narrow lanceolate to narrow elliptic-oval, 11–16 (18)mm long, 3–5 (6)mm wide.   **90**

90a Young branches and leaves with thick grey to thin hair; leaves rarely more than four per ring; stipules deciduous, not callous when fresh; 1.5–2mm long, 0.4–0.5mm wide.
South Colombia and Ecuador   **F. dependens**
90b Young branches and leaves densely to thinly haired; leaves mostly more than four per ring; stipules thick and callous when fresh, persistent, bent on older buds 2.5–4mm long, about 3mm wide.
Central Colombia   **F. crassistipula**

91a Flowers more or less in bunches, not plumes; flower stalks 10–53mm long.
North Peru   **F. rivularis**
91b Flowers in panicles; flower stalks 44–12mm long.   **92**

92a Young branches and leaves roughly to thinly haired.
Central Colombia   **F. hirtella**
92b Young branches and leaves finely haired to bare.
Ecuador and south Colombia   **F. polyantha**

93a Fifteen to twenty-five side veins on each side of main vein.   **94**
93b Seven to fifteen side veins on each side of main vein.   **95**

94a Leaf stalks 4–10mm long; sepals not reflexed after blooming; flower stalks diverging and standing.
Peru   **F. abrupta**
94b Leaf stalks 20–70mm long; sepals strongly bent back after blooming; flower stalks pendent.
Bolivia   **F. boliviana**

95a Petals clearly shorter than sepals.   **96**
95b Petals almost as long or longer than sepals.   **98**

96a Flower tube 55–76mm long.
Central Peru   **F. sanmartina**
96b Flower tube 22–40mm long.   **97**

97a Flowers closely together in bunches 0.5–3cm long; petals 2.5–4mm wide.
South Ecuador   **F. lehmannii**

97b Flowers not close together; bunches 4–15cm long; petals 4–6mm wide.
Hispaniola   **F. triphylla**

98a Leaf stalk 10–48mm long.   **99**
98b Leaf stalk 2–10mm long.   **100**

99a Flower stalks mostly short 9–11 (25)mm long; ovary cylindrical, 7–10mm long; leaves softly haired, 7–18cm long; stipules pale, 3–5mm wide, persistent.
North Peru   **F. wurdackii**
99b Flower stalks 12–40mm long, ovary egg-shaped, mostly thinner at top, 5–7mm long; leaves herb-like, almost bare to thinly haired 3.5–12cm long; stipules dark 1.5–2mm long, often deciduous.
Venezuela   **F. gehrigeri**

100a Leaves mostly in rings of four; thirteen to fifteen side veins on each side of main vein; sepal tops mostly free and divergent in bud; stamens narrow oblong 4–4.5mm long.
North Peru   **F. rivularis**
100b Leaves mostly in rings of three; seven to twelve veins on each side of main vein; sepal tops linked in bud; stamens oblong 2–3.5mm long.   **101**

101a Young branches and leaves with dense hair, often reddish; leaves narrow elliptical to short oblong, often more or less bent to one side; not shiny.
North Peru   **F. mathewsii**
101b Young branches and leaves bare to covered with fine erect hair, never reddish; leaves elliptical, symmetric, shiny on both sides.
Colombia and Venezuela   **F. venusta**

Section 2a, Ellobium (Lilja)
Breedlove, Berry and Raven Comb. Nov.

This group has bisexual flowers with well-developed style, stigma and stamens with good pollen in each. The plants do not form really wooden stems. They normally grow in the soil or sometimes as epiphytes (i.e., on rocks or tree trunks without roots in soil). Sometimes they have clearly thickened tuber roots. The leaves stand crosswise or in rings of three on the stalk; they are herb like, elliptic-oval or heart shaped. The flowers stand in the leaf axils, sometimes in plumes. The flower tube is longer than the sepals. Petals are mostly half as long or less than sepals. The honey gland has no lobes but is a smooth strip 0.3–0.5mm thick filling the lowest part of the flower tube. Stamens stand erect, shorter than the sepals or protrude less than 5mm. Stamens in front of sepals are longer than those in front of the corolla. The stigma is green. Berries are ellipsoidal to narrow, tube shaped, and large; between fifty and one hundred seeds, laterally compressed, oval to scalene triangular, 1–2mm long, 0.5–1mm wide.

Habitat

In the evergreen misty woods and in humid oak and coniferous forests of north Costa Rica to Mexico at 1,450–3,400 metres.

There are three species: *F. splendens*, with large edible berries, Mexico, Guatemala, San Salvador; *F. fulgens*, with thickened roots often epiphytic, Mexico to Costa Rica; *F. decidua* (Standley), with tuber roots, Mexico. *F. decidua* has flowers in branched plumes, and blooms in the leafless period (previously classified under Hemsleyella). This species has not yet been grown in the Netherlands. The other two are very decorative and have therefore long been planted in gardens; they have formed hybrids that did not occur in the wild, because the two species are not found in the same regions. One of these is *F. speciosa* cult.

Section 3, Kierschlegeria (Spach)
Species *F. lycioides* (Andrews 1807)

The type species has a clear wooden knot growing to a thorn at the foot of the leaf stalk, a form now present in the Netherlands; those that used to be called such were often hybrids probably with *F. magellanica* as the other parent. They lack thorns and have oblong berries. In the true species the berry is small, spherical and black. Five or six flower buds are formed in the leaf axils. Along with the very short stalk limbs the result is a mass of flowers on a small piece of stalk, very conspicuous although the flowers are small. The bisexual flowers (with good pistils and stamens) have a cylinder-shaped flower tube, at the top four sepals and four small petals. Female flowers, with good pistil and stamens without pollen, have a shorter and wider open tube 1.5–3mm long and a style of 6–10mm. The larger bisexual flowers sometimes have a badly developed style and stigma, so that they appear as male. The pistil flowers give many berries, the bisexual ones rather fewer per plant. The humming-bird that brings about pollination is a very small species, found only in the habitat of *F. lycioides*.

Section 4, Skinnera de Candolle

The four fuchsias in this group occur only in New Zealand and Tahiti. *F. cyrtandroides* from Tahiti, is not yet grown in the Netherlands. In New Zealand we find *F. colensoi* (a hybrid of *F. excorticata* and *F. perscandens*) and the species *F. excorticata*, *F. perscandens* and *F. procumbens*. *F. kirkii*, which used to be regarded as a separate species, merely carries the staminate flowers of *F. procumbens* and is not, therefore, a true species. The first three species are grown in the Netherlands.

Key for Section 4, Skinnera de Candolle

1a Petals 2–4mm long; plant very lignified, sometimes a climbing liana, shrub or tree; leaves whitish on underside 1–9cm long.   2
1b No petals, small plant, creeping with very thin wiry branches; leaves less white on underside, 0.5–11.8cm long.   5

2a Trees; leaves 2–9cm long, about ten large veins on each side of main vein.   3
2b No trees; leaves 1–4cm long with three to nine side veins.   4

3a Leaves oblong, oval, pointed to sharp at top, hairy along main vein on underside.
New Zealand   **F. excorticata**
3b Leaves elliptical to inverted elliptic-oval, rounded or blunt at top, underside bare.
Tahiti   **F. cyrtandroides**

4a Erect shrub; leaves oblong, oval, mostly 2–4cm long.
New Zealand   **F. colensoi**
4b Liana; leaves almost circular, 1–2cm long.
New Zealand   **F. perscandens**

5a Sepals pointed; style as long as stamens, flower tube tube-shaped to spread out, 7–8mm long.
New Zealand   **F. procumbens**
5b Sepals blunt, style shorter than flower tube, which is spread out 6–7mm long.   **F. kirkii**

Section 5, Hemsleyella Munz

Mexico, Bolivia, Peru, Venezuela. There are eleven known species in this group. Berry has claimed that here are fourteen but gives no name for the last three. The eleven are: *F. apetala*, *F. cestroides*, *F. garleppiana*, *F. hirsuta*, *F. juntasensis*, *F. macrantha*, *F. membranacea*, *F. salicifolia*, *F. tuberosa*, *F. tunariensis* and *F. unduavensis*. They are peculiar and very conspicuous. They have no petals, but a flower tube sometimes 14cm long and four sepals. Besides, they mostly flower on the bare wood, when the plants carry no leaves. They are climbing shrubs, often epiphytes (not rooted in soil), growing on rocks and tree trunks. They may grow well in soil suitable for orchids.

Key for Section 5, Hemsleyella Munz

1a Flower tube less than 2cm long, thirteen to sixteen side veins on each side of main vein.
Peru   **F. cestroides**
1b Flower tube longer than 2.5cm; leaves with five to ten large side veins on each side of the main vein.   **2**

2a Flower tube at least four or five times longer than sepals (inclusive of the lower part which is grown together).   **3**
2b Flower tube 1.5–3 times longer than sepals (inclusive as in 2a).   **4**

3a Leaves unroll when flowers appear; leaf stalks 3–7cm long; flower stalks 3–5cm long; flower tube 10–14cm long.
Bolivia   **F. garleppiana**
3b Mostly leafless when flowers appear; leaf stalks 1–3cm long; flower stalks 0.5–2.5cm long; flower tube 6–12 cm long.
Peru   **F. macrantha**

4a Flower tube without external hair.   **5**
4b Flower tube not bare outside under a magnifying glass.   **7**

5a Leaves spread, lance to egg-shaped, mostly two to four times longer than wide; flower tube 8–12mm wide; sepals greenish.
Peru   **F. tuberosa**
5b Leaves crosswise; elliptical to oval egg-shaped, not more than twice as long as wide; flower tube 5–8mm wide; sepals red.   **6**

6a Leaves mostly fallen off when flowering; sepals 18–22mm long; stamens longer than sepals; pistil 1–1.5cm longer than stamens.
Bolivia   **F. juntasensis**
6b Leaves present when flowering; stamens shorter than sepals; style nearly protrudes above stamens.
Venezuela   **F. membranacea**

7a Leaves elliptical to oval, branches not bare.   **8**
7b Leaves lance-shaped to oval; branches bare; flower tube little to lightly haired with gland hair.
Peru   **F. salicifolia**

8a Leaves crosswise; with fine short downy hairs; flower tube 5–8mm wide.   **F. tunariensis**
8b Leaves spread; branches with long hair; flower tube 7–11mm wide.**9**

9a Stamens longer than sepals; flower stalk 1.5–2.5cm long; inflorescence with short hair.   **F. apetala**
9b Stamens shorter than sepals; leaf stalk 1–1.5cm long, inflorescence with rough hair.   **10**

10a Leaves fall off when flower opens; white hairs, 0.5–1mm long. Peru and Brazil   **F. hirsuta**
10b Leaves present during flowering; brown hairs 1–1.5cm long. Bolivia   **F. unduavensis**

Section 6, Schufia (Spach) Munz 1943

This group contains two species: *F. arborescens* (Sims, 1825) and *F. paniculata* (Lindley, 1856); both are grown in the Netherlands and flower in gardens all year. The flowers are small, the leaves crosswise or in rings of three or four. Flowers stand erect in branching, erect panicles up to 25cm long and 20cm wide. The surface of the almost spherical berries has a waxy bloom, like that seen on grapes.

F. arborescens has whole leaves and is bisexual; stamens with pollen and pistil are well developed in each flower. Flowering starts early. When one might be thinking about trimming spring shoots, the plants are fully in bud – so do not trim! Flower tube and calyx pink violet, petals lilac. Habitat: Mexico, to a height of 1,750–2,500 metres.

F. paniculata has saw-toothed leaves and female besides bisexual flowers. Flowers are somewhat lighter in colour than those of *F. arborescens*, and also smaller and slimmer. Female flowers have short stamens without pollen. Ovary, style and stigma are well developed. Habitat: southeast Mexico to Panama, to a height of 1,200–3,000 metres.

Section 6a, Jimenezia Breedlove, Berry, Raven, 1967

Fuchsia jimenezii is the one species in this group grown in the Netherlands. Like group 6, it has many flowers in erect bunches. Stamens stand in front of petals and are bent back in the flower tube. Flower pink-red and petals pink.

Section 7, Encliandra (Zucc) Endlicher
Mexico and Central America

Small shrubs with small to very small leaves. Flowers very small. The group, which is also called Breviflora, has given much trouble to those concerned with their nomenclature. Munz describes sixteen species. After the 1969 revision by Breedlove only four remain, together with two new species and one natural hybrid: *F. encliandra*, *F. microphylla*, *F. obconica*, *F. parviflora*, *F. ravenii*, *F. thymifolia* and the natural hybrid *F. × bacillaris* cult.

This group is dioecious (male and female flowers are borne on different plants, or complete flowers on one plant and flowers with only pistils or only stamens are borne on another). These were once incorrectly described as separate species because the plants were clearly different. To identify a plant, begin by cutting a flower lengthwise (use a strong steel pin) and use a magnifying glass to see if it is complete, male or female. Next, use the appropriate key.

Key for Complete Flowers (Pistil and stamens)

1a Flower tube white when blooming, blunt, sepals bent back.　2
1b Flower tube red or red-violet on blooming, cylinder shaped; sepals erect to spread.　4

2a Leaf roughly dentate, herb-like; young branches with golden-brown hair.　**F. microphylla** subsp. **hidalgensis**
2b Leaf saw-toothed, leathery; young branches with white hairs or bare.　3

3a Flower tube 2.5–4mm long; leaf 30–60mm long.
Mexico (Chiapas) to Guatemala　**F. thymifolia** subsp. **minimiflora**
3b Flower tube 4–6mm long, leaf 10–25mm long.
Mexico (Durango to Oaxaca)　**F. thymifolia** subsp. **thymifolia**

4a Leaves 35–65mm long, downy hairs, dull on upper side.　**F. ravenii**
4b Leaf 6–30mm long, bare and shiny on upper side.　5

5a Leaf edge whole, flower tube red.　6
5b Leaf roughly dentate; tube red to violet red.　7

6a Flower tube with downy hair; leaf flat.
　　　　　　　　　　　　　　　F. microphylla subsp. **aprica**
6b Flower tube bare; leaf somewhat curled.
　　　　　　　　　　　　　　F. microphylla subsp. **quercetorum**

7a Flower tube 7–9.5mm long, red, cylindrical.
Costa Rica and Panama   **F. microphylla** subsp. **hemsleyana**
7b Flower tube 9–12mm long, red-violet, cylindrical.
Mexico (Hidalgo and Jalisco) to Honduras   8

8a Mexico (Hidalgo and Jalisco to Oaxaca)
                    F. microphylla subsp. **microphylla**
8b Mexico (Chiapas) to Honduras   **F. microphylla** subsp. **aprica**

Key for Male Flowers

1a Flower tube white.   **F. obconica**
1b Flower tube red.   2

2a Petals white.   3
2b Petals red.   5

3a Sepals white.   **F. parviflora**
3b Sepals red.   4

4a Leaf 9–20mm long.
Mexico (Hidalgo and Guerrero to Oaxaca)
                    F. encliandra subsp. **encliandra**
4b Leaf 35–110mm long.
Mexico (Chiapas) to Nicaragua   **F. encliandra** subsp. **tetradactyla**

5a Leaf 30–75mm long, felt to downy haired.
Mexico (Durango to Guerrero)   **F. parviflora**
5b Leaf 9–110mm long; bristly to downy hair.   6

6a Leaf 9–20mm long.
Mexico (Hidalgo and Guerrero to Oaxaca)
                    F. encliandra subsp. **encliandra**
6b Leaf 35–110mm long.
Mexico (Chiapas) to Nicaragua   **F. encliandra** subsp. **tetradactyla**

Key for Female Flowers

1a Flower tube white.   2
1b Flower tube red or purple.   5

2a Leaf roughly dentate; herb-like; young branches with golden-
brown hair.   **F. microphylla** subsp. **hidalgensis**
2b Leaf saw-toothed, leathery, small branches with white hair or bare.3

3a Flower tube 2.2–3.1mm long; honey gland with 4 lobes.
                                               F. obconica
3b Flower tube 1.2–3.1mm long; honey gland with 8 lobes.   4

4a Leaf 10–25mm long.
Mexico (Durango to Oaxaca)   **F. thymifolia** subsp. **thymifolia**
4b Leaf 30–60mm long.
Mexico (Chiapas) and Guatemala   **F. thymifolia** subsp. **minimiflora**

5a Leaf leathery.   6
5b Leaf herb-like.   9

6a Leaf 9–20mm long.
Mexico (Hidalgo and Guerrero to Oaxaca)
                                  F. encliandra subsp. **encliandra**
6b Leaf 30–110mm long.   7

7a Felty hair.
Mexico (Durango to Guerrero)   **F. parviflora**
7b Bristly hair.   8

8a Seeds 2.9–3.5mm long.
Mexico (Chiapas) to Nicaragua   **F. encliandra** subsp. **tetradactyla**
8b Seeds 1.8–2.9mm long.
Mexico (Oaxaca)   **F. ravenii**

9a Leaf edge whole, flower tube red.   10
9b Leaf coarsely dentate, flower tube red to violet red.   11

10a Flower tube lightly haired; flat leaves.
                                  F. microphylla subsp. **aprica**
10b Flower tube bare; leaves curly.
                                  F. microphylla subsp. **quercetorum**

11a Flower tube 7–9.5mm long, red, cylindrical.
Costa Rica and Panama   **F. microphylla** subsp. **hemsleyana**
11b Flower tube 9–12mm long, violet red, cylindrical.
Mexico (Hidalgo and Jalisco) to Honduras   12

12a Mexico (Hidalgo and Jalisco to Oaxaca)
                                  F. microphylla subsp. **microphylla**
12b Mexico (Chiapas) to Honduras   **F. microphylla** subsp. **aprica**

Key for Plants without Flowers, Sterile or only with Berries

1a Leaf coarsely dentate   2
1b Leaf edge smooth to saw-toothed.   5

2a Young branches with brown hair.
                                  F. microphylla subsp. **hidalgensis**
2b Young branches with white hair.   3

3a Mexico (north of the isthmus of Tehuantepec)
F. microphylla subsp. **microphylla**
3b Mexico (south of the isthmus of Tehuantepec)   **4**

4a Mexico (Chiapas) to Honduras   **F. microphylla** subsp. **aprica**
4b Costa Rica and Panama   **F. microphylla** subsp. **hemsleyana**

5a Leaf herb-like, side branches at right angles to stem.   **6**
5b Leaf leathery, side branches at acute angles to stem.   **8**

6a Leaf curly.   **F. microphylla** subsp. **quercetorum**
6b Leaf flat.   **7**

7a Mexico (Chiapas) to El Salvador
F. microphylla subsp. **hemsleyana**
7b Costa Rica to Panama   **F. microphylla** subsp. **hemsleyana**

8a Leaf large, 30–110mm long.   **9**
8b Leaf small, 9-25mm long.   **11**

9a Felty hair.
Mexico (Durango to Guerrero)   **F. parviflora**
9b Bristly hair.   **10**

10a Mexico (Chiapas) to Nicaragua
F. encliandra subsp. **tetradactyla**
10b Mexico (North of isthmus of Tehuantepec)   **12**

11a Mexico (Jalasco)   **F. obconica**
11b Mexico (Hidalgo and Guerrero to Oaxaca)
F. encliandra subsp. **enclandria**

12a Mexico (Sierra de Miahuatan Oaxaca)   **F. ravenii**
12b Trans-Mexican volcanic belt   **F. obconica**

In addition to the true species there are hybrids, both natural and cultivated. The hybrids often bloom more profusely than the species, and they
also have larger flowers.

Description of species

Key: T = flower tube; S = sepal; C = corolla; Syn. = synonym;
Gr. = group; H3 = half winter-hardy. Numbers in square brackets [...]
refer to plates.

F. abrupta (Johnston 1925) Gr. 2
Syn. *F. aspiazui* (Macbride 1943)
Climbing to erect shrub, 1–3 metres high.
Flowers in overhanging bunches. T and S
bright orange-red; C orange-red.
Habitat: central Peru rain forests, 1,500–
2,700 metres.

F. acynifolia (Scheidw.) Gr. 7
See *F. encliandra* subsp. *encliandra*

F. affinis (Cambess. 1829) Gr. 1
See *F. regia* var. *affinis*

F. alpestris (Gardner 1843) Gr. 1
See *F. regia* var. *alpestris*

F. alternans (Sessé and Monico 1828)
Gr. 7
See *F. thymifolia*

F. ampliata (Bentham 1845) Gr. 2
Syn. *F. ayavacensis* sensu Munz,
F. canescens sensu Munz.
Erect to climbing shrub 1–3 metres high
with upward branches. Flowers in leaf
axils, mostly few. T and S bright scarlet to
orange-red; C red to orange-red.
Habitat: Ecuador and south Colombia to
heights of 3,000–3,500 metres.

F. ampliata (Kris) Gr. 2
See *F. ayavacensis* sensu Munz

F. apetala (Ruiz and Pavón 1802) Gr. 5
Syn. *F. insignis* (Hemsley 1876)
Climbing shrub, often epiphytic; about 1
metre high. Few flowers at top of twigs;
T orange-red, S red-orange, spread out.
Habitat: Venezuela and Ecuador.

F. apiculata Gr. 2
See *F. loxensis*

F. aprica (Lundell 1940) Gr. 7
See *F. microphylla* subsp. *aprica*

F. araucana (Phil. 1876) Gr. 1
See *F. magellanica* var. *typica*

F. arborea (Sessé and Mocino 1888) Gr. 6
See *F. arborescens*

F. arborescens (Sims 1825) 143 Gr. 6
Syn. *F. arborea* (Sessé and Mocino)

Bisexual, upright shrub or small tree, 3–8
metres high, leaves somewhat leathery,
smooth edge. Flowers upright, many
flowers in two-or three-branched panicles;
T and S pink violet; C lavender. Flowers
especially in dry periods.
Habitat: Mexico, in damp clefts in forest
areas, 1,750–2,500 metres high.

F. arborescens var. **megalantha**
(Donnel Smith 1893)
F. arborescens var. **syringaeflora**
(Lemaire 1848)
F. arborescens forma **tenuis** (Munz
1943)
F. arborescens forma **parva** (Munz
1943)
See *F. paniculata*

F. aspiazui (Macbride 1941) Gr. 2
See *F. abrupta* (Johnston 1925)

F. asplundii (Macbride 1941) Gr. 2
See *F. ayavacensis*

F. atrorubra (Johnston 1929) Gr. 2
See *F. sylvatica* (Bentham 1845)

F. austromontana (Johnston 1929) Gr. 2
Syn. *F. serratifolia* (Hook 1845)
T light red; S red; C red-violet when
drying. Loose shrub, leaf 2–10 × 1–3cm.
Habitat: Peru at heights of 2,000–4,000
metres.

F. ayavacensis (Humboldt, Bonpland and
Kunth 1823) Gr. 2
Syn. *F. townsendii* (Johnston 1925);
F. asplundii (Macbride 1941)
Slack to climbing shrub, 1–4 metres high
with long flexible branches. T, S and C
orange-red.
Habitat: Peru and south Ecuador at
heights of 1,900–3,200 metres.

F. ayavacensis (sensu Munz 1943 and
1974. Both partly) Gr. 2
See *F. vulcanica*

F. × bacillaris (Lindley 1832) Gr. 7
F. microphylla subsp.
thymifolia × F. thymifolia subsp.
microphylla

Syn. *F. cinnabarina* and *F. reflexa* cult.
T red, S rosy and spread or bent back,
C pink; berry round, flower complete or
female. Shrub to 2 metres high. Small
leaves. A natural hybrid, cultivated forms
bloom better than forebears.
Habitat: Mexico.

F. boliviana (Carr 1876) [131] Gr. 2
Syn. *F. corymbiflora* (Ruiz and Pavón
1802); *F. corymbiflora* var. *alba* (Harrison
1849); *F. boliviana* var. *luxurians* (Johnston
1925); *F. cuspidata* (Fawcett and Rendle
1926); *F. boliviana* forma *puberulenta*
(Munz 1943)
Erect shrub or small tree, 2–4.5 metres
high. Many flowers hanging from
end,sometimes branched plumes. T and S
pale pink to bright scarlet, sometimes pale
white C red and sharp at top (crumpled or
folded). Berry cylindrical, dark violet,
hairy, edible.
Habitat: north Argentina to south Peru;
occurring in many parts of South America
at heights of 1,000–3,000 metres.

F. campos-portoi (Pilger and Schulze
1935)
Steeply rising shrub, young branches very
slim, leaf with glands at top of dentation.
T and S red. Flowers single in leaf axils.
Habitat: Brazil.

F. canescens (sensu Munz 1943, partly)
Gr. 2
See *F. vulcanica*

F. caracasensis (Fielding and Gardner
1844) Gr. 2
Natural hybrid of *F. nigricans* and
F. gehrigeri.
Habitat: Venezuela.

F. chiapensis (Brandegee 1940) Gr. 7
See *F. microphylla* subsp. *aprica*

F. chonotica Gr. 1
See *F. reflexa* cult.; *F. × bacillaris*

F. coccinea (Soland 1789) Gr. 1
Syn. *F. coccinea* (J. D. Hooker 1868);
F. elegans (Salisbury 1791); *F. pendula*
(Salisbury 1796); *F. pubescens* (Cambess.
1829); *F. montana* (Cambess. 1829);
F. glazioviana (Taub. 1892).
See also *F. magellanica* var. *macrostema*
Shrub to 1 metre and climbing to 3 metres.
T and S red, C violet. First fuchsia to
come to Europe.
Habitat: wild in Jamaica.

F. coccinea var. **macrostema** (Lindl.
1827)
See *F. magellanica* var. *macrostema*

F. coccinea var. **robustior** (Hook.1847)
Gr. 1
See *F. magellanica* var. *typica*

F. colensoi (Hooker 1867) Gr. 4
Small erect shrub, leaf 1.4 × 0.5–2cm. T
red or dark violet; S greenish to reddish
reflexed; C purple.
Habitat: New Zealand, both islands.

F. colimae (Munz 1943) Gr. 7
See *F. thymifolia* subsp. *thymifolia*

F. conica (Lindl. 1827) Gr. 1
See *F. magellanica* var. *typica*

F. cordifolia (Hooker 1842) Gr. 2a
See *F. splendens*

F. corymbiflora (many authors; notably
Ruiz and Pavón 1802) Gr. 2
See *F. boliviana*

F. corymbiflora var. **alba** 128 Gr. 2
See *F. boliviana*, white and red blooming.

F. corymbosa (Pritzel 1886) Gr. 2
See *F. corymbiflora* (*corymbosa* is a
misspelling)

F. crassistipula (P. Berry 1979) [142]
Gr. 2
Slack to climbing shrub 1–3 metres high.
Many flowers in terminal and lateral ears
or on branched, erect plumes. T shiny
pink-red, S same colour but dull purple
near top, C dark red.
Habitat: central Colombian rain forests to
heights of 2,600–3,000 metres.

F. curviflora (Bentham 1845) Gr. 2
See *F. petiolaris*

F. cuspidata (Fawcett and Rendle 1926)
Gr. 2
See *F. boliviana*

F. cylindracea (Lindley 1838) Gr. 7
See *F. parviflora* (Lindley)

F. decussata (Ruiz and Pavón 1802) Gr. 2
Syn: *F. scandens*, *F. fusca*
Slack to climbing shrub 1–3 metres high.
Flowers in leaf axils; T red; S red with dull
green top; C red to orange red.
Habitat: Peru, in rain forests to heights of
2,900–3,000 metres.

F. denticulata (Ruiz and Pavón 1802) [144] Gr. 2
Syn. *F. serratifolia* (Ruiz and Pavón 1802); *F. leptopoda* (K. Krause 1905); *F. siphonata* (K. Krause 1905); *F. tacsoniiflora* (K. Krause 1905)
Erect to climbing shrub 1.5–4 metres high. Flowers in leaf axils, hanging. T whitish pink; S pink to light red with light green to whitish top and edges (sometimes wholly whitish green); C orange to scarlet with violet stripes when drying.
Haibtat: Peru to heights of 2,800–3,500 metres and Bolivia to heights of 2,200–3,100 metres.

F. dependens (Hooker 1837) Gr. 2
Syn. *F. corymbiflora* (sensu Macbride)
Erect to climbing shrub 2–10 metres high with bent hanging branches. Many flowers in dense hanging terminal plumes. T orange-red to red, S likewise but dull green at top. Mainly in hedges.
Habitat: south Colombia and central Ecuador to heights of 2,400–3,300 metres.

F. discolor (Lindl. 1835) Gr. 1
See *F. magellanica* var. *typica*

F. encliandra subsp. **encliandra** (Steudel 1840) Gr. 7
Syn. *F. acynifolia* (Scheidw.)
Shrub 0.5–2.5 metres high. Male flower long stalk to 20mm; T, S, C red. Female flower stalk 8–10mm; T red to violet-red; S red; C white or red.
Habitat: Mexico to north Nicaragua to heights of 1,800–2,600 metres.

F. encliandra subsp. **tetradactyla** (Lindley 1846) Gr. 7
Syn. *F. striolata*; *F. seleriana*; *F. tetradactyla*
Shrub to 2.5 metres. Male flower T and S red, C pink red.
Habitat: Mexico, Guatemala, San Salvador and Nicaragua.

F. excorticata (Forster 1776) [133] Gr. 4
Syn. *Skinnera excorticata* (Forster 1776)
Broad tree to 1 metre with papery sliding light-brown bark. Berry about 1cm, dark. T and S first green, then purple-red, C dark violet standing 2–4mm. Blue pollen.
Habitat: New Zealand, both islands.

F. excorticata purpurescens Gr. 4
Form with defintely purple leaf and silvery underside.
Habitat: New Zealand.

F. fisheri (Macbride 1940)
See *F. mathewsii*

F. fulgens (De Candolle 1828) Gr. 2a
Syn. *F. fulgens pumila* (Carrière 1881); *F. fulgens racemosa* (Sessé and Mocino 1888)
Shrub, little lignified, 0.5–3 metres high, with thickened lumpy roots, often epiphytic on trees or rocks. Flowers in hanging bunches; T pink to dull red; S pale red and yellow-green near top; C bright red.
Habitat: Mexico to heights of 1,450–2,300 metres.

F. fulgens var. **gesneriana** (Barbet 1964, cult.?) Gr. 2a
Shorter T and slacker growth.
Habitat: Guatemala.

F. fulgens pumila (Carrière 1881) Gr. 2a
See *F. fulgens*

F. fulgens racemosa (Sessé and Mocino 1888) Gr. 2a
See *F. fulgens*

F. fulgens var. **rubra grandiflora** [135] Gr. 2a (No author or year, cult.?)
Larger flower than ancestor, very handsome.
Habitat: Guatemala and El Salvador.

F. fusca Gr. 2
See *F. decussata*

F. gehrigeri (Munz 1943) [130] Gr. 2
Syn. *F. jahnii* (Munz 1943)
Erect to climbing shrub 2–5 metres. Flowers borne in leaf axils at top of branches sometimes in panicles; T and S red; C red violet.
Habitat: Venezuela; Andes along Colombian border in rain forests to heights of 2,200–2,800 metres.

F. glazioviana (Taub. 1802) Gr. 1
See *F. coccinea*

F. globosa
See *F. magellanica* var. *globosa* cult.

F. gracilis var. **multiflora** (Lindl. 1827)
F. gracilis var. **tenella** (Lindl. 1828) Gr. 1
See *F. magellanica* var. *typica* and *F. m.* var. *macrostemma*

F. grandiflora (Ruiz and Dahlgren 1940) Gr. 2
See *F. denticulata*

F. hamellioides (Sessé and Mocino 1832)
Gr. 6
See *F. arborescens*

F. hartwegii (Bentham 1845) Gr. 2
Low shrub to small tree 0.5–4m high.
Bisexual flowers or only female, flowering
profusely in the top of branches or
branching iin panicles, flowering stems
5–20cm; T and S shiny orange-red to
bright red; C red.
Habitat: Colombia, rain forest to 2,300–
2,700 metres.

F. hemsleyana (Woodson and Siebert
1937) Gr. 7
See *F. microphylla* subsp. *hemsleyana*
Breedlove comb. nov.

F. heterotricha (Lundell 1940) Gr. 7
See *F. microphylla* subsp. *aprica*

F. hirtella (Humboldt, Bonpland and
Kunth 1823) Gr. 2
Climbing shrub 2–5 metres. Pendent
inflorescence or hanging plume at top of
branches; T and S shiny lavender to pink
red; C somewhat darker, carmine.
Habitat: Colombia to a height of 2,500–
3,300 metres.

F. hitchcockii (Johnston 1925) Gr. 2
See *F. vulcanica*

F. insignis (Hemsley 1876) Gr. 5
See *F. apetala* (Ruiz and Pavón 1802)

F. integrifolia (Cambess. 1829) Gr. 1
See *F. regia* var. *typica*

F. intermedia (Hemsley 1878) Gr. 2a
See *F. splendens*

F. jahnii (Munz 1943) Gr. 2
See *F. gehrigeri* (Munz)

F. jimenezii (Breedlove, Berry and Raven
1967) Gr. 6a
Flowers in erect branching bunches with
two or three side branches; T and S red to
pink; C pink.
Habitat: Panama and Costa Rica to heights
of 1,500–1,900 metres.

F. juntasensis (Kuntze 1898) Gr. 5
Syn. *F. mattoana*; *F. steinbachii*
Climbing mostly epiphytic shrub 50cm
high and more. Freely borne flowers,
together in terminal bunches, sometimes
with short side branches. T pink to flesh
coloured, tube to funnel-shaped; S
reddish; C green.
Habitat: Bolivia at 3,000 metres.

F. kirkii (Hooker 1868) Gr. 4
Grows and looks like *F. procumbens*. Male
plant of the dioecious *F. procumbens*.
Habitat: New Zealand.

F. lampadaria (Wright 1978) Gr. 2
See *F. magdalenae*

F. leibmannii (Léveillé 1912) Gr. 6
See *F. paniculata*

F. leptopoda (Krause 1905) Gr. 2
See *F. denticulata*

F. longiflora (Bentham 1845) Gr. 2
See *F. macrostigma* (Bentham 1844)

F. loxensis (Humboldt, Bonpland and
Kunth 1823) Gr. 2
Syn. *F. umbrosa* (Bentham 1845);
F. apiculata (Johnston 1923); *F. hypoleuca*
(Johnston 1933)
Climbing or erect shrub or tree 1.5–6
metres high with many side branches.
T and S bright red-orange; C dull red-
orange. A variable species.
Habitat: Ecuador, along paths and fields,
in thickets, dry valleys, but also on moister
east and west slopes to heights of 2,500–
3,500 metres.

F. lycioides (Andrews 1807) Gr. 3
Syn. *F. rosea* (Ruiz and Pavón 1802)
Erect shrub with stout stem and branches,
knotty. Lowest part of leaf stalk grows into
a thorn. T red; C violet.
Habitat: Chile

F. lycopsis Gr. 7
See *F. thymifolia*

F. macropetala (Presi 1835) Gr. 2
See *F. corymbifolia*

F. macrophylla (Johnston 1925) Gr. 2
Erect to climbing shrub, 1–3 metres high.
Flowers borne on short side branches, ears
2–10cm long, T red; S red with green top;
C scarlet.
Habitat: central and south Peru, rain forest
to subtropical zone, to heights of 1,200–
2,000 metres.

F. macrostema Gr. 1
See *F. magellanica* var. *macrostema*

F. macrostigma (Bentham 1844) [146]
Gr. 2
Syn. *F. longiflora* (Bentham); *F. spectabilis*
(Hooker and Lindley); *F. macrostigma* var.
pubens (Johnston)
Shrub standing 0.5–1.5 metres high.
Flowers rare, in the highest leaf axils;
T pale to dark red; S red with dull green

top; C bright red and shorter than sepals.
Habitat: Colombia and Ecuador, in moist
rain forest on west slopes to heights of
1,000–2,500 metres.

F. macrostigma var. **pubens** (Johnston
1925) Gr. 2
See *F. macrostigma*

F. magdalenae (Muna 1943) [141] Gr. 2
Syn. *F. lampadaria* (Munz)
Shrub 2–5 metres high. Flowers pendent,
single in highest leaf axils when opening;
T violet at foot and orange-red upwards;
S shiny orange-red with green top; C
orange-red round to inverted oval.
Habitat: northeast Columbia to heights of
3,000–3,350 metres.

F. magellanica (Lamarck 1788). Gr. 1
[76]
Three varieties: *F. m. typica*, *F. m.
macrostema* and *F. m. molinae*.
Habitat: Chile and Argentina.

F. magellanica var. **alba** Gr. 1
See *F. magellanica* var. *molinea* cult.

F. magellanica var. **conica cult.** 1825
Gr. 1
T and S red, C violet. Thicker and
rounder bud.
Habitat: Chile.

F. magellanica var. **corallina** (Pince
1844)
cult. *F. cordifolia* × *F. globosa*
T and S red; C dull violet. According to
Wood, bronze-green leaf, lax growth. H3.
According to Lynch (1883), synonym for
F. exoniensis. According to Pince (1842),
F. radicans × *F. exoniensis*.

F. magellanica var. **discolor** Gr. 1
Dwarf form. Flower red and light violet,
good winter hardy. Grown from seed from
Port Famin, Straits of Magellan.

F. magellanica var. **globosa** (Lindley
1833)
Cult, probably *F. magellanica* × var. *conica*.
Formerly all bred forms were called
F. globosa. Strong build, somewhat larger
flowers, thicker flower bud. S thus wider;
T and S red; C violet.

F. magellanica var. **gracilis** cult. 182
Gr. 1
Single flower red and violet. Form: leaf
multicoloured. Silvery multicoloured leaf
also grown.
Habitat: Chile.

F. magellanica var. **longipedunculata**
cult. Gr. 1
Long narrow flower on long stalk. C lilac-
mauve.

F. magellanica var. **macrostema** (Ruiz
and Pavón 1802) Munz comb. nov.
Syn. *F. macrostema* (Ruiz and Pavón 1802);
F. gracilis var. *multiflora* (Lindl. 1827);
F. coccinea var. *macrostema* (Hook. 1847);
F. coccinea (Curtis 1789); *F. decussata*
(R. Grah. 1824); *F. gracilis* (Lindl. 1824);
F. macrostema var. *recurvata* (Hook. 1836)
T and S red; C violet; stamens reddish.
Leaf 25–50mm by 10–20mm. Flower and
leaf bigger than in *F. typica*.
Habitat: Chile and Argentina.

F. magellanica var. **molinae** (Espinosa
1929) Gr. 1
T, S, C lilac-pink. Stamens and style pink.
F. magellanica var. *molinae alba* cult. white
inflorescence.
Habitat: Chile, wild and cultivated.

F. magellanica var. **myrtifolia** (Koehne
1893) cult. Gr. 1
.Single flower red and lilac, form of
F. macrostema, very small. Good for rock
garden.

F. magellanica var. **riccartonii** (John
Young 1833) cult. Gr. 1
Best known winter-hardy garden fuchsia.
F. globosa × *F. macrostema discolor*. Single
flower, red and violet. To about 2.75
metres high. H3 cult.

F. magellanica var. **tricolori** cult. Gr. 1
According to Delen a seedling of *F. gracilis
variegata*. Leaf silvery, multicoloured with
pink sheen. H3.

F. magellanica var. **typica** (Munz 1943)
new name. Gr. 1
Many hybrids with *F. macrostema*.
Syn. *F. gracilis* var. *multiflora*
(Lindl.1827); *F. gracilis* var. *tenella* (Lindl.
1828); *F. conica* (Lindl. 1827); *F. multiflora*
(Lodd. 1828); *F. discolor* (Lindl. 1805);
F. chonotica, *F. araucana*, *F. coccinea-
robustior* (Hook. 1847). T deep red; C
violet. Filaments reddish. Leaf 15–22mm
by 4–10mm. Flower stalk 2–3.5cm red.
Habitat: Chile and Argentina.

F. mathewsii (Macbride 1940) Gr. 2
Syn. *F. fisheri* (Macbride 1940); *F. storkii*
(Munz 1943)
Half-climbing shrub, 1–3 metres high.

Many flowers close together at top of hanging end bunches or plumes. T and S pale pink to lavender or light red; C somewhat darker (bright red to light violet).
Habitat: north Peru at heights of 2,700–3,350 metres.

F. mattoana (Krause 1906) Gr. 5
See *F. juntasensis*

F. mexiae (Munz 1943) Gr. 7
See *F. parviflora*

F. michoacanensis (Sessé and Mocino 1887–90) Gr. 7
See *F. microphylla* var. *aprica*; *F. parviflora*

F. microphylla (H. B. Kris 1823) Gr. 7
Subspecies: *F. microphylla*; *F. hidalgensis*, *F. quercetorum*, *F. aprica*, *F. hemsleana*.
All accepted because it is not clear which are grown in the Netherlands. Complete flowers and female ones.

F. microphylla subsp. **aprica** (Lundell) Breedlove. comb. nov. Gr. 7
Syn. *F. aprica* (Lundell 1940);
F. microphylla var. *aprica* (Munz 1943); *F. chiapensis* (Brandegee 1914); *F. heterotricha* (Lundell 1940)
Munz describes this subsp. under
F. michoacanensis, *F. striolata*,
F. × *bacillaris*, *F. microphylla* var. *aprica*
Shrub 1–3 metres high, leaf narrow and lanceolate to wide oval. T red; S red to violet red; C red to light pink-red.
Habitat: Mexico, Guatemala, El Salvador and Honduras.

F. microphylla subsp. **microphylla** Gr. 7
Syn. *F. mixta* (Hemsley); *F. minutiflora* (Hemsley); *F. uniflora* (Sessé and Mocino)
Complete flower: T and S red-violet; C light violet-red. Shrub of 0.5–3 metres.
Habitat: Mexico to a height of 2,100–3,200 metres.

F. microphylla subsp. **hidalgensis** Gr. 7
Syn. *F. minutiflora* var. *hidalgensis* (Munz 1943)
Complete and female flower: T, S, C white.
Habitat: Mexico to a height of 1,600–2,200 metres.

F. microphylla subsp. **quercetorum** (Breedlove 1969) Gr. 7
Munz identified this as *F. michoacanensis*,

F. striolata and *F. microphylla* var. *aprica*
Complete flower: flower stalk, T red or red-violet; S and C red. Female flower: T, S, C red.
Habitat: Mexico and Guatemala to a height of 1,500–2,200 metres.

F. microphylla subsp. **hemsleyana** (Woodson and Seibert 1937) Breedlove comb. nov. 1969 Gr. 7
Syn. *F. hemsleyana* (Woodson and Seibert); *F. pulchella* (Woodson and Seibert); Munz describes it as
F. hemsleyana or *F. michoacanensis*
Complete flower: T red; S red turned back to spread out and top pointed; C red.
Female flower: T, S, C red.
Habitat: Costa Rica and north Panama.

F. microphylla var. **typica** Gr. 7
See *F. microphylla* subsp. *microphylla*
Complete flowers.

F. minimiflora (Hemsley 1878) Gr. 7
See *F. thymifolia* subsp. *minimiflora*

F. minutiflora (Hemsley 1878) Gr. 7
See *F. microphylla* subsp. *microphylla*
Male flower.

F. minutiflora var. **hidalgensis** (Munz) Gr. 7
See *F. microphylla* subsp. *hidalgensis* (Munz)

F. mixta (Hemsley 1878) Gr. 7
See *F. microphylla* subsp. *microphylla*

F. mollis (Krause 1906) Gr. 1
See *F. regia* var. *alpestris*

F. montana (Cambess.) Gr. 1
See *F. coccinea*

F. multiflora (Lodd. 1828) Gr. 1
See *F. magellanica* var. *typica*

F. munzii (J. F. Macbride 1941) Gr. 2
See *F. corymbiflora* (Ruiz and Pavón 1941)

F. nigricans (Linden and Plancon 1849) [147] Gr. 2
Shrub 1–3 metres, branches erect or standing out. Flowers in leaf axils or in branching bunches; T and S pale pink to lavender or light red; C much darker violet.
Habitat: Venezuela and Colombia to heights of 2,100–2,650 and 1,700–2,700 metres.

F. notarisii (Lehm 1852) Gr. 7
See *F. microphylla* subsp. *microphylla*

F. obconica (Breedlove 1969) sp.nov.
Gr. 7
Dioecious. Male flower: T hairy outside,
greenish-white; S narrow white; C white.
Female flower: T and S greenish-white; C
white. Munz calls the female plant
F. pringlei and the male plant *F. thymifolia*
and *F. tacanensis*.
Habitat: Mexico to heights of 1,700–2,400
metres.

F. paniculata (Lindley 1856) [143] Gr. 6
Syn. *F. arborescens* (author not Sims 1825,
Essig in Munz); *F. arborescens* var.
syringaeflora (Lemaire 1848); *F. arborescens*
var. *megalantha* (Donnell Smith 1893);
F. aborescens forma *tenuis* (Munz 1943);
F. arborescens forma *parva* (Munz 1943);
F. leibmannii (Léveillé 1912)
Plants bisexual or female. Erect shrub or
small tree, 3–8m high, mostly bare. Leaf
edge finely to roughly saw-toothed.
Complete flower: T and S pink-violet;
C lavender. Female flower: anther
undeveloped.
Habitat: Mexico and Panama in cloudy
zones to heights of 1,200–3,000 metres.

F. parviflora (Lindley 1827) Gr. 7
Syn. *F. cylindracea* (Lidley 1838);
F. michoacanensis (Sessé and Mocino
1888); *F. mexiae* (Munz 1943)
Dioecious. Male flower: T red hairy; S and
C white or red, ovary undeveloped.
Female flower: much resembles
F. encliandra subsp. *encliandra* but has
larger leaves, smaller seeds and loosely
haired small branches. Munz (1943) called
it *F. michoacanensis*, *F. cylindracea* and
F. mexiae.
Habitat: Mexico.

F. pendula (Salisbury 1796) Gr. 1
See *F. coccinea*

F. perscandens (Cockayne and Allen
1927) [132] Gr. 4
Climbing shrub little branching. Flower
resembles that of *F. excorticata*.
Habitat: New Zealand (North Island).

F. petiolaris (Humboldt, Bonpland and
Kunth 1823) Gr. 2
Syn. *F. quinduensis* (Humboldt, Bonpland
and Kunth 1823); *F. curviflora* (Bentham
1845); *F. smithii* (Munz 1943); *F. petiolaris*
var. *bolivarensis* (Munz 1943)
Low shrub, 0.5–2 metres high, climbing in
trees to 5 metres. Flowers in leaf axils,

flower stalk hanging; T dull red; S mostly
lighter and sometimes with greenish top; C
bright pink-red.
Habitat: Colombia and Venezuela at
heights of 2,900–3,900 metres.

F. petiolaris var. **bolivarensis**
(Humboldt, Bonpland and Kunth 1823)
Gr. 2
See *F. petiolaris*

F. pringlei (Robinson and Seaton 1893)
Gr. 7
See *F. thymifolia* subsp. *thymifolia*

F. pringsheimii (Urban 1899) Gr. 2
Erect to climbing shrub 0.5–2 metres high.
T and S bright to pink-red; C red to pink
red.
Habitat: Hispaniola (Haiti and Dominican
Republic) to heights of 1,400–2,500
metres.

F. procumbens (Cunningham 1839)
[139], [140] Gr. 4
Syn. *F. prostata*
T yellow-green; S green, bent back,
narrow and pointed, top red; C green.
Pollen blue. Berry large, light red with
silvery haze, very attractive. Flower erect.
Creeping plant with wiry, thin twigs.
Good for rock gardens in Britain. Winter-
hardy. *F. kirkii* is the male plant with only
good stamens, pistil absent or
rudimentary.
Habitat: New Zealand (North Island).

F. prostata (Baill. 1880) Gr. 4
See *F. procumbens*

F. pubescens (Cambess. 1829) Gr. 1
See *F. coccinea* (Soland) and *F. bracellina*
(Munz)

F. pulchella (Woodson and Seibert 1937)
Gr. 7
See *F. microphylla* subsp. *hemsleyana*

F. putumayensis (Munz 1943) Gr. 2
Shrub 1–3 metres high. Many flowers
mostly in short bunches. T and S bright
orange to coral red; C orange-red.
Habitat: Colombia and Ecuador to heights
of 1,400–2,100 metres.

F. pyrifolia (Presl.1858) Gr. 1
See *F. regia* var. *radicans*

F. quinduensis (Humboldt, Bonpland
and Kunth 1823) Gr. 2
See *F. petiolaris*

F. radicans (Miers 1841) Gr. 1
See *F. regia* var. *radicans*

F. ravenii (Breedlove 1969) Gr. 7
T red and hairy; S and C red. Munz called
this *F. tetradactyla*.
Habitat: Mexico to heights of 2,600
metres.

F. reflexa cult.
F. reflexta cult. Gr. 7
See *F. cinnabarina*

F. regia (Vandeli 1825) (Munz. nov.
comb.) Gr. 1
Syn. *F. integrifolia*
Large, semi-climbing shrubs to 6 metres
with long branches. Single flowers borne
in leaf axils. T dark red 3–15mm; S red;
C violet red.
Habitat: Brazil.

F. regia var. **affinis** (Vand. Munz 1825)
Gr. 1
Young branches and leaf densely haired.
Habitat: east Brazil.

F. regia var. **alpestris** (Munz 1843) Gr. 1
Young branches and leaf with soft hairs.
Habitat: east Brazil.

F. regia var. **radicans** (Vand. Miers,
Munz, comb. nov. 1841) Gr. 1
Wholly bare. Seed was imported from
Brazil by de Groot who called it Burilibra
de Brazil. Ancestor of winter-hardy
seedlings.
Habitat: east Brazil.

F. regia var. **typica** (Vand. Munz) Gr. 1
Bare. De Groot got seed from Brazil and
called the seedlings Mantancira Rio de
Janeiro. Ancestor of semi-hardy winter
cultivars.
Habitat: east Brazil.

F. rivularis (J. F. Macbride 1940) Gr. 2
Syn. *F. woytkowskii* (J. F. Macbride 1941)
Climbing shrub or liana, to 10 metres high
with long, flexible, unbranching side
branches. Few flowers, hanging in the
topmost leaf axils. T and S bright violet-
red, C orange-red.
Habitat: north Peru to heights of 1,900–
2,650 metres.

F. rosea (Ruiz and Pavón 1802)
F. rosea var. **spinosa** (Reiche 1897) Gr. 3
See *F. lycioides*

F. salicifolia (Hemsley 1887) Gr. 5
Epiphytic shrub; few flowers borne in leaf
axils.
Habitat: Bolivia to heights of 2,450 metres
and perhaps also in Peru.

F. sanctae-rosae (O. Kuntze 1898) Gr. 2
Syn. *F. boliviana* (Bull 1876); *F. britonii*
(Johnston 1925); *F. weberbeuri* (Krause
1905); *F. filipes* (Rusby 1925)
Semi-wooden to herb-like, 30–50cm high
to shrubs 2–3 metres. Many flowers borne
in leaf axils, with somewhat smaller leaf.
T and S red; C orange-red. Not winter-
hardy in the Netherlands.
Habitat: Bolivia and Peru to heights at
2,000–3,000 metres.

F. scabriuscula (Bentham 1845) Gr. 2
Creeping or erect shrub 0.5–2.5m high.
Few flowers, borne singly in the axils of
the highest leaves. T and S whitish-pink to
red; C pink to scarlet.
Habitat: Ecuador and south Colombia to
heights of 1,400–2,750 metres.

F. seleriana (Loesener 1913) Gr. 7
See *F. encliandra* subsp. *tetradactyla*

F. serratifolia Gr. 2
See *F. denticulata* (Ruiz and Pavón 1802)

F. sessilifolia (Bentham 1845) Gr. 2
Shrub or small tree. Blooms in bunches
hanging from end. T red; S greenish-red;
C red.
Habitat: Colombia and Ecuador.

F. simplicicaulis (Ruiz and Pavón 1802)
Gr. 2
Climbing shrub 2–5 metres high. Flowers
in hanging bunches with three or four
flowers per ring of leaves; T and S light
pink-red; C red.
Habiat: central Peru to heights of 2,200–
2,500 metres.

F. siphonata (Krause 1905) Gr. 2
See *F. denticulata*

F. skutchiana (Munz 1943) Gr. 7
See *F. thymifolia* subsp. *minimiflora*

F. speciosa (Prest) [17] Gr. 2a
According to Van Delen a cultivar of
F. fulgens × *F. splendens*.

F. spectabilis (Hooker and Lindley 1848)
Gr. 2
See *F. macrostigma* (Bentham 1844)

F. spinosa (Prel. 1835) Gr. 3
See *F. lycioides*

F. splendens (Zuccarini 1832) Gr. 2a
Syn. *F. cordifolia* (Bentham 1841);
F. intermedia (Hemsley 1876)
Shrub 0.5–2.5 metres high, sometimes
epiphytic on tree trunks. Flowers in leaf
axils of young branches. T pink to bright
red; S green with red tip. In flower all
year.
Habitat: Mexico to Costa Rica at heights
of 2,000–3,400 metres.

F. steinbachii (Johnston 1925) Gr. 5
See *F. juntasensis*

F. storkii (Munz 1943) Gr. 2
See *F. mathewsii*

F. striolata (Lundell 1940) Gr. 7
See *F. encliandra* subsp. *tetradactyla*

F. sylvatica (Bentham 1845) Gr. 2
Syn. *F. nigricans* (Linden 1849);
F. atrorubra (Johnston 1925)
T pink or light red; S likewise and
standing out; C dark red to purple-red.
Flowers in terminal or lateral pendent
bunches.
Habitat: Ecuador, Venezuela and
Colombia.

F. syringaeflora (Carr. 1873) Gr. 6
See *F. arborescens* forma *typica*

F. tacanensis (Lundell 1940) Gr. 7
See *F. thymifolia* subsp. *minimiflora*

F. tacsoniiflora (Krause 1905) Gr. 2
See *F. denticulata*

F. tetradactyla (Lindley 1846) Gr. 7
See *F. encliandra* subsp. *tetradactyla*

F. thymifolia (H. B. Kris 1823) Gr. 7
Two subspecies: *F. thymifolia* subsp.
thymifolia and *F. thymifolia* subsp.
minimiflora.
Habitat: Mexico and Guatemala.

E. thymifolia subsp. **minimiflora** Gr. 7
T, S, C white. Differs from subsp.
thymifolia. Subsp. *microphylla* has larger
leaves and shorter T.
Habitat: Mexico and Guatemala to heights
of 2,100–2,500 metres.

F. thymifolia subsp. **thymifolia**
(H. B. Kris 1823) Gr. 7
Syn. *F. pringlei* (Robinson and Seaton
1893); *F. colimae* (Munz 1943)
T and S pink-white; C pink-white but
violet after pollination. Munz called the

female plants from the Mexican volcanic
area *F. pringlei*, and from the volcano
Colima *F. colimae*.
Habitat: Mexico.

F. tincta Gr. 2
See *F. vargasiana*

F. townsendii (Johnston 1925) Gr. 2
See *F. ayavacensis*

F. tricolor cult. Gr. 1
See *F. magellanica* var. *tricolor*

F. triphylla (Linnaeus 1753) Gr. 2 [86]
T and S red; C red but lighter at base.
Low shrub. Difficult to grow. The first
fuchsia found by Charles Plumier. Earlier
called *F. triphylla flore coccinea*.
Habitat: Haiti and San Domingo.

F. umbrosa Gr. 2
See *F. loxensis*

F. uniflora (Sessé and Mocino 1888) Gr. 7
See *F. microphylla* subsp. *microphylla*

F. vargasiana (Munz ex Vargas 1946)
Gr. 2
Syn. *F. tincta*
Erect shrub 1–2 metres high. Flowers
three to ten on terminally branching
inflorescence. T red; S green with reddish
base; C red.
Habitat: Peru at heights of 1,700–2,300
metres.

F. velutina (Johnston 1925) Gr. 2
See *F. corymbiflora*

F. venusta (H. B. Kris 1823) Gr. 2
Sometimes climbing shrub. Flowers in
bunch hanging at end. T tube-shaped and
red; S red; C carmine.
Habitat: Colombia at heights of 1,800–
2,300 metres.

F. vulcanica (André 1888) Gr. 2
Syn. *F. hitchcockii* (Johnston 1925);
F. ayavacensis (sensu Munz 1943 and 1974
for his part); *F. canescens* (sensu Munz
1943 for his part and 1974)
Standing to climbing shrub 0.4–3.5 metres
high, sometimes semi-epiphytic on mossy
tree trunks. Flowers mostly fewer than
twelve per branch, borne in leaf axils and
hanging. T and S shiny, red, violet or
orange-red; S sometimes with dull red top;
C red.
Habitat: south Colombia and Ecuador at
boundary of tree growth at heights of

3,400–4,000 metres. Some populations at lower levels down to 2,500 metres.

F. woykowskii (J. F. Macbride 1941) Gr. 2

See *F. rivularis*

F. wurdackii (Munz 1964) Gr. 2

Standing shrub 1–1.5 metres high.

Flowers in branching, pendent end bunches. T and S coral-red; C red. Habitat: north Peru to heights of 2,100–2,400 metres.

Skinnera excorticata Gr. 4

See *F. excorticata*

Glossary of specific names

abruptus/a – broken off, ending suddenly

acynifolia – leaves pointed on both sides

affinis – related to, similar to

albus/a – white

alpestris – alpine, of the mountains

alternans – alternating

ampliatus/a – speading out

apetalus/a – without petals

apiculatus/a – terminated by short, but not stiff, point

apricus/a – sunny

araucan/usa – named after the Colombian province Arauca

arboreus/a – tree-like

arborescens – becoming tree-like

aspiazui – named after R. Aspiazu c.1930, doctor and collector in Lima, Peru

asplundii – named after E. Asplund (1888–1974), Swedish botanist, collector in South America

atrorubrus/a – dark red

austromontan/usa – south of the mountains

ayavacensis – named after Ayabaca in northwest Peru

bacillaris – stick-like

bolivianius/a; boliviensis – Bolivian

campos-portoi – a place in Brazil

canescens – greyish, hoary

caracensis; caracasanus/a – from Caracas

chiapensis – from Chiapa, Mexico

chonotica – from the Chonos archipelago, Chile

cinnabarinus/a – vermilion, cinnabar red

coccineus/a – scarlet

colensoi – named after the Rev W. Colenso (1811–99), missionary and botanist in New Zealand

colimae – from the Colima volcano, Mexico

conicus/a – conical, cone-shaped

corallinus/a – coral-red

cordifolius/a – with heart-shaped leaf

corymbiflorus/a – with blooms in corymbs

crassistipulus/a – with thick stipules

curviflorus/a – with bent flower
cuspidatus/a – narrowing to a point
cylindraceus/a – tube-shaped, cylindrical, long and round
decussatus/a – with crosswise leaves, at right-angles
denticulatus/a – finely dentate
dependens – hanging down
discolor – of several colours
elegans – graceful
encliandra – with bent stamens
excorticata – without a bark or cortex
fisheri – probably named after Paul Fisher, a Swiss photographer
fulgens – shining; often applied to scarlet plants
fuscus/a – dark
gehrigeri – named after W. Gehriger, botanist collecting in Venezuela *c.*1930
glaziovii/iana – named after A. F. M. Glaziou (1828–1906), French gardener,
    successful landscape architect in the Imperial Gardens, Rio de Janeiro, Brazil
globosus/a – spherical
gracilis – slender
grandiflorus/a – with large flowers
hamelloides – bucket-shaped
hartwegii – named after C. T. Hartweg (1812–71), collector for the Royal
    Horticultural Society
hemsleyanaus/a – named after W. B. Hemsley (1843–1924), keeper of the
    herbarium at Kew Gardens
heterotricha – with various sorts of hair
hidalgensis – from Hidalgo, Mexican state
hirtella – somewhat hairy
hitchcockii – named after A. S. Hitchcock (1865–1935), American botanist,
    collector for Bureau of Plants
hybridus/a – hybrid
hypoleucus/a – whitish underside
insignis – striking, remarkable
integrifolius/a – with smooth-edged leaf
intermedius/a – intermediate
jahnii – named after A. Jahn (1867–1940), botanist who worked in Venezuela
jimenezii – named after A. Jimenez
juntasensis – found near Rio Juntas in Bolivia
kirkii – named after Thomas Kirk (1828–98), botany lecturer in Wellington,
    New Zealand
lampadarius/a – torch-shaped
leibmannii – after a collector called Leibmann
leptopodus/a – with slack leaf stalks
longipedunculatus/a – with long flower stalk
longiflorus/a – with long flower
loxensis – from Loya in Ecuador
lycioides, lyciopsis – resembling boxthorn

macrophyllus/a – large leaved
macrostema – with long stamens
macrostigma – with large stigma
magdalenae – from the department of Magdalena in Colombia
magellanicus/a – named after the Straits of Magellan, Chile
mathewsii – named after A. Mathews (*fl.*1848); also Matthew, grower and
    collector for the Royal Horticultural Society
mattoana – named after Dr D. Matto
mexiae – named after Mrs D. R. Ynez Mexia
michoacanensis – from the state of Michoacan, Mexico
microphyllus/a – small leaved
minimiflorus/a – with very small flowers
minutiflorus/a – with small flowers
mixtus/a – mixed
mollis – soft
montanus/a – of the mountains
multiflorus/a – with many flowers
munzii – named after P. A. Munz (1892–1974), American taxonomist
nigricans – blackish
notarisii – named after Giuseppe de Notaris (1805–77), Italian botany professor
paniculatus/a – with flowers in panicle
parviflorus/a – with small blooms
pendulus/a – hanging down, pendent
perscandens – strongly climbing
petiolaris – with leaf stalks
pringlei – named after C. G. Pringle (1838–1911), botanist from USA who
    collected more than 20,000 new species in Central and South America
pringsheimii – named after C. G. Pringsheim (1823–94), noted German botanist
procumbens – ground-hugging
prostratus/a – prostrate but not rooting
puberulentus/a – downy
pubescens – covered with downy hair
pulchellus/a – pretty
pumilus/a – low or small
purpurascens – becoming purple
putumayensis – from the province of Putumayo, Colombia
pyrifolius/a – pear-shaped leaves
quercetorum – growing in oak forests
racemosa – arranged in racemes
radicans – with rooting stems
ravenii – named after P. H. Raven, American botany professor, director of
    Missouri Botanical Garden
reflexus/a, reflextus/a – bent back harply, reflexed
regius/a – regal
riccartonii – probably after Riccarton (Ayr or Roxburgh), Scotland
rivularis – growing along streams

Fuchsia Species   191

robustior – strongly growing
rosea – rose-coloured
salicifolia – with willow-like leaves
sanctae-rosae – probably named after the Bolivian plant Santa Rosa
scabriusculus/a – somewhat rough
scandens – climbing
serratifolia – saw-toothed leaf
sessilifolia – stalkless leaf
simplicicaulis – with undivided stalks
siphonata (should be *siphonantha*) – tube-shaped
skutchiana – named after A. F. Skutch (b. 1904), biologist and collector in South
   America
smithii – named after the botanist A. C. Smith
speciosus/a – very showy, good looking
spectabilis – worth seeing
spinosus/a – with thorns
splendens – gleaming
steinbachii – probably named after the botanist J. Steinbach Kemmerich (1876–
   1930), collector in South America
storkii – named after H. E. Stork (b.1890), botany professor at University of
   California
striolatus/a – marked with fine lines and ridges
sylvaticus/a – growing in forest
syringaeflorus/a – flower shaped like lilac
tacanensis – from the Mexican volcano Tacana
tacsoniiflorus/a – flowers as in Tacsonia, an obsolete name of a genus, now called
   Passiflora, a hanging plant from South America
tenellus/a – delicate
tetradactylus/a – with four fingers
thymifolius/a – shaped like thyme leaf
tinctus/a – coloured
townsendii – named after C. H. Townsend
tricoloris – with three colours
triphylla – with three leaves
umbrosa – growing in the shade
uniflorus/a – with single flower
vargasianus/a – named after J. C. Vargas Calderon (b.1900), botany professor at
   Cuzeo University, Peru
venustus/a – lovely,graceful
vulcanicus/a – volcanic
woytkowskii – named after F. Woytkowski, botanist collector in Peru *c.*1938
wurdackii – named after J. Wurdack (b.1921) botanist–curator of the National
   Herbarium in Washington

chapter 21

Fuchsia Cultivars

As an aid to selecting suitable plants, the following is a list of some 500 cultivars.
The descriptions have been compiled from the list of cultivars available in the
Netherlands and produced by the Technical Section of the Dutch Circle of Fuchsia Lovers.
This is a selection of the most widely grown cultivars.

After the name of the plant the name of the grower, the year in which the new
cultivar became known and the country of origin are given. If information is
uncertain, it is followed by a question mark. In many cases the name of the parent
plants of the cross are given in the form (female × male). If only one parent is
known, the information is given in the form (*F.* × not known).

Abbreviations
T = flower tube; S = sepals; C = corolla; numbers in square brackets [...] refer to plates.
If a plant is described as hardy, it may be overwintered outdoors, with care, in temperate
areas of northern Europe.
Flowers are described as: single = 4–5 petals; semi-double = 5–7 petals; and double = 8 or
more petals.

126 Species from section 5, Hemsleyella

127 The as yet unnamed species shown in Plate 126 was found in Venezuela in 1985 near the road from Bocono to Guaramacal about 12.5 metres from Bocono at a height of 2,800 metres

128 *F. boliviana* var. *luxurians* 'Alba'

129 *F. fulgens* var. 'Goselli'

130 *F. gehrigeri* × *F. nigricans*

131 *F. boliviana* var. *luxurians*

132 *F. perscandens*

133 *F. excorticata*

134 'Dominyana'

135 *F. fulgens* var. *rubra grandiflora*

136 *F. boliviana* var. 'Pink Cornet'

137 'Northumbrian Pipes'

Abbé Farges [47]
Lemoine, France, 1901
Single or semi-double. T and S light red;
C lilac; filaments and style light red. Leaf
small and mid-green; flower small but
profuse. Growth erect and compact.
Branches fragile. Hardy.

Achievement [89]
Melville, UK, 1886
Single. T and S carmine; C red-violet,
scarlet at base; filaments and style carmine.
Yellow-green leaf. Growth erect; self-
branching. Easy plant. Hardy.

Aika
Bogemann, Germany, 1984
(*F. magdalenae* × 'Ting-a-Ling')
Single. T pale pink, long and with pink-
red blush depending on location and with
dark red stripes; S pink-red, gradually
merging via pale pink into green tips,
darker stripes; C violet-red, of notable
shape with three points, sometimes partly
curled; veins red, pink at base; filaments
and style pale pink. Leaf dark green,
lighter on undersurface and slightly
serrated. Medium-sized flowers appear to
be semidouble, because of the form of the
petals. Moderately upright growth.

Alaska
Schnabel, USA, 1963
Double. T and S white; S with green,
slightly upturned tips; C white; filaments
pale pink; style white. Dark green leaf.
Large flower. Very free-flowering for a
double white. In the sun the flower turns
pale pink. Sturdy, self-branching growth;
may need staking.

Alice Hoffmann
Klese, Germany, 1911
Semi-double. T and S pale red; C white
with pale veins; filaments and style light
red. Profuse, but small, flowers. Small
bronze-green leaves. Compact, upright
growth.

Alison Ewart [124]
G. Roe, UK, 1977
Single. T and S pink-red; S with green
tips; C mauve (soft violet) with red blush.
Small, freely borne flowers. Bronzegreen
leaves. Upright, self-branching shrub.

Alison Ryle
Ryle, UK, 1968
('Lena Dalton' × 'Tennessee Waltz')
Semi-double. T and S bright pink; T

short; S with paler tips; C deep lavender-
blue with pale mauve blush and pink
veins; darker along edges; filaments
crimson; style pink. Leaves mid-green to
dark green. Medium-sized flowers, freely
borne. Can stand full sun. Vigorous, erect,
self-branching growth.

Ambassador
W. Jones, UK and Machado, USA; 1962
Single. T and S madder red with white
blush, white fading to pink; underside of S
darker pink; C violet, fading to peony red;
filaments and style pink. Leaves mid-
green. Large, freely borne flowers. Strong,
fast-growing, self-branching shrub.

Amélie Aubin [38]
Eggbrecht, Germany, 1884
Single. T and S waxy white; S with green
tips; T long and thick; C pink-carmine;
filaments pale pink; style white. Light
green leaves. Medium-sized, freely borne
flowers. Vigorous growth but somewhat
lax shrub; suitable trailer. Pinching out
necessary to keep in shape.

Andenken an Heinrich Henkel [85]
Rehnelt, Germany, 1897
(*F. triphylla* × 'Edelstein'?)
Single. T and S pale carmine pink with
faint vermilion blush; T very long; short
C bright carmine. Free-flowering. Leaves
dark reddish-green with violet-red glow.
Growth erect but somewhat slack.

Andromeda
De Groot, Netherlands, 1972
(*F. regia* var. *typica* × 'Upward Look')
Single. T and S light red; S standing out;
C lilac with red veins. Leaves mid-green.
Small to medium-sized flowers.
Freeflowering, upright shrub.

Angela Leslie
Tiret, USA, 1959
Double. T and S pink; S green tips and
darker pink underside, recurving; C pale
pink with darker pink patches and veins;
filaments and style pink; sometimes a small
petal present instead of anther. Leaves
mid-green. Strong upright, woody growth.
Especially suitable for a cool greenhouse.
Large, freely borne flowers. Self-
branching, upright shrub.

Angel's Flight
George Martin, USA, 1957
Double. T white to soft pink; S pink,

deeper colour at base and edge, and curled over against T; C white, pale pink veins; filaments pink; style white. Mid-green leaves. Free-flowering, self-branching bush; growth lax (needs staking) or suitable for hanging-basket.

Annabel [71]
Ryle, UK, 1977
('Ingram Maid' × 'Nancy Lou')
Double. Fairly long T white with pink stripes; S white with soft pink blush and pink at base; wide with tips curled and recurved; long and fairly full C white with pink veins; style pale pink; filaments pink. Leaves fairly light green. Large flowers borne in clusters. Bushy, upright shrub, though somewhat lax.

Ann Howard Tripp
Clark, UK, 1982
('Lady Isobel Barnett' × 'Joy Patmore')
Single to semi-double. T and S white, S with a touch of pale pink at edges and green tips; C with faint pink veins. Leaves light green. Strong, self-branching growth.

Applause
Stubbs, USA 1978
Double. T light carmine, short and thick; S carmine, quite wide and bending slightly as the flower ages; numerous, deep orange-red C and widely spread. Leaves dark green. Large, very handsome blooms. Strong upward growth but weight of flowers makes staking necessary. Best in shaded conditions.

Aquarius [74]
Soo Yun, USA, 1971
Single or semi-double. T and S pale pink; S green tips and darker pink on underside; C pink with deep red veins; filaments and style pink. Leaves mid-green with serrated edges. Fairly large, bell-shaped flower. Upright shrub.

Arcadia [99]
Tolley, UK, 1979
Single. T and S cherry red; S long and slightly recurved; C bright red, long and strong, but not out-turned. Large flowers. Pale green leaves. Upright shrub.

Archie Owen [79]
Stubbs, USA, 1977
Double. T soft pink, medium length and width; S soft pink, medium length, somewhat pointed and turning back as the

flower ages; many, soft pink P. Medium-sized to small, dark green leaves with a hint of red and red veins. Suitable for hanging-basket.

Army Nurse
Hodges, USA, 1947
Semi-double. T and S carmine; C violet, pink at base and with pink veins; filaments and style bright pink. Mid-green leaves. Flowers rather small but profuse. Easy to grow. Vigorous, upright growth. Hardy.

Athela
Whiteman, UK, 1942
('Rolla' × 'Mrs Rundle')
Single. T creamy pink; S pink; C salmon pink, deeper at base and pale pink at edge. Medium-sized flower. Flowers borne profusely and early. Upright shrub.

Auntie Jinks
J. W. Wilson, UK, 1970
('Checkerboard' × not known)
Single. T pink-red; S white with cherry red edge; C red-violet with white shading; filaments pale pink; style pink. Leaves small, mid-green and pointed. Fairly small, freely borne flowers. Suitable for hanging-basket.

Aunt Juliana
Hanson, USA, 1950
(sport of 'Uncle Jones')
Double. T and S carmine; T short; S reflexed; C pale lavender; style red. Leaves mid-green. Flowers large. Free-flowering and self-branching shrub or hanging-basket.

Autumnale
Meteor, Europe, 1880(?)
Single. T and S red; C reddish-violet; filaments and style red. Variegated leaves, yellow and green, turning copper-red. Stiff growth but lax habit; much nipping out required. Medium-sized flowers, borne late in year. May be the same as 'Burning Bush', with which it is often confused.

Baby Chang [102]
Hazard and Hazard, USA, 1950
T and S deep orange-red; C orange-red; inside orange; filaments salmon pink; style pink; stigma orange-red. Tiny flowers, borne profusely. Small leaves mid-green. Natural trailer with untidy habit.

Balkonkönigin
Neubronner, Germany, 1896
Single. T and S pale pink; S with green
tips; C pink; filaments pale pink; style
white. Leaves mid-green with carmine
central vein and side veins. Pendent habit;
not self-branching.

Barbara
Tolley, UK, 1973
('Display' × not known)
Single. T soft pink; S pink, darker on
underside; filaments deep pink; style pink.
Leaves mid-green. Flowers medium size
and profuse, but not long lasting; seedpods
falling at same time. Strong, self-
branching upward-growing plant. Can be
grown in full sun.

Baroness van Dedem
De Groot, Netherlands, 1980
Single. T and S red; C violet. Flowers
small to medium size, petals out-turned.
Small shrub or pot plant.

Baroque Pearl [115]
De Graaff, Netherlands, 1980
Double. T greenish-white, fading to pink;
S ivory with pink blush and green tips,
pink on underside; C pale violet-lilac, pink
at base, fading to deep pink-lilac; filaments
light red; style white. Medium-size
flowers. Leaves mid-green. Upright, self-
branching shrub. Do not grow in full sun.

Beacon
Bull, UK, 1871
Single. T and S scarlet; C bright violet-
pink; filaments pale red; style pink. Freely
borne, early flowers. Leaves dark green
with wavy edge. Growth upright, compact
and self-branching.

Beacon Rosa [4]
Burgi-Ott, Switzerland, 1972
Single. T and S pink-red; T fairly long;
C pink with light red veins; filaments and
style pink; short style. Leaves dark green.
Medium-sized flower. Upright, self-
branching growth.

Belle de Lisse [116]
De Graaff, Netherlands, 1977
('Trail Blazer' × not known)
Double. T and S white with some pink;
S with green tips; C lilac pink, outermost
ones shorter than the inner ones; filaments
and style pink. Large flowers. Fairly large,
mid-green leaves. Erect shrub or semi-
trailer.

Belle de Spa [42]
Author unknown, 1988
Single. T and S orange-pink; S lighter
towards ends, green tips; T long; C
orange-red and fairly short; filaments and
style pink. Medium-sized, profusely borne
flowers. Upright or trailing habit.

Belsay Beauty
Ryle, UK, 1975
Semi-double. Short T deep pink; short,
fleshy S deep pink on underside, whitish
on upperside with deep pink shading; C
violet fading to red-violet. Few small violet
petaloids with deep pink stripes. Pleasing
contrast between old and new flowers.
Mid- to light green leaves. Bushy, trailing
habit.

Berba [56]
Bats, Netherlands, 1979
('Mevr. Goyaerts' × not known)
Semi-double. T white, very long (to 5cm);
erect S pink, deep pink on underside,
green tips; C deep pink-red, darker at
edges and lighter at base, with salmon pink
spots at base; filaments red; style pale pink.
Large flowers. Mid-green, medium-sized
leaves. Self-branching; good for hanging
basket; grow out of direct sun.

Berbanella
Bats, Netherlands, 1981
('La Campanella' × not known)
Double. T and S pink; S with green tips;
C various pink tones with lilac spots.
Sturdy, mid-green leaves. Medium-sized
flowers that do not fade. Best grown in a
hanging-basket.

Berba's Trio
Bats, Netherlands, 1983
('La Campanella' × 'Bridesmaid')
Single to semi-double. T white with pink
blush; S pink-red with light tinge and
small green tips, underside crepey texture
and erect; C three possibilities on one
plant: white with violet-blue and spots;
white with red veins at base; blue-violet
with red veins at base; filaments white to
pink. Fairly small, mid-green leaves.
Flowers medium-sized, the spotted variety
identifiable by sharp border between white
and blue-violet and many transitions from
simple white to simple blue-violet. Lax
shrub or hanging-basket subject. To
maintain plants with three kinds of
flowers, take cuttings from stems with
multicoloured flowers.

Bergnimf ('Mountain Nymph') [25]
S. A. Appel, Netherlands, 1981
(*F. sessifolia* × *F. fulgens*)
Single. T from ovary to S runs from dull
pink-red to bright deep pink-red; S bright
deep rosy-red; C red. Blooms at end of
each branch in large clusters. Dark green
leaves. Strongly upward-growing, self-
branching plant.

Bernadette [51]
Schnabel, USA, 1950
Double. T and S light red; C veronica-
blue. Small leaves dark green. Medium-
sized flowers. Erect shrub, but with stiff
side branches. Will not overwinter below
10°C.

Beth Robley
Tiret, USA, 1971
Double. T greenish-white; S white with
pink blush and green tips, salmon pink on
underside; C dark orange-red, white at
base; filaments carmine; style white to
salmon. Mid-green leaves. Large flowers.
Pendent habit.

Bicentennial [13]
Paskesen, USA, 1976
Double. T thin and white; long S salmon
orange on outside, orange on inside; C
bright red inside corolla and orange petals
and petaloids; filaments light red. The
orange comes out best if the plant gets
some sun. Free-flowering, semipendent,
self-branching habit

Billy Green
Rawlins(?), UK, 1966(?)
Single. T, S and C salmon pink; T long.
Olive-green leaves. Vigorous, upright
growth. Parents may have included: *F.
triphylla*, 'Andenken an Heinrich Henkel'
and 'Leverkusen'.

Blanche Regina [81]
Clyne, UK, 1974
('La Campanella' × 'Flirtation Waltz')
Double. T and S white; S reflexed, crepey
underside; C violet, turning purple with
age; pink blush at base; filaments bright
pink, long; style white, long. Leaves mid-
green. Medium-sized, freely borne
flowers. Strong, self-branching, pendent
growth.

Blue Pearl [112]
Martin, USA, 1955
Double. T and S pink; S heavy, wide,
curved, green tips; C violet-blue. Good

quality, flat flowers. Fairly freeflowering,
pendent habit.

Blue Ribbon [69]
Fuchsia-la Nursery, USA, 1967
Double. T pale pink; S pink, lying against
corolla; C white with some pink, square;
filaments and style pale pink. Large, freely
borne flowers. Large, mid-green leaves.
Slow-growing, slack habit.

Blush o' Dawn [119]
Martin, USA, 1962
Double. T greenish-white; S white, green
tips, soft pink on underside; C pale silvery
grey-lilac, pale pink at base; filaments light
cerise pink; style white. Freely borne,
medium-sized flowers. Mid-green leaves.
Semi-trailer and not very vigorous.

Bobby Shaftoe
Ryle-Atkinson, UK, 1973
Semi-double. T, S and C frosty white with
pale pink blush; T short; S crepey on
underside and with lemon-yellow tip; C
with pink veins, flared and ruffled to form
four grooves. Medium-sized, freely borne
flowers, appearing late in year. Leaves
mid- to light green. Self-branching,
upright habit.

Boerhaave [92]
V. Wieringen, Netherlands, 1970
Single. T and S dark red; T long; C dark
rose to pink-purple; filaments cerise; style
dark pink. Largish flowers, freely borne.
Mid-green leaves. Erect habit.

Bon Accorde ('Erecta Novelty')
Crousse, France. 1861
Single. T and S waxy white; C soft violet
with white blush; filaments soft pink; style
white. Mid-green leaves. Fairly small,
erect flowers, freely borne. Stiff, upright
habit but needs much nipping out.

Bon Bon
Kennet, USA, 1963
Double. Long T greenish-white; S pale
pink, darker pink on underside; C pale
pink; filaments pink; style white. Medium-
sized, freely borne flowers. Fairly small,
mid-green leaves. Self-branching,
vigorous habit; needs pinching out.
Suitable for hanging-basket.

Border Queen
Ryle-Atkinson, UK, 1974
('Leonora' × 'Lena Dalton')
Single. T pale pink, short and thin; S pink

with green tips; C violet; filaments bright
pink; style pale pink. Medium-sized, bell-
shaped flowers, freely borne. Mid-green
leaves with reddish stems. Erect, self-
branching shrub.

Border Reiver
Ryle, UK, 1980
Single. T and S deep pink; S half-reflexed,
vermilion on underside; C deep scarlet;
filament and anthers red; style pink.
Beautifully coloured, medium-sized
flowers. Dark green leaves, medium to
large, oval, tip blunt, base lobed, edges
serrated. Free-flowering, vigorous, erect
shrub. Can be grown in full sun.

Bornemann's Best
Bornemann, Germany, c.1926
Single. T pink-red, long, fairly thick,
broadening from ovary; S pink-red, small,
pointed, salmon pink on underside; C
orange, small, pointed; filaments and style
salmon pink, slightly protruding.
Medium-sized flowers of Triphylla type.
Large leaves dark green with dull green
underside. Vigorous, erect, self-branching
shrub.

Bouffant
Tiret, USA, 1949
Single. T and S red; long C white with red
veins; filaments and style red. Large, freely
borne flowers. Mid-green leaves. Strong
growth, pendent habit. Suitable for
hanging-basket.

Bountiful
Munkner, USA, 1963
Double. T white; S pale pink with green
tips, deep pink on underside; C milky with
fine pink veins; filaments pink; style
wholly pale pink. Large, freely borne
flowers, appear early. Growth vigorous
and erect; support flowering stems. Grow
as bush or semi-trailing subject.

Bow Bells
Handley, UK, 1972
Single or semi-double. T greenish-white;
S white, green tips, long and strong;
C magenta, carmine edges, white at base;
filaments pale pink; style white. Large,
early flowers, freely borne. Fairly large
light green leaves. Self-branching, upright
growth. Can be grown in full sun.

Brandt's 500 Club
Brandt, USA, 1955
Single. T and S pale pink; S long; C same

colour but with orange blush. Large, self-
coloured flowers, freely borne. Midgreen
leaves with serrated edges. Upright habit.
Needs sun.

Brenda
Ryle, UK, 1980
Double. T pale pink, short and thick; S
with a touch of pink and reflexed; C two
shades of pink; filaments red. Dark green,
medium to large oval to heart-shaped
leaves with sharp points and slightly
crinkled. Freely borne, medium-sized to
large flowers. Large, erect, self-branching
shrub.

Bridesmaid
Tiret, USA, 1952
Double. T and S white with carmine
blush; T thick; S wide and recurved;
C pale lilac-violet, deeper at edges with
typical sheen. Medium-sized flowers.
Upright, bushy habit. Can be prone to
botrytis.

Brilliant
Bull, UK, 1865
Single or semi-double. T and S scarlet;
T long; C violet-magenta with red veins;
filaments and style pink. Mid-green leaves.
Strong, erect growth. Not self-branching
and needs frequent nipping out. Suitable
for bedding.

Brookwood Joy
Gilbert, UK, 1983
('Stanley Cash' × 'Joan Gilbert')
Double. T white, medium length; S white
with green tips, pink blush on underside,
held out horizontally with recurved tips;
C hyacinth blue with pink spots, quite full;
filaments deep pink; style pale pink. Large
flowers with heart-shaped buds. Mid-
green leaves. Lax shrub or stiff trailer.

Brunette
De Graaff, Netherlands, 1982
('Mephisto' × not known)
Single. T creamy white, long and slim; S
white with pink blush, green tips; C runs
from pale pink base through orange to
smoky, brownish-orange. Lasting,
medium-sized flowers borne at ends of
stems. Medium-sized leaves have light
green veins and serrated edges. Semi-
pendent or pendent; suitable for hanging-
basket.

Bunny
Need, UK, 1965
Semi-double. T and S cerise; C lilac-pink
with darker violet-pink edge. Erect, woody
growth.

Buttercup
Paskesen, USA, 1976
Single. T and S soft pink; T short; S
orange on underside, held horizontally and
slightly bent inwards at tips; C orange.
Medium-sized flower. Erect, bushy habit.
Grows best in shade.

Caledonia
Lemoine, France, 1899
Single. T and S cherry red; T long; C
crimson; filaments and style cherry red.
Almost self-coloured, medium-sized
flowers, freely borne. Mid-green leaves.
Low, upright bush (to 60cm). Hardy.

Callaly Pink
Ryle, UK, 1974
('Mrs Lawrence Lyons' × not known)
Single. T and S white; T with shell pink
stripes; S with pink blush, pale pink on
underside, green tips, slightly upturned; C
shell pink with darker pink veins; filaments
pink; style pale pink. Handsome, compact,
medium-sized flowers. Mid-green leaves.
Erect habit; needs regular pinching out.

Cambridge Louie [63]
Naphten, UK, 1977
Single. T and S pinkish-orange; S darker
tint on underside; T thin; C pink, darker at
edges. Medium-sized flowers, very freely
borne. Fairly small, light green leaves.
Erect bush, vigorous and self-branching.

Cara Mia
Schnabel, USA, 1957
Semi-double. T greenish-white, fairly
long; S pale pink with green tips, long,
pointed and reflexed; C dark crimson to
vermilion, white at base, around calyx;
filaments pale pink; style white to pale
pink. Medium-sized, freely borne flowers.
Mid-green leaves. Vigorous, trailing habit.

Cardinal
Evans and Reeves, USA, 1938
('Santa Monica' × 'President')
Single to semi-double. T, S and C red,
almost self-coloured; filaments dark pink;
style pink. Large flowers. Large, fairly
light green leaves. Vigorous, upward
growth but not selfbranching.

Cardinal Farges
Rawlins, UK, 1958
(sport of 'Abbé Farges')
Single or semi-double. T and S pale cerise;
C white with some cerise veins; filaments
and style pale cerise. Small flowers, freely
borne. Small mid-green leaves. Erect, stiff
and woody growth; branches break easily.
Self-branching.

Carillon van Amsterdam
V. Wieringen, Netherlands, 1970
Single. T and S red; T long and slim;
S long and slim, green tips, held out
horizontally; C dark red; filaments and
style pink. Medium-sized flowers. Mid-
green leaves. Lax habit; suitable for
hanging-basket.

Carmel Blue [11]
Hodges, USA, 1936
Single. T and S white; T long; S spread
out, pink blush, green tips; long C blue,
becoming purple as flowers age; filaments
pink; style white. Fairly large flowers.
Mid-green leaves. Vigorous growth, erect
and woody; self-branching and
freeflowering. Do not grow in full sun.

Carmen Maria
Breitner, USA, 1970
(sport of 'Leonora')
Single. T and S pink; S long, narrow and
erect; C pink with deep pink veins.
Vigorous self-branching and free-
flowering, erect shrub.

Carnival
Tiret, USA, 1956
Double. Long T from white to crimson;
S white with green tips, long and curling
back; C bright red, very long; filaments
pink; style white. Graceful flowers, early in
year and freely borne. Mid-green leaves.
Lax habit; trailing; not selfbranching.

Caroline [125]
Miller, UK, 1967
('Citation' × not known)
Single or semi-double. T pink; S pale
pink, green tips, deeper pink on underside;
C pale lavender, pale pink at base;
filaments pink; style pale pink. Large
flowers freely borne. Mid-green leaves.
Large flower. Upright habit. Not an easy
plant.

Cascade

J. B. Lagen, USA, 1937

('Rolla' × 'Amy Lye')

Single. T and S white with carmine blush;
S long; C deep carmine; filaments and
style pink. Medium-sized flowers, freely
borne. Fairly light green leaves. Pendent,
selfbranching habit.

Celadore

Hall, UK, 1981

('Pink Galore' × 'Blush o' Dawn')

Double. T deep pink; S bright deep pink
on upperside, crepey, deep pink on
underside, green tips, held out
horizontally; C bright deep pink. Medium-
sized flower. Heart-shaped leaves deep
green, with wide, central vein with pink
tint. Vigorous trailing habit.

Celia Smedley [57]

Roe, UK, 1970

Single to semi-double. T greenish-white;
S pinkish-white with pink blush; C bright
currant red with some white at base;
filaments pink; style white. Striking
flowers, slightly larger than medium size,
freely borne early in the year. Mid-green
leaves fairly large with red central vein.
Vigorous, selfbranching, upright habit,
but needs pinching out regularly.

Chang [5]

Hazard and Hazard, USA, 1946

F. cordifolia hybrid. Single. T and S
orange-red; S green tips, paler on
underside; C bright orange; filaments pale
pink; style white. Small, freely borne
flowers. Fairly light green, large leaves.
Vigorous, erect growth, but needs regular
pinching out.

Chartwell

Gadsby, UK, 1977

('Christine Clement' × 'Cloverdale Pearl')

Single. T white; S pink with green tips,
long and recurved, standing out from
calyx; C violet-blue, lighter at base;
Medium-sized flower. Erect, self-
branching bush that will do well in full
sun. Likes warmth. Hardy.

Checkerboard [59 and 60]

Walker and Jones, USA, 1948

Single. T red; S white; C red, white at
base; style white; filaments wholly pale
pink. Profuse, medium-sized flowers borne
early in the year. Vigorous, erect habit.

Checkmate

Tolley, UK, 1980

(Sport of 'Checkerboard')

Double. T pale coral pink; S coral pink,
wide, with sharp points, pale pink stripes
at centre; C Indian magenta; filaments and
style same as P. Medium-sized flowers.
Mid-to dark green leaves. Free-flowering
but lax habit; selfbranching but needs
pinching out regularly.

Chillerton Beauty

Bass, UK, 1847

Single. T and S pale pink; S green tips,
deeper pink on underside; C violet,
becoming pinkish as flowers age, pink
veins; filaments white to pinkish-violet;
style pink. Small, freely bone flowers.
Mid-green leaves. Erect habit; easy to
grow.

China Lantern

Grower unknown, USA(?), 1953(?)

Single. T shiny reddish-pink; S white with
green tips; C dark pink shading to
vermilion, with white at base; filaments
and style cerise. Medium-sized flowers late
in year. Dark green leaves. Rather lax,
upright growth.

Cicely Ann

Holmes, UK, 1977

Single. T and S crimson; T long and thin;
S upturned with yellow-green tips and
crimson underside; C light magenta, pink
at base; filaments carmine; style pink.
Medium-sized flowers. Mid-green leaves.
Vigorous, self-branching, natural trailing
habit. Can be grown in full sun.

Citation

Hodges, USA, 1953

Single. T and S light red-pink; S
upturned; C white, pink veins, flaring
widely; filaments and style light red-pink.
Large, well-shaped, profuse flowers. Fairly
light green leaves. Erect, busy habit; prone
to botrytis. Best grown in shaded
greenhouse.

Cliff's Hardy

Gadsby, UK, 1966

('Athela' × 'Bon Accorde')

Single. T and S light crimson; S long, with
green tips; C pale violet, red veins, lighter
at base; filaments cherry red; style pink.
Small to medium-sized erect flowers,
freely borne. Dark green leaves. Erect,
bushy growth. Hardy.

Cliff's Unique
Gadsby, UK, 1976
Double. T pale pink, short and thick; S waxy white with pink blush, green tips, wide and thick; C gentian blue shading to violet-pink as flowers age. Medium-sized, well-formed flowers, erect especially on plants grown in cool setting or in the open, appearing early in the year and freely borne. Upright, self-branching habit.

Cloverdale
Gadsby, UK, 1972
Single. T and S crimson; C blue-violet, turning violet as flowers age; filaments cherry red; style light red. Small flowers held horizontally from plant. Small, mid-green leaves. Compact, free-flowering, dwarf shrub.

Cloverdale Jewel
Gadsby, UK, 1974
('Cloverdale' × 'Lady Isobel Barnett')
Semi-double. T and S pink; C blue-violet, pink veins, darkening as flowers age; filaments pink; style white. Long-lasting, medium-sized flowers, appearing early and continuing until late in year. Small, mid-green leaves. Vigorous, small, erect shrub. Small petaloids distinguish this cultivar from the previous one.

Cloverdale Pearl [121]
Gadsby, UK, 1974
(unnamed seedling × 'Grace Darling')
Single. T white; S pink shading to white, green tips; C white; filaments pink; style pale pink. Medium-sized, well-shaped flowers. freely borne. Small leaves, mid-green to dark green. Self-branching, upright shrub. Gives best colour if grown in shade.

Coachman
Bright, UK, 1920(?)
Single. T and S salmon pink; T fairly long; C vermilion-orange; filaments pink; style pale pink. Medium-sized flowers, very freely borne early in the year. Fairly light green leaves. Vigorous, self-branching habitat; can be grown in hanging-basket.

Come Dancing [12]
E. Handley, UK, 1972
Double. T deep pink; S deep pink, long and wide, with yellowgreen tips; C magenta, salmon pink at base. Large flowers borne over a long period.

Bright green leaves, crinkled and rounded. Semi-pendent habit.

Constance [77]
Berkley Hort. Nursery, USA, 1935
(sport of 'Pink Pearl')
Double. T pale pink; S pink with green tips, deeper pink on underside; C reddish-violet, pink at base; filaments and style pink. Medium-sized flowers. Mid-green leaves. Free-flowering, upright habit. Easy to grow.

Contramine
De Graaff, Netherlands, 1978
('La Campanella' × not known)
Single. T pale pink; S white with pink blush, green, recurved tips; C pale violet-blue, pink at base; filaments pink, anther dark red; style white. Medium-size, profuse blooms, semi-erect. Mid-green leaves with dark red-brown stems. Upright habit.

Coquet Bell
Ryle, UK, 1973
('Lena Dalton' × 'Citation')
Single to semi-double. T and S dark pink; T short; S slightly green tips; C pale mauve with pink-mauve blush at base and red veins; bell-shaped with slightly wavy edges; filaments deep pink; style white to pale pink. Medium-sized flowers, freely borne. Mid-green leaves. Vigorous, self-branching bush; short stem sections.

Corallina
Pince, UK, 1844
(*F. cordifolia* × *F. globosa*)
Single. T and S scarlet; S long, drooping over calyx; C violet, pink at base; filaments and style scarlet. Medium-sized flowers. Leaves dark green-bronze. Vigorous but rather lax growth; branches spread horizontally. Hardy.

Cornelis Steevens
Steevens, Netherlands, 1968
Single or semi-double. Long T and S white with soft pink; S with green tips; C deep pink-red, lighter at base; filaments and style pink. Medium to large flowers. Fairly dark green leaves. Naturally trailing habit.

Countess of Aberdeen
Dobbie Forbes, UK, 1888
Single. T creamy white; S white, pale pink in sun; C white with soft pink blush, quite

soft pink in shade, rich pink in sun; filaments pale pink; style white. Small, graceful flowers. Small, mid-green leaves. Needs to be grown in shade for best colour. Prone to botrytis. Upright, self-branching habit. Not an easy plant to grow.

Crackerjack
Fuchsia-la Nursery, USA, 1961
Single or semi-double. T and S white with soft pink blush; long C pale lilac, white at base, red veins; filaments pink; style white. Large, freely borne flowers. Large, light green leaves with red central vein. Vigorous, self-branching cultivar, good for hanging-basket.

Cross Check [58]
Brouwer, Netherlands, 1982
('Checkerboard' × 'Achievement')
Single. T pink-red shading to pink, fairly long; S pink-red, pink at ends, upturned; C violet-red with red-orange edges; filaments and style deep pink. Medium to large flowers. Light green leaves. Upright but lax growth; suitable for hangingbasket. Grow in full sun.

Crystal Stars
Mrs I. Clyne, UK, 1974
(('La Campanella' × 'Flirtation Waltz') × 'Ting-a-Ling')
Semi-double. T and S white; T thick, greenish-white with red blush; S with red blush, recurved; C white. Medium to fairly small flower. Medium to small, mid-green leaves. Self-branching, upright habit.

Curly Q
Kennet, USA, 1961
Single. T and S white flushed with carmine; S recurved and typically rolled against T; C violet, four rolled up in corolla; filaments pink; style white. Fairly small, freely borne flowers. Mid-green, small leaves. Lax, self-branching, trailing habit.

Curtain Call
Munkner, USA, 1961
Single. T and S pinkish-carmine; C varies from deep pinkishbengal red to carmine, with serrated edges. Large flowers, freely borne, four from each leaf axil. Lax habit.

Daisy Bell [34]
Author unknown, USA, 1975(?)
Single. Long T deep scarlet; S red, pink

on underside, green tips; C carmine red to carmine pink. Medium-sized, freely borne flowers. Unusual multi-coloured leaves, olive-green above, paler below with heavy red veins. Vigorous, self-branching, naturally trailing habit.

Danny Boy
Tiret, USA 1961
Double. T and S pale red; C red. Very large flower. Largish, mid-green leaves. Upright, self-branching habit, but must be nipped out regularly.

Dark Eyes
Erickson, USA, 1958
Double. Short T and S deep red; S upturned; C violet-blue, curled and rolled. Medium-sized flowers, freely borne. Self-branching, woody growth.

Dark Secret
Hodges, USA, 1957
Double. T short, greenish-white; S heavy, wide, upturned, waxy white outside, pale pink and crepey on underside; deep violet corolla, outermost C marked red-lilac. Medium-sized flowers. Dark green leaves. Bushy, upright, self-branching habit.

Dark Spider
De Graaff, Netherlands, 1979
('Brutus' × not known)
Single to semi-double. T and S red; S spider-type; C dark violet, violet-red spots at base; fades to burgundy red; C somewhat toothed; filaments dark red; style red. Medium-sized to large flowers. Mid-green leaves, paler undersides, with evident red veins. Self-branching, vigorous, trailer. Needs full light.

Dee Copley
Copley Gardens, USA, 1964
Double. T and S deep carmine; C soft deep violet with carmine and pink spots; filaments and style carmine. Large, profuse flowers. Mid-green leaves with carmine central vein. Large flower. Sturdy, self-branching, upright growth.

Delice
De Graaff, Netherlands, 1984
('Pink Galore' × not known)
Single to semi-double. T quite light red; S pale pink, somewhat lighter underside, semi-erect; C pink-violet on opening, somewhat more violet as flowers age; filaments and style pink. Medium-sized

flowers. Mid-green, dentate and oval, medium-size leaves with red veins and stalks. Trailing habit; needs regular pinching out.

Delta Beauty
Felix, Netherlands, 1982
(*F. rubra grandiflora* × 'Blue Veil')
Double. T creamy white; S pink, spread, with green tips; C lilac-pink, darker pink along edges; short corolla. Moderate grower, but must be nipped out. Semi-pendent habit.

Delta Pearl
Felix, Netherlands, 1982
('Blush o' Dawn' × 'Blush o' Dawn')
Double. T greenish-white; S white to pale pink, long and narrow; C pale lilac. Medium-sized flowers, freely borne. Narrow, rather small, light green leaves. Pendent habit. Do not grow in full sun.

Deltaschön
Felix, Netherlands, 1982
(sport of 'Tausendschön')
Double. T and S red; C white with pink blush and veins; filaments and style red. Medium-sized flowers, freely borne early in the year. Mid-green leaves with red central vein and stalks. Upright, bushy growth.

De Pleiaden
De Groot, Netherlands, 1974(?)
('Saturnus' × 'Bon Accorde')
Single. T, S and C pinkish-white; mid-green leaves. Smallish, freely borne flowers, held more or less erect. Small, erect shrub.

Derby Imp
Gadsby, UK, 1974
Single. T and S cherry red; C blue-violet, turning purple as flowers age, pink at base, cherry red veins; filaments and style cherry red. Small flowers early in the year. Small, mid-green leaves. Vigorous, free-flowering and self-branching.

Diana Wills [44]
Gadsby, UK, 1971
Double. T greenish-white; S white, green tips; C bluish-purple (red-purple as flowers age), white and dark pink spots; filaments and style pale pink. Large flowers, freely borne. Mid-green leaves. Self-branching, slack growth. Needs staking.

Dilly Dilly
Tiret, USA, 1963
Double. T white to pale pink, darker on underside, green tips; C bright lilac, pink at base; filaments pink; style pale pink. Fairly large flowers. Mid-green leaves. Upright, rather lax habit. Easy to grow.

Dirk van Delen
Steevens, Netherlands, 1971(?)
('Frau Ida Noak' × not known)
Single. T and S pink; S with green tips; C pale violet-pink. Medium-sized, freely borne flowers. Dark green leaves. Vigorous, upright shrub; can be trained as a standard.

Display
Smith, UK, 1881
Single. T and S pink-red; C a little darker; filaments pinkred; style dark pink. Medium-sized, bell-shaped flowers, freely borne. Mid-green leaves. Upright, self-branching habit.

Dollar Princess [94]
Lemoine, France, 1912
Double. T and S cherry red; C rich violet. Fairly small flowers, profusely borne. Small to medium mid-green leaves. Self-branching, upright and vigorous habit. Easy to grow. Good garden plant.

Dominyana [134]
Dominy, UK, 1852
(*F. macrostigma* × *F. denticulata*)
Single. T and S scarlet; T long; S small; C small and scarlet. Long, trumpet-shaped self-coloured flowers, borne in clusters. Dark green-bronze leaves. Upright habit. Does best in greenhouse.

Drame
Lemoine, France, 1880
('Ricartonii' × not known)
Single or semi-double. T and S scarlet; C reddish-violet, scarlet at base; filaments dark red; style light scarlet. Medium-sized flowers, freely borne. Small to medium, yellowish-green leaves. Vigorous, self-branching, upright shrub. Hardy.

Dulcie Elizabeth
Clyne-Aimes, UK, 1974
('Tennessee Waltz' × 'Winston Churchill')
Double. T and S pink; flaring C blue with deep pink spots and shell pink. Medium-sized flowers, freely borne, rather late in year. Mid-green leaves. Self-branching,

vigorous shrub. Colour of flowers does not depend on sun or shade.

Dusky Beauty
Ryle/Fuchsiavale, UK, 1981
Single. T and S deep pink; T medium length; S held horizontally; C pale violet with pink blush, deeper pink at edges. Small flowers, freely borne. Mid-to dark green, small to medium leaves. Upright, vigorous and self-branching habit.

Dusky Rose
Waltz, USA, 1960
Double. T deep pink to red; S deep pink with green, upturned tips; C pink, fading to raspberry red with coral spots; filaments and style dark pink. Fairly large flowers, freely borne. Mid-green leaves. Self-branching, lax habit. Stands heat well.

Dutch Firebird
De Graaff, Netherlands, 1977
('Mevr. Goyaerts' × not known)
Single. Long T light red; S light red (spider type); C red with a touch of violet; filaments and style pink. Medium-sized flowers, very freely borne. Mid-green leaves. Stiff, trailing habit.

Dutch Flamingo
De Graaff, Netherlands, 1977
('Mephisto' × not known)
Single. T and S salmon pink; T long; S lighter towards green tips; C salmon pink. Flowers small, almost self-coloured. Dark green leaves. Erect shrub.

Dutch Mill
Peterson, USA, 1962
Single. T and S bright light red; S long and curled; C pale violet. Medium-sized flowers, very freely borne. Mid-green leaves. Erect, vigorous and self-branching.

Earl of Beaconsfield
Laing, UK, 1878
(*F. fulgens* × 'Perfection')
Single. T and S salmon pink; T long; S with green tips; C salmon orange; filaments pink; style salmon pink. Fairly large flowers. Light green leaves. Free-flowering, upright and vigorous but not self-branching.

El Camino
Lee, USA, 1955
Double. T and S pink-red; S short, wide and recurved; C white with strong pink blush and pink veins; filaments and style

pink-red. Fairly large flowers, freely borne. Mid-to dark green leaves. Self-branching, erect habit. Easy to grow.

Eleanor Leytham
Roe, UK, 1973
('Countess of Aberdeen' × 'Pink Darling')
Single. T and S white with pink blush; C pink, deeper at edge. Small flowers, profusely borne. Small, mid-green leaves. Upright, compact habit, but not easy to grow.

Elfriede Ott [82]
Nutzinger, Austria, 1977
('Koralle' × *F. splendens*)
Triphylla hybrid. T and S dark pink-red, deeper on underside. T very long; S long for a Triphylla; C dark pink-red, more intense than T and S, white edge, short compared with T and S; filaments and style pale pink. Large flowers, freely borne in clusters. Mid-green leaves with red central vein. Upright, vigorous shrub.

Elizabeth
Whiteman, UK, 1941(?)
Single. T and S opal pink; T very long; S with green tips; C deep pink with salmon pink tinge; filaments and style pink. Compact flowers, very freely borne. Mid-green leaves. Vigorous, not self-branching bush.

Ellen Morgan
Holmes, UK, 1976
('Phyllis' × not known)
Double. T and S salmon pink; S with green tips; C rich magenta, salmon pink at base; filaments and style light red. Medium-sized flowers, freely borne. Mid-green leaves. Upright, vigorous habit. Easy to grow.

El Matador
Kennet, USA, 1965
Semi-double or double. T pink; S white with pink blush and green tips, salmon pink on underside; C violet to wine red with salmon spots, white at base; filaments pink; style white to pink, very long. Large to medium-sized, freely borne flowers. Fairly light green leaves. Natural trailing habit; vigorous. Suitable for hanging-basket.

Elsie Mitchell
Ryle, UK, 1980
Double. T pink; S pink at base shading to

white and with green tips; C lavender with a touch of pink. Medium-sized flowers, with stamens and pistil not protruding. Small to medium, mid-green leaves. Upright and self-branching bush. Best colours in shade.

Emile de Wildeman 'Fascination'
Lemoine, France, 1905
Double. T dark carmine; erect S carmine; C pink, deep pink and cherry red veins; filaments and style cherry red. Fairly large flowers, freely borne. Mid-green leaves. Self-branching, bushy and vigorous habit.

Empress of Prussia
Hoppe, UK, 1868
Single. T and S scarlet; C reddish-violet or magenta, paler at base; filaments and style deep pink. Medium-sized, freely borne flowers. Mid-green, slightly serrated leaves. Upright, self-branching, sturdy growth. Hardy. Rediscovered in a UK garden after 60 years.

Estelle Marie [111]
Newton, USA, 1973
Single. T and S greenish- white; T short and thick; recurving S with green tips; C blue-violet, violet as flowers age, white at base; filaments white to pale pink; style white. Small to medium-sized, erect flowers. Mid-green to dark green leaves. Erect, self-branching and vigorous habit.

Eternal Flame
Paskesen, USA, 1971
Semi-double. T and S dark salmon pink; S with green tips and orange on underside; C smoky pink with orange stripes, salmon pink at base; filaments pink; style salmon pink. Medium-sized flowers, freely borne. Fairly dark green leaves. Bushy, vigorous and upright habit.

Eusebia [46]
Stubbs, USA, 1982
Double. T white; S long, recurved, white shading to pink; C deep red. Rather short, fully flaring flowers. Long, dark green leaves. Self-branching, free-flowering, upright bush.

Evensong
Colville, UK, 1967
Single. T pink; S white with green tips, a trace of pink at base; C white; filaments pale pink; style white. Medium-sized, freely borne flowers. Pale green leaves. Erect, self-branching and vigorous habit.

Falling Stars [26]
Reiter, USA, 1941
(old cultivar resembling 'Morning Mist' × 'Cascade')
Single. T pale pinkish-red, fairly long; S reddish-pink, salmon pink on underside, green tips; C turkish red with pale orange tint; filaments pink; style pale pink. Medium-sized flowers. Light green leaves. Lax, upright habit; needs regular pinching out.

Fanfare [22]
Reiter, USA, 1941
(*F. denticulata* × *F. leptopoda*)
Single. T red-pink with small carmine lines, very long. S redpink with green tips, short; C orange; filaments and style pink. Long flowers appearing late in year. Deep green, large leaves. Untidy, vigorous habit, with drooping stems.

Fenna [18]
Bögemann, Germany, 1984
('Leverkusen' × not known)
Single. T pink-red, fairly long at beginning of S; S red-pink, gradually shading to whitish-green tips (typical of the flower), pale pink on underside, held downwards; C orange-pink with darker veins; filaments and style pale pink. Medium-sized leaves with red veins. Lax, upright shrub.

Fiery Spider [23]
Munkner, USA, 1960
Single. T carmine, long; S salmon with green tip, long; filaments pink; style pale pink. Freely borne, long flowers. Pale green leaves. Natural trailing habit; vigorous. Colour is best in full sun.

Filigrain
Brouwer, Netherlands, 1982
('Madame Cornelissen' × 'Caledonia')
Single. T deep red, thin; S deep red, long and narrow, with recurved tips held horizontally and slightly turned; C violetpink with darker veins; filaments dark violet-red; style red and very long. Medium-sized, slender flowers, freely borne. Long, narrow, mid-green leaves with red stems. Upright, vigorous habit.

Fiona
Clark, UK, 1958
Single. T and S white; S long with green tips; C blue, reddish-violet as flowers age,

flared white at base; filaments pink; style white. Large, elegant flowers, very freely borne. Mid-green leaves. Upright, vigorous habit, rather lax.

First Kiss
De Graaff, Netherlands 1978
('La Campanella' × not known)
Semi-double. T and S creamy white, can become reddish in full sun; C pale pink. Medium-sized flowers. Mid-green leaves. Self-branching, erect shrub.

First Success
Weeda, Netherlands, 1982
(*F. splendens* × *F. paniculata*; primary cross)
Flowers not only January to end May in frost-free greenhouse, but also in summer in a shady spot in the garden. T violet pink; S reddish to wine red; C pale lilac. Flowers borne in clusters. Erect, vigorous habit.

Flash
Hazard and Hazard, USA, 1930(?)
Single. T and S pale red; C red; filaments and style red. Small flowers, almost self-coloured. Small pale green leaves. Erect, vigorous habit.

Flashlight
Gadsby, UK, 1968
('Flash' × *F. magellanica alba*)
Single. T pale pink with green tips; C mauve-pink; filaments pale pink; style white. Freely borne, small flowers. Small, pale green leaves. Upright, self-branching bush.

Flim Flam
De Graaff, Netherlands, 1977
Single. T and S creamy white with pink blush; S deeper blush pink; T fairly long; C deep salmon pink with darker orange edges; filaments pink; style white. Profuse, medium-sized flowers. Fairly dark, small leaves. Self-branching, upright bush.

Flirtation
Leitner, USA, 1946
(sport of 'Lucky Strike')
Double. T and S pale pink; S deeper pink on underside; C pale pinkish-mauve; filaments pink; style white. Freely borne, medium-sized flowers. Longish, mid-green leaves. Selfbranching, upright bush.

Flirtation Waltz
Waltz, USA, 1972
Double. T and S white; S green tips, pale pink on underside; C pale pink; filaments pink; style white. Medium-sized flowers, freely borne. Pale green, medium-sized leaves. Vigorous, selfbranching, erect habit.

Flora
Tolley, 1971, UK
Semi-double. T and S bright cherry red; S long and upturned; C pale violet with pink veins. Large, bell-shaped flowers, freely borne. Yellowish-green leaves with red veins. Vigorous, self-branching and upright habit.

Floral City
Holmes, UK, 1974
Double. T and S pale pink; C pale lilac. Profuse, medium-sized flowers. Lax, erect habit.

Flowerdream
M. Rijf, Netherlands, 1983
('Merry Mary' × 'Bora Bora')
Double. T white with wide carmine strips, shading to lilac; S white, quite recurved, carmine spot on underside; C white with carmine rings and spots, increasing from 12 in spring and autumn to 20 in summer. Dull mid-green leaves with red stems. Free-flowering, pendent or semi-pendent habit; self-branching. Achieves best colour in the sun.

Flying Cloud
Reiter, USA, 1949
Double. T white; S white with green tips, soft pink on underside; C white, a touch of pink at base; filaments pale pink; style white. Fairly large flowers. Dark green leaves. Upright, vigorous habit but somewhat lax.

Forget-me-not
Banks, UK, 1866
Single. T and S pale flesh-coloured pink; C pale blue. Small flowers, freely borne, early in the year. Small to medium, pale green leaves. Vigorous, upright habit. Requires regular pinching out.

Foxtrot [48]
Tolley, UK, 1974
('Tennessee Waltz' × not known)
Semi-double. T and S pale cherry red; T short; S held out from corolla, green tips;

C pale lavender, pink at base. Medium-sized flowers, semi-flared. Small to medium-sized, pale green leaves. Vigorous, free-flowering, self-branching habit.

François Villon
De Graaff, Netherlands, 1978
('La Campanella' × not known)
Single. T and S white, tinted pink-red; S held up; C bright red. Smallish, compact flowers, very freely borne. Fairly small, mid-green leaves. Self-branching, vigorous trailer.

Franz Noszian
Nutzinger, Austria, 1976
Semi-double. T and S pink-red; T short, round and deeper colour than S; C soft pink with pink-red veins; filaments and style pink-red. Medium-sized, freely borne flowers. Fairly small mid-green leaves. Self-branching, vigorous growth.

Frau Ida Noak
Lemoine, France, 1911
Double. T and S red; C violet; filaments red. Dark green leaves. Erect, woody growth.

Frederike
Felix, Netherlands, 1979
(seedling × 'Wassernymph')
Single to semi-double. T white with pink blush; T spherical; S pink with green tips, spherical. C deep bordeaux red, salmon pink at base (sometimes orange-red petaloids). Medium-sized flowers. Mid-green leaves. Self-branching, erect shrub.

Frosted Flame [45]
Handley, UK, 1975
Single. T and S white; S with green tips and pale pink underside, long and narrow, stands out well, upward curled tips; C bright fire red with darker edge and soft pink at base; filaments and style pink-red. Long, large and spindle-shaped flower, overlapping petals, profusely borne. Mid-green leaves. Natural trailing habit, self-branching. Grow in shade for best colour. Suitable for hanging-basket.

Galadriel [105]
De Graaff, Netherlands, 1982
('Mephisto' × 'Countess of Aberdeen')
Single. T waxy white, short; S waxy white shading to pink-red halfway, darker edge, green tips, flared; C pale orange-red, short; filaments pink; style white. Small flowers,

freely borne. Small mid-green leaves. Vigorous, upright bush, easily shaped. Grow in sun for best blooms.

Gartenmeister Bonstedt [87]
Bonstedt, Germany, 1905
(*F. triphylla* × not known)
Single. T, S and C orange-red; T long, *triphylla*-type. Dark bronze-red-green leaves. Strong erect, free-flowering habit.

Gay Fandango
Nelson, USA, 1951
Double. T and S pink carmine, large; C pink-claret, of different lengths. Large flowers, freely borne. Medium to large leaves, mid-green leaves. Vigorous, upright habit; semi-pendent.

Gay Parasol
Stubbs, USA, 1979
Double. T ivory green, short and thick; S ivory with fine red stripes near edges, shading into pure ivory with a hint of red, lifting like a parasol above corolla; C dark violet, turning to bright burgundy red as flowers age. Fairly short flowers, opening flat as they mature. Pale buds contrast well with dark, open flowers. Mid-to dark green leaves with red veins. Upright, self-branching bush.

General Monk
Author unknown, France, 1844(?)
Double. T and S light red; C blue, fading to mauve. Medium-sized flowers, freely borne. Mid-green, medium-sized leaves. Vigorous, self-branching bush.

Genii
Reiter, USA, 1951
Single. T and S cherry red; C dark violet, turning reddishpurple as flowers age; filaments and style cherry red. Pale yellowish-green leaves. Free-flowering, self-branching, upright bush. Good for sunny position.

Georgana
Tiret, USA, 1955
Double. T and S pink; C soft pastel blue and lilac checkered. Very large, profuse flowers. Large, bright green leaves. Vigorous, upright habit.

Glitters
Erickson, USA, 1963
Single. T and S salmon pink, paler towards green tips; C salmon orange;

filaments and style pink. Medium-sized, compact flowers, freely borne. Mid-green leaves. Vigorous, erect bush.

Golden Dawn
Haag, USA, 1951
Single. T and S salmon; C pale orange to light red; filaments pink; style pale pink. Medium-sized flowers. Fairly pale green leaves. Free-flowering, vigorous, upright habit.

Golden Glow
Munkner, USA, 1958
Single. T and S pale carmine, salmon blush; T long; C yellowish-orange. Medium-sized flower. Large, often curled leaves. Pendent habit.

Golden la Campanella
See 'La Campanella' for flowers and growth, but this cultivar has multicoloured leaves, which come out best in sun.

Golden Lena
Nottingham, UK, 1979
(sport of 'Lena')
Semi-double. For flower and growth see 'Lena', but this cultivar has leaves in various shades of green and goldenyellow.

Golden Marinka
Weber, USA, 1959
(sport of 'Marinka')
Single. T and S red; C deep red; filaments and style red. Medium-sized flowers, freely borne. Multicoloured green and golden leaves with red veins. Vigorous, trailing growth. Needs good light.

Golondrina
Niederholzer, USA, 1941
Single. T light red; S scarlet; C dark magenta, fading to light red at base, sometimes with pink stripes; filaments pale pink, almost invisible; style pale pink. Medium-sized flowers, very freely borne. Mid-green leaves. Vigorous, pendent habit. Suitable for hanging-basket.

Göttingen [83]
Bonstedt, Germany, 1904
May be a Triphylla hybrid. Single. T and S salmon orange; C vermilion. Upright and slow-growing habit.

Grasmere [24]
S. Travis, UK, 1964
(*F. cordifolia* × *F. lycioides*)
Single. T and S coral red; T long and thin;

S green tips; C deep coral pink. Flowers almost self-coloured; very freely borne in clusters. Deep green leaves. Self-branching, naturally trailing habit.

Greenpeace
De Graaff, Netherlands, 1981
('Speciosa' × 'Ting-a-Ling')
Single. T very short, pale green, pink blush in sun; S pale green tending to pale greenish-pink, tips upturned; C pale pink, no coloured veins; filaments pinkish-white; anthers small pale green leaves with pink tips; style pink-white; very large pistil. Medium-sized flowers, turning reddish in sun. Rough, mid-green leaves. Vigorous, but lax, upright habit. Requires regular pinching out.

Groene Kan's Glorie
Steevens, Netherlands, 1972
Single. T dark salmon; S salmon, salmon orange on underside, green tips; C orange; filaments and style orange-pink. Fairly large flowers, freely borne. Pale green leaves. Upright, bushy, habit.

Gruss aus dem Bodethal
Teupel, Germany, 1892
('Cupido' × 'Creusa')
Single or semi-double. T and S carmine; C quite dark violet; filaments and style crimson. Medium-sized to small flowers, freely borne. Mid-green leaves. Self-branching, erect, bush. Easy to grow.

Harebell
Felix, Netherlands, 1983
('Nancy Lou' × 'Joy Patmore')
Semi-double. T white with salmon touches and pale pink stripes; S pale pink, paler towards tips, held well out; C mauve-violet; filaments pale carmine; style white. Medium-sized flowers, freely borne early in year. Mid-green, medium-sized leaves. Vigorous, upright growth.

Harriet
Soo Yun, USA, 1971
Double. T pinkish-white; S white, green tips, a hint of pink on underside, upright when flower is in full bloom; C pale blue, deeper blue at edges and white at centre; filaments pink; style white. Large flowers, freely borne. Fairly dark green leaves. Naturally trailing habit. Suitable for hanging-basket.

Harry Gray
Dunnett, UK, 1981
('La Campanella' × 'Powder Puff')
Double. T deep pink stripes, relatively
short and medium thick; S white shading
to deep pink at base, green tips, somewhat
recurved; C white shading to pink at base,
turning pale pink as flowers age; filaments
pink; style long and white. Small to
medium-sized flowers, prolific for double.
Small, dark green leaves with red stems.
Short segments. Self-branching, lax
growth. Suitable for hanging-baskets. Best
colour in semi-shade.

Heather Hobbs [108]
R. Holmes, UK, 1972
('Hugh Morgan' × not known)
Single. T crimson, short; S crimson, paler
on underside, yellow tips, long and
narrow, sometimes turned up and twisted;
C white, neon pink veins with hint of pink;
calyx bell-shaped. Yellow-green leaves,
small, oval and somewhat dentate.
Vigorous, free-flowering, erect, self-
branching growth.

Heinrich Henkel [85]
See 'Andenken an Heinrich Henkel'

Hellas
Van Tuyl, Netherlands, 1982
Semi-double. T quite pale pink; S
somewhat darker pink with darker pink
spots and darker underside; C white with
pale pink veins at base; filaments and style
pink. Medium-sized flowers. Dark green,
fairly small leaves. Upright, vigorous
habit. Suitable for small standard.

Hendrikje Stoffels
Brouwer, Netherlands, 1983
('Checkerboard' × 'Papa Bleuss')
Double. T pink-red and thick; S white,
flamed with pink, standing out
horizontally, long and narrow; C deep
wine red, darker at edges, pink with some
salmon at base; filaments and style pink.
Large flowers. Mid-green leaves. Trailing
habit. Requires regular pinching out. Not
easy to grow. Suitable for hanging-basket.

Henriette Ernst
Ernst, Germany, 1841
Single. T and S bright red; C blue-violet.
Medium-sized flowers. Mid-green,
medium-sized leaves. Slow-growing,
upright, self-branching habit.

Henri Poincaré
Lemoine, France, 1905
Single. T and S red; S recurved; C violet,
red veins, wavy edge; bell-shaped calyx;
filaments and style red. Longish flowers.
Fairly dark green leaves. Rather lax habit.
Needs to be pinched out regularly.

Heron
Lemoine, France, 1891
Single. R and S scarlet; C bluish-magenta,
often striped pink in middle, scarlet veins;
filaments cherry red; style pale cherry red.
Mid-green leaves. Free-flowering, self-
branching, vigorous and erect habit.
Hardy.

Heydon
Clitheroe, UK, 1981
('Nancy Lou' × 'The 13th Star')
Double. T and S white with pink blush; S
green tips; C pale pink at base, violet-blue
at edges. Large flowers, freely borne for
double plant. Deep green leaves; wood red
as plant ages. Medium, upright growth.
Suitable for standard.

Hiawatha
Van Wijk, Netherlands, 1984
('La Campanella × not known)
Single. T white with some pink, short and
square; S white with a little pink, pink on
underside, somewhat recurved; C deep
dark red; filaments red; very long style
pink. Fairly small flowers, freely borne.
Mid-green leaves. Erect, self-branching
shrub.

Hidcote Beauty
Webb, UK, 1949
Single. T and S waxy cream, green tips;
C pale salmon pink, pale pink flush.
Medium-sized flowers, freely borne. Pale
green leaves. Self-branching, vigorous and
erect habit.

Highland Pipes
De Graaff, Netherlands, 1983
(*F. magdalenae* × *F. excorticata*)
Single. Long T glowing beetroot-violet
with darker stripes from dark base; small S
yellow-green with beetroot-violet stripes
and base; C almost same colour as T but
somewhat shorter than S; style beetroot-
violet. Oblong, mid-green leaves with pale
underside and red central vein, apparently
in rings of 3; stems clearly paler. Vigorous,
fairly free-flowering, upright growth. Best
kept growing in winter.

Hindu Belle
Munkner, USA, 1959
Single. T and S white; S with green tips,
pink blush on underside; C rich wine red,
fading to red; filaments pink; style white.
Medium-sized flowers, freely borne. Mid-
green leaves. Vigorous, upright growth.
Needs carefully pinching out.

Hobson's Choice
Hobson, UK, 1976
Double. T and S pink; C paler pink with
fine shadings. Medium-sized flowers borne
in profusion. Upright, bushy shrub.

Hula Girl
Paskesen, USA, 1972
Double. T and S dark pink; S slightly
reflexed; C white with pink blush at base,
dark pink veins; filaments pink-red; style
white to pale red. Very large, full flowers,
freely borne. Mid-green leaves, red central
vein. Bushy, naturally trailing habit.

Hummeltje
Appel, Netherlands, 1979
(*F. microphylla* subsp.
aprica × *F. microphylla*)
Single. Flowers of Encliandra type, quite
small (5mm), deep red; inner surface of C
pink. Flowers early and profuse. Small,
fairly dark green leaves close together.
Upright, self-branching habit. Needs
careful pinching out.

Hurrycane
Rijff, Netherlands, 1983
('First Kiss' × 'Pink Bon Accorde')
Single. T pale pink, deeper on underside;
C red to lilac, inner side darker with hint
of pink.

Iced Champagne
Jennings, UK, 1968
('Miss California' × 'Jack Ackland' or 'Jack
Shahan'). Single or semi-double. T and S
pink; S with green tips; C pale pink, pink
veins; filaments pink; style pale pink.
Longish, medium-sized flowers with loose
petals. Large, mid-green leaves with red
central vein. Self-branching, free-
flowering, upright habit.

Igloo Maid
Holmes, UK, 1972
Double. T white; S white with green tips;
C white with faint pink tint; filaments and
style white. Medium to large flowers.
Yellowish-green leaves. Self-branching,
free-flowering, upright habit.

Impudence [40]
Schnabel, USA, 1957
Single. T and S carmine; S long and
slender; C white with carmine veins, held
out horizontally; filaments and style
carmine. Medium-sized flowers, freely
borne. Mid-green leaves. Upright and
vigorous habit. Requires regular nipping
out.

Ina
De Groot, Netherlands, 1973
('Bon Accorde' × 'Venus')
Single. T greenish-white; S white with
green tips; C pink, violet-red edge,
forming strong contrast; filaments and
style pale pink. Medium-sized flowers,
held out horizontally. Medium-sized, mid-
green leaves. Shrub.

Indian Maid
Waltz, USA, 1962
Double. T and S scarlet; S very long and
recurved; C rich violet, handsome on
opening. Large, freely borne flowers. Dark
green leaves. Lax habit, but will make
bush if pinched out regularly.

Ingram Maid
Ryle, UK, 1976
(('Pink Cloud' × 'Lena Dalton') × 'Sonata')
Single. T and S white; S pale pink blush
on underside, held out horizontally; C
creamy white; filaments and style red.
Medium-sized flowers, tube-shaped calyx.
Best colour achieved in sun. Tall, upright
shrub.

Iris Amer
Amer, UK, 1966
('Empress of Prussia' × not known)
Semi-double. T pale pink; S with green
tips, pink blush on underside; C reddish-
pink with pink spots; filaments pink; style
white to pale pink. Profuse, medium-sized
flowers, 4–6 in each leaf axil. Mid-green
leaves. Upright, vigorous growth. Short-
jointed stems; needs little nipping out.

Isis
De Groot, Netherlands, 1973
Single. T and S red; T short; C violet,
fading to violet red; filaments red; style
light red. Medium-sized flowers, freely
borne. Small to medium-sized, dark green
leaves with red veins; young leaves brown.
Self-branching, free-flowering upright
habit.

Jack Ackland
Haag and Son, USA, 1952
Single. T and S bright pink; C deep pink-red, darkening as flowers age. Freely borne, large to medium-sized flowers. Midgreen leaves. Self-branching, upright habit.

Jack King [49]
R. Holmes, UK, c.1978
(sport of 'General Monk')
Double. T and S crimson; S inside pink-red and crepey; C lilac, pink red veins, some covered with pale pink at base shading to red-violet. Medium-sized flowers, freely borne. Upright, self-branching and vigorous habit.

Jamboree
Reiter, USA, 1955
Double. T pinkish-white; S salmon pink, deeper pink on underside, white at base; C salmon pink to bright carmine; filaments pink; style white. Medium-sized to large flowers, freely borne. Fairly dark green, medium-sized leaves. Upright, stiff growth; nip out when young.

Jan Bremer [98]
Bremer, Netherlands, 1973
Single. T, S and C light red; T fairly long. Medium-sized flowers, freely borne on each leaf axil. Mid-green leaves. Quick-growing, rather lax habit.

Janny Appel
Appel, Netherlands, 1979
(*F. microphylla* × *F. helmsleyana*)
Single. Flowers of Encliandra type, pale pink, growing darker as they age; borne early and over long period. Leaves small. Strong, self-branching growth.

Jean Ewart
G. Roe, UK, 1981
('Mipam' × 'Carol Roe')
Single. T and S china-rose; T short; S short, pointed and curled back; C pink. Medium-sized flowers, very freely borne. Small to medium-sized, mid-green leaves. Strong, self branching, upright growth.

Je Maintiendrai
De Graaff, Netherlands, 1979
('Speciosa' × not known)
Single. T and S pink-red; S green tips; C brown-orange. Medium-sized flowers. Stiff, trailing habit. Suitable for hanging-basket.

Jessimae
White, UK, 1980
('Countess of Aberdeen' × not known)
Single. T and S china-rose; T short; S wide; C pale plumviolet. Medium-sized flower, freely borne. Upright, bushy habit.

Joan Gilbert
W. Gilbert, UK, 1977
Double. T and S deep pink; S with clear green tips, wide and spherical, waxy; C peculiarly fixed to outermost petaloids, so that full flower spreads to show curled and folded innermost ones; calyx multicoloured, rich violet at base, many salmon spots, always so at top of petaloids and innermost petals. Upright, short-jointed and self-branching.

Joan Pacey
Gadsby, UK, 1972
T white, tinged with pink; S pink; C lilac-pink with pale green tips, long and narrow; filaments deep pink; S light red. Medium-sized, freely borne flowers. Mid-green, medium-sized leaves with serrated edges. Upright, self-branching, bushy growth. Can be grown in full sun.

Johanna Roemerman
Van de Beek, Netherlands, 1982
('Swingtime' × not known)
Semi-double. T pink-red, short; S pale pink-red, shading to white with a white spot at base, red striped and green tips, underside crepey and recurved; C neat white with pink-red veins from base; filaments and style pale pink red. Medium-sized flowers. Yellow-green leaves, with red central vein and stems. Erect, stiff habit. Requires much nipping out at first and can be grown in partial shade.

Joker
De Graaff, Netherlands, 1977
('Lena' × not known)
Semi-double. T and S pink-red; S paler towards green tips; C multicoloured red with blue; numerous petaloids; filaments and style pink. Medium-sized, open flowers, freely borne and longlasting. Mid-green leaves, with red stems and central veins. Natural trailing habit but can be grown as upright bush; selfbranching. Prefers semi-shade.

Joy Patmore
Turner, UK, 1961
Single. T and S white; T short; S green tips, curling outwards; C red-pink, darker at edges, white at base; filaments pink; style white. Medium-sized, bell-shaped flowers, freely borne. Mid-green leaves. Self-branching, upright habit. Easy to grow.

Julie Horton
Gagnon, USA, 1962
Semi-double. T pale pink, long; S pale pink, green tips, long and narrow; C pink, wide, overlapping. Fairly large flowers, freely borne. Medium-sized, dark green, leathery leaves. Vigorous trailer.

Kaboutertje
De Graaff, Netherlands, 1983
('Minirose' × 'Whiteknight's Blush')
Single. T and S crimson; C ruby red; stamen crimson. Small flowers. Small green leaves, lighter on underside. Stiff, slow-growing trailing habit.

Karina
De Groot, Netherlands, 1977
Single. T and S red; S held out gracefully; C violet, red veins, pink at base; filaments and style pink-red. Small to medium-sized flowers, freely borne. Medium-sized, mid-green leaves. Erect habit.

Kathy Louise
Antonelli, USA, 1963
Double. T and S carmine; upperside of S shiny, underside crepey; C lilac-pink, pink veins, pink blush; filaments and style pink. Medium-sized flowers. Fairly small, dark green leaves. Trailing, vigorous habit. Suitable for hanging-basket.

Kegworth Carnival
Smith, UK, 1979
Double. T and S white, fairly long; C violet, fading to bengal red, fairly short. Medium-sized flowers, freely borne. Midgreen, medium-sized leaves. Lax, upright, vigorous habit. Suitable for hanging-basket.

Keukenhof
De Graaff, Netherlands, 1979
Single. T and S pale pink-red; C cherry red to orange. Mediumsized, freely borne, spider-type flowers. Medium-sized leaves. Upright, free-flowering and vigorous. Good subject for hanging-basket.

Kiwi
Tiret, USA, 1966
Double. T and S greenish-white, S edge green, base white; filaments pink; style white. Fairly large flowers, freely borne. Mid-green leaves. Trailing, vigorous habit. Suitable for hanging-basket or can be trained as bush. Easy to grow.

Kocarde
De Groot, Netherlands, 1983
('Kwintet' × 'Cardinal')
Single. T red with some stripes in paler shades; S red, deeper on underside and pale pink tips, recurving slight; C deep red, a little paler at base; filaments red; style pink. Medium-sized, long-lasting flowers, freely borne in clusters. Dark green leaves. Vigorous, erect habit. Easy to grow.

Kon Tiki
Tiret, USA, 1965
Double. T and S white; C violet-pink. Medium-sized flowers, freely borne. Midgreen, medium-sized leaves. Lax branches, sometimes weighed down with weight of flowers; vigorous growth.

Koralle [88]
Bonstedt, Germany, 1905
(*F. triphylla* × not known)
Single. T, S and C salmon orange; T long; C short. Long flowers. Dark, bluish-green leaves. Free-flowering, vigorous and upright habit. Sometimes known as 'Coralle'.

Kwintet [96]
Van Wieringen, Netherlands, 1970
Single. T and S dark pink; C red-pink; filaments and style dark pink. Medium-sized, almost self-coloured flowers, freely borne early in the season. Mid-green, small to medium-sized leaves. Self-branching, erect and vigorous habit.

La Bergère
De Graaff, Netherlands, 1978
('La Campanella' × not known)
Semi-double. T and S white but a bit pinker than 'Le Berger' (see below); S upstanding; T shorter than in 'Li Berger'; S upturned; C creamy white. Medium-sized flower, freely borne. Mid-green leaves. Lax, bushy habit. Suitable for hanging-basket.

La Campanella
Blackwell, UK, 1968
Semi-double. T pink; S white with pink blush, pink on underside; C violet, white at base, cherry red veins; filaments pink; style white. Small,flowers, very freely borne. Small, mid-green leaves. Vigorous, lax growth. Very suitable for hanging-basket.

Lace Petticoats
Tiret, USA, 1952
Double. T and S white; S recurved with green tips; C with touch of pink at base; filaments whitish-pink; style white. Fairly large, full flowers, freely borne and white than most other white cultivars. Fairly dark green leaves. Upright, somewhat lax habit.

Lady Boothby [93]
Raffill, UK, 1939
(*F. alpestris* × 'Royal Purple')
Single. T and S crimson; C blackish-violet, pink at base, cherry red veins; filaments and style crimson. Small flowers. Fairly dark green leaves. Vigorous, upright growth. Long stem sections and needs frequent pinching out.

Lady Isobel Barnett
Gadsby, UK, 197
('Caroline' × 'Derby Belle')
Single. T and S pink-red; C pale purple, red veins. Medium-sized, freely borne, open flowers, held semi-erect. Mid-green leaves. Vigorous, upright and bushy growth.

Lady Kathleen Spence
Ryle, UK, 1974
('Bobby Shaftoe' × 'Schneewittchen')
Single. T and S white; S green tips and pale pink on underside, long, thin, standing out well; C lavender shading to lilac; filaments pink; style pale pink. Medium-sized flowers. Large, mid-green leaves. Fairly upright habit; can be trained for hanging-basket. Colour best when grown in shade.

Lady Thumb
Roe, USA, 1966
(sport of 'Tom Thumb')
Semi-double. T and S carmine pink; C with pink veins; filaments and style carmine. Small flowers, very freely borne. Small, mid-green leaves. Self-branching, upright, bushy habit.

Laga
Felix, Netherlands, 1979
(sport of 'Spring Bells')
Single. T and S bright red; S stand out gracefully; C white,red veins; filaments and style deep pink. Medium-sized flowers. Small, dark green leaves. Self-branching, low-growing habit.

Lakeland Princess
Mitchinson, UK, 1981
('Eden Lady' × 'Norman Mitchinson')
Single. T carmine, short; S white with carmine blush at base of outer side, quite recurved; C violet and white at base; filaments bright carmine. Medium-sized, attractive flowers, freely borne. Mid-green, medium-sized leaves. Erect, vigorous growth.

La Neige
Tiret, USA, 1965
Double. T white, touch of pink; S green tips, quite pale pink on underside; C creamy white; filaments pale pink; style white. Medium-sized flowers, freely borne. Mid-green leaves. Upright but rather lax growth; self-branching.

La Rosita
Erickson-Lewis, USA, 1959
Double. T and S carmine; C orchid pink, cherry pink veins; filaments and style pink red. Medium-sized flowers, colour depending on whether grown in sun or shade. Mid-green leaves. Upright, rather lax growth.

Lazy Lady
Martin, USA, 1960
Semi-double. T and S light red; S extra long and curled; C blue shading to pale blue at base. Freely borne, medium-sized flowers. Mid-green, medium-sized leaves. Natural trailing habit. Suitable for hanging-basket.

Le Berger [7]
De Graaff, Netherlands, 1977
('La Campanella' × not known)
Semi-double. T pink; S white, with green tips; C white with some pink; filaments pink; style white. Medium-sized flowers, larger than those of 'La Campanella', freely borne. Medium-sized or small leaves. Natural trailing habit, rather lax. Keeps colour best in shade.

Lena
Bunney, UK, 1862
Semi-double. T and S pale flesh-coloured
pink; S deeper pink on underside, green
tips; C violet, paler at base, pink blush;
filaments and style pale pink. Medium-
sized flowers, very freely borne. Fairly pale
green leaves. Lax, self-branching, vigorous
habit. Hardy.

Lena Dalton
Reimers, USA, 1953
Double. T pale pink; S pale pink, white in
shadow, recurved; C blue, pinkish-mauve
as lowers age; filaments pink; style white.
Medium-sized flowers, freely borne. Dark
green, small to medium-sized leaves.
Erect, self-branching habit. Flower size
and colour can vary.

Leonora
Tiret, USA, 1960
Single. T and S pink; S green tips; C pink,
bell-shaped calyx; filaments pink; style
pale pink. Medium-sized, almost self-
coloured flowers, freely borne. Mid-green
leaves. Upright, self-branching growth.
One of best of US single fuchsias.

Leverkusen
Rehnelt, Germany, 1902
(F2 of the cross *F. triphylla* × 'Andenken
an Heinrich Henkel')
Single. T, S and C pinkish-cherry red; T
long; S short and drooping. Shorter flower
than in most Triphylla hybrids. Midgreen
leaves. Vigorous, erect habit, but quickly
sheds buds and flowers if weather
conditions change.

Liemers Lantaern
Giesen, Netherlands, 1983
(sport of 'Dusky Rose')
Double. T dark pink with paler sheen,
fairly long; S dark pink shading to pink
green with pale shades and white dots;
C dark pink with somewhat darker veins at
the salmon pink base; sometimes white
spots at extremities; filaments and style
dark pink. Very large flowers; oblong buds.
Natural trailing habit; lax growth. Suitable
for hanging-basket.

Lilac Lustre
Munkner, USA, 1961
Double. T ad S pink-red; T short; S wide
and recurved; C soft blue to bright lilac.

Beautiful, medium-sized to large flowers.
Rich green leaves. Free-flowering, self-
branching and vigorous habit.

Lilac Queen
Raiser unknown, Europe, date unknown
Double. T and S bright crimson; C white
with lilac blush and small veins. Large
flowers, freely borne. Erect and bushy
habit.

L'Ingenue
De Graaff, Netherlands, 1983
('Loeky' × 'Mazda')
Single. T and S carmine; C ruby and held
well out; filaments and style light ruby.
Freely borne, medium-sized flowers like
those of 'Loeky' (see below). Mid-green,
medium-sized leaves. Vigorous, self-
branching, upright growth.

Lisa
Antonelli, USA, 1965
Double. T and S bright pink; C rich
lavender. Large, freely borne flowers.
Mid-green leaves. Vigorous, trailing habit.
Suitable for hanging-basket.

Little Beauty [97]
Author unknown, USA(?), year unknown
Single. T and S flesh-coloured; C lavender
blue. Small, compact flowers, appearing
early and freely borne. Compact, bushy
growth. Colour best when grown in shade.

Liz
Holmes, UK, 1970
Double. T greenish-white; S pale pink,
darker on underside with green tips;
C pale pink, with deep pink veins and
spots; filaments pink; style whitish-pink.
Medium-sized flowers, freely borne. Mid-
green leaves with crimson central vein.
Vigorous, erect habit.

Lochinvar
Mitchinson, UK, 1983
(seedling × 'Valerie')
Double. T pale pink; S pale pink on
upperside, deeper underside, held out
horizontally with recurved tips; C violet,
pale pink base, darker edge, loose and
slightly flared; filaments and style pink.
Medium-sized flowers, freely borne.
Medium-sized, dark green leaves with
paler underside; green veins. Self-
branching, vigorous growth. Prefers cool
climate.

Loeky [41]
De Graaff, Netherlands, 1979
('Joy Patmore' × 'Impudence')
Single. T and S pink; S curling up to T; C
pink-lilac, red veins, held out horizontally;
filaments pink-red; style pink. Medium-
sized flowers, opening almost flat and
freely borne. Mid-green leaves with red
centre veins and stems. Upright, bushy,
self-branching habit.

Lolita
Tiret, USA, 1963
Double. T and S whitish-pink; S green
tips, pink underside; C porcelain blue,
paler at base, turning lilac as flowers age;
filaments and style pale pink. Medium-
sized flowers, freely borne. Leaves mid-
green. Naturally trailing habit. Tender.

Lord Lonsdale [35]
Author unknown, UK, date unknown
Single. T and S pale apricot; C peach-
orange. Medium-sized flowers, freely
borne. Leaves light green and crinkled.
Upright, vigorous growth.

Lottie Hobby
Edwards, UK, 1939
Single. T and S dull scarlet; S has lighter
tips; C scarlet. Small flowers, freely borne
late in season. Mid- to dark green leaves.
Bushy, vigorous habit. Although often
regarded as a cultivar, really a *breviflora*
hybrid.

Loveliness
Lye, UK, 1869
Single. T and S creamy white; S recurved;
C pink carmine. Medium-sized flowers,
freely borne early in season. Mid-green
medium-sized leaves. Upright, self-
branching bush. Can be trained as
standard.

Lunters Roem 'Lunter's Glory'
Appel, Netherlands, 1984
('Carmel Blue' × 'Pennine')
Double. T white; S white with green tips
and soft pink blush on underside, curved
up towards tube and ovary; C blue-lilac,
shading to violet-lilac; each petal pale at
base and getting darker towards edge;
petals unequal lengths; filaments pink;
style white. Medium-sized flowers, freely
borne. Mid-green leaves with light green
veins. Upright and vigorous habit.

Lynn Ellen
Erickson, USA, 1962
Double. T and S bright pink; S wide and
upturned; C pinkviolet, turning bright
pink as flowers age, with salmon pink
spots; filaments and style pink. Medium-
sized, loose-petalled flowers, freely borne.
Mid-green, medium-sized leaves.
Vigorous, erect bush. Can withstand heat.

Machu Picchu [19]
De Graaff, Netherlands, 1977
('Speciosa' × not known)
Single. T and S pale salmon orange; T
fairly long; S with green tips; C salmon
orange; hairy filaments and style pale
salmon orange. Medium-sized flowers,
freely borne and fairly long-lasting. Mid-
green leaves with red central vein and
reddish stems. Lax grower, needs pinching
out to maintain shape. Hardy.

Madame Cornelissen
Cornelissen, Belgium, 1860
Single to semi-double. T and S rich
scarlet; C white with cherry red veins;
filaments and style cherry red. Fairly small
flowers, freely borne. Small, dark green
leaves. Self-branching, vigorous, upright
growth. Hardy.

Magic Flute
Handley, UK, 1975
Single. T waxy white and quite thick; S
white with pink tips, narrow and thick,
held out at right angles to T; C bright
coral pink, white near T. Freely borne,
medium-sized, funnel-shaped flowers
appear early in season. Medium-sized,
bright green leaves. Vigorous, self-
branching and naturally trailing. Suitable
for hanging-baskets.

Major Heaphy
Author unknown, UK, year unknown
Single. T and S orange-red; S with green
tips; C brick red;filaments red; style pink.
Small flowers, freely borne. Medium-
sized, mid-green elves. Upright, self-
branching habit. Do not allow to dry out,
or flowers and buds will drop.

Mandarin [101]
Schnabel, USA, 1963
Semi-double. T pale salmon pink with
deep pink stripes; S salmon pink with
green stripes, deeper pink on underside; C
orange carmine; filaments pink; style pale

pink. Medium-sized flowers, freely borne. Dark green, medium-sized leaves. Lax but vigorous habit.

Mantilla [84]
Reiter, USA, 1984
('Mrs Victor Reiter' × (*F. triphylla* × *F. pringsheimii*))
Triphylla hybrid. T, S and C rich carmine; T long and narrow; S and C quite small. Attractive, long flowers, borne in clusters. Bronze-green leaves. Free-flowering, trailing habit. Tender. The first cultivar to be registered by the American Fuchsia Society (A. F. S. No. 1).

Marco Boy
Bats, Netherlands, 1979
('La Campanella' × not known)
Semi-double. T white with pink blush, fairly long; S with green tips and pink underside; C violet-blue, lighter at base and with pink spots at base; filaments red; style pale pink. Medium-sized flowers. Fairly dark green, smallish leaves. Self-branching, lax but upright habit. Suitable for hanging-basket. Do not grow in full sun.

Margaret [61]
Wood, UK, 1937 or 1943
(*F. magellanica* var. *alba* × 'Heritage')
Semi-double. T and S carmine to scarlet; S reflexed over T; C violet, pink at base, cherry red veins; filaments and style cherry red. Medium-sized flowers, freely borne. Leaves mid-green. Vigorous, erect habit. Hardy.

Margaret Roe
Gadsby, UK, 1968
Single. T light red; S pink with green tips; C pale violet, deeper shade at edges, pale pink at base, pink veins; filaments pale pink; style pink. Erect, medium-size flowers, very freely borne. Mid-green leaves. Upright, self-branching habit.

Margaret Rose
N. D. Hobbs, UK, 1976
Single. T deep pink, short and thick; S deep pink with green tips, held horizontally; C deep pink with red edge. Medium-sized flowers, freely borne. Mid-green leaves. Upright, vigorous growth. Colour best in shade.

Marie Punselie [65]
Van der Post, Netherlands, 1981
('Lady Boothby' × 'Lord Lonsdale')
Single. T pink red; S red; C violet; filaments and long style pink-red. Medium-sized flowers borne on long stems. Squarish bud green with white stripes. Dark green leaves with red central vein. Naturally trailing habit. Suitable for hanging-basket. Grow in good light.

Marin Glow
Reedstrom, USA, 1954
Single. T and S waxy white; S with green tips; C violet, fading to magenta, pink at base; filaments pink; style white. Medium-sized flowers, freely borne. Mid-green, medium-sized leaves. Upright, self-branching and vigorous habit. Easy to grow.

Marinka
Rozain-Boucharlat, France, 1902
Single. T and S rich red; C a bit darker but the flowers are almost self-coloured. Medium-sized flowers, profusely borne. Mid- to dark green leaves to reddish veins. Vigorous, bushy habit. Easy to grow and suitable for hanging-basket.

Marjon Wit
Steevens, Netherlands, 1972
Single. T and S red; C dark blue. Flowers borne early season. Does best in shade.

Marlies
Van de Beek, Netherlands, 1986
('Swingtime' × 'Celebrity')
Double. Short T bright red with lighter touches; S bright red with pale touches, reflexed and often curled; C white, wavy with pink veins; outer petals often light red to pink; filaments and style light red. Very large, rose-shaped flowers, quite freely borne. Conical red buds. Dark green, oval leaves with red central veins and stems. Vigorous, naturally trailing habit. Requires regular pinching out. Suitable for hanging-basket. Reasonably resistant to sun.

Mary
Bonstedt, Germany 1894
(*F. triphylla* × *F. corymbiflora*)
Single, *triphylla* type. T, S and C bright scarlet; T long; S short. Dark green leaves with reddish-purple veins and underside. Free-flowering, upright habit. Does not overwinter well.

Mary Fairclo
Fairclo, USA, 1955
Single. T, S and C deep pink; almost self-coloured. Conspicuous bell-shaped flowers becoming dish-shaped on opening. Naturally trailing habit. Needs regular nipping out.

Masquerade
Kennett, USA, 1963
Double. T and S flesh-coloured to pink, both short; C violet, outer ones upturned and with pink spots. Large flowers, loose petalled and freely borne. Leaves fairly dark green. Vigorous trailing habit. Suitable for hanging-basket.

Mazda
Reiter, USA, 1947
Single. T and S pale orange-pink; C carmine orange, lighter at base; filaments and style pink. Medium-sized flowers, freely borne. Mid-to dark green leaves. Upright, vigorous habit. Likes warm, sunny position and requires regular nipping out.

Meadowlark
Kennett, USA, 1971
Double. T and S white; T long; S upturned and standing out horizontally overhanging corolla; C violet to bright pink, white stripes; filaments and style white. Large flowers, freely borne. Mid-green leaves. Naturally trailing habit. Suitable for hanging-basket.

Medusa
De Graaff, Netherlands, 1977
('Centrepiece' × not known)
Single. T and S red; C white with pink veins; under petals, red and white petaloids stand out from corolla;filaments light red; style pink. Fairly large flowers, freely borne. Mid-green leaves. Vigorous, trailing habit. Suitable for hanging-basket.

Melody
Reiter, USA, 1942
('Patty Evans' × 'Mrs Victor Reiter')
Single. T and S light red-pink; S reflexed; C pale cyclamen; filaments and style pink. Medium-sized, freely borne flowers. Bright green leaves. Upright, bushy growth. Easy to grow.

Menna [20]
Bögemann, Germany, 1984
('Leverkusen' × not known)
Single. T pink, long and round; S pink, held horizontally, salmon red on underside; C orange-red; filaments and style pink. Medium-sized to large flowers, freely borne. Mid-green leaves. Upright habit. Will grow in full sun.

Mephisto
Reiter, USA, 1941
(F. lycioides × 'Mrs Rundle')
Single. T and S scarlet; T long; C deep crimson; almost self-coloured; filaments cherry red; style pink. Fairly small flowers, very freely borne. Mid-green leaves. Vigorous upright habit.

Mercurius
De Groot, Netherlands 1971
(F. regia var. typica × 'Beacon')
Single. T and S red; T short; S fairly long and wide; C violet fading to violet-red; filaments and style red. Medium-sized flowers. Mid-green leaves with red central vein and metallic sheen. Upright, vigorous, somewhat horizontal, growth.

Mevr Goyaerts
Goyaerts, Netherlands, c.1970
Semi-double or double. T and S white with pink blush; S long, green tips; inner C deep purple; outer C shorter and orangeed with lighter spots; filaments pink; style soft pink. Large flowers. Mid-green leaves. Lax bush or trailing habit.

Mia van der Zee [36]
De Graaff, Netherlands, 1978
('La Campanella' × not known)
Single. T and S pink; C purple. Lax upright or stiff trailing habit.

Micky Goult
Roe, UK, 1981
('Bobby Shaftoe' X 'Santa Barbara')
Single. T and S pale to deeper pink; T short; S horizontal; C violet-pink. Small, sturdy flowers that do not fade as they age. Mid-green, small to medium-sized leaves. Upright, vigorous and self-branching habit.

Mieke Meursing
Hopwood, UK, 1968
(Seedling of 'R. A. F. ')
Single to semi-double. T and S carmine; pink with cherry red veins; filaments and

style carmine. Medium-sized flowers, very freely borne. Mid-green leaves. Upright, vigorous, self-branching growth. Very easy to grow; regarded as one of best single cultivars; good for exhibition purposes.

Mimi Kubischka
Nutzinger, Austria, 1976
Double. T and S pink; T short and round; C white with pink veins; filaments light red; style pink. Medium-sized flowers appear early in season. Mid-green, fairly small leaves. Compact, self-branching, vigorous shrub.

Minirok
Steevens, Netherlands, 1970
Single. T and S red; S long; C violet. Small flowers. Small, fairly dark green leaves. Lax growth. Suitable for hanging-basket.

Minirose
De Graaff, Netherlands, 1981
('Rose of Castile' × not known)
Single. T white with pink blush, shading to white, stands out star-like; C light red-violet with pale pink base; filaments pale red; style pale pink. Flowers profuse and long-lasting. Medium-sized leaves with lighter veins. Upright, vigorous growth. Needs careful pinching out.

Miss California
Hodges, USA, 1952
Semi-double. T and S pink; S long and pointed, deep pink blush; C white with soft red glow inside and pale pink veins at base; filaments and style ink. Medium-sized, long flowers, freely borne. Mid-green, narrow leaves. Self-branching, erect habit.

Mission Bells
Walker and Jones, USA, 1948
Single or semi-double. T and S scarlet; C violet with cherry red spots at base; filaments cherry red; style cherry pink. Medium-sized to large, bell-shaped flowers, freely borne. Mid-green leaves. Upright, vigorous and self-branching habit. Suitable for bedding.

Molesworth
Lemoine, France, 1903
Double. T and S bright cherry red; C creamy white, cherry red veins; filaments and style cherry red. Medium-sized, full flowers, very freely borne. Mid-green,

small to medium-sized leaves. Lax, self-branching habit. Needs staking if grown as bush.

Monstera [14]
Reedstrom, USA, 1956
Semi-double. T and S dark crimson; C all shades of magenta, lighter at base. Medium-sized flowers with long, different length stems. Naturally trailing habit.

Montezuma
Fuchsia-la Nursery, USA, 1967
Double. T and S carmine pink; S green tips; C pink or rink-red with dull red edge and carmine at base. Large flowers, freely borne. Vigorous trailing habit. Suitable for hanging-basket.

Moonraker [120]
Clitheroe, UK, 1979
('Northumbrian Bell' × 'Blush o' Dawn')
Double. T and S off-white with deep pink blush; T long; S green tips, underside white to pink at base, held well out; C pale blue; pale blue petaloids on P, which stand out as petals rise; petals and petaloids have unusual ragged edges. Loose but attractive flowers, freely borne. Mid-green, oval leaves. Vigorous, upright growth. Needs careful pinching out.

Morgenrood
Steevens, Netherlands, 1978
Single. T and S white with pink blush; S fairly long, deeper pink on underside, green tips; C lilac-red; filaments pink; style white. Medium-sized flowers appear early in season. Light green leaves. Upright growth.

Morning Light
Waltz, USA, 1960
Double. T coral pink; S white, green tips, coral pink along edges and at base, pale pink underside, wide and recurved; C lavender with pale pink and deep pink spots; filaments pink; style white. Large, freely borne flowers, which discolour quickly. Golden-green leaf with crimson central vein. Lax, upright growth. Prone to botrytis.

Moth Blue
Tiret, USA, 1949
Double. T and S red; T short; S long; C deep lilac-blue. Fairly large flowers, freely borne. Dark green leaves. Vigorous trailing habit. Suitable for hanging-basket.

Mountain Mist
Crockett, UK, 1971
Double. T greenish-white; S white with
pale pink blush at tops; C silver-grey-
mauve, more pinkish at base; filaments
bright pink; style white. Large, unusually
coloured flowers, freely borne. Mid-green,
small to medium-sized leaves. Upright,
bushy habit. Does best in cool, airy, shade.

Mrs Lovell Swisher
Evans and Reeves, USA, 1942
Single. T flesh-coloured pink; S pinkish-
white, green tips, light reddish underside;
C light carmine, paler at base; filaments
carmine red; style light red. Small flowers,
very freely borne, appear early in the year.
Mid-green, medium-sized leaves.
Vigorous, upright, self-branching habit.

Mrs Popple
Elliott, UK, 1899
Single. T and S scarlet; C violet, cherry
red at centre, cherry red veins; filaments
and style cherry red. Freely borne,
medium-sized flowers. Small, dark green
leaves. Upright, vigorous bush. Hardy.

Mrs W. P. Wood
Wood, UK, 1949
('Margaret' × hybrid of *F. magellanica* var.
alba)
Single. T and S pale pink; C clear white;
filaments pale pink; style white. Small
flowers, freely borne. Light green, small
leaves. Upright, vigorous habit. Hardy.

Mrs W. Rundle [2]
Rundle, UK, 1883
('Earl of Beaconsfield' × 'Lady
Heytesbury')
Single. T and S flesh-coloured pink;
T quite long; S recurved; C orange-
vermilion; filaments and style pink.
Largish flowers, freely borne. Light green
leaves. Vigorous bush. Needs regular
nipping out to keep in shape.

Multa [53]
Van Suchtelen, Netherlands, 1968
Single. T and S red; C violet. Fairly small
flowers, freely borne in each leaf axil. Lax
growth. Easy to grow.

Muriel
Author unknown, UK, 1930(?)
Single or semi-double. T and S scarlet;
T long; S recurved with green tips; C light
violet, paler at base, cherry red veins;

filaments and style cherry red. Long
flowers, freely borne. Mid-green leaves.
Lax, vigorous growth. Suitable for
hanging-basket.

Nancy Lou
Stubbs, USA, 1971
Double. T pale pink; S light red, brighter
red underside, green tips; C bright white;
filaments bright, light red; style pale pink.
Erect flowers, large and freely borne.
Leaves mid-green and serrated. Vigorous,
upright growth.

Native Dancer
Tiret, USA, 1965
Double. T and S bright red; C deep violet.
Larger flower, very freely borne. Mid-to
dark green leaves. Vigorous, lax growth.
Requires staking if grown as bush. Easy to
grow.

Nellie Nuttall
Rose, UK, 1977
('Snowcap' × 'Mieke Meursing'(?))
Single. T and S deep crimson; C white.
Profuse, medium-sized, erect flowers.
Light green leaves. Upright, bushy habit.
Short stem segments.

Nellie Wallace
De Graaff, Netherlands, 1983
('Fiona' × not known)
Semi-double to double. T light green with
darker strips; S with touch of pink and
green tips, long and spidery; C creamy
white with pale pink veins, rather short
and compress; filaments pink; style pale
pink. Larger flowers. Olive-green leaves.
Naturally trailing habit. Needs careful
pinching out. Suitable for hanging-basket.

Nicolaas Aalhuizen
Steevens, Netherlands, 1973
Single. T and S red; C violet; filaments
and style red. Profuse, long-lasting, small
flowers. Small, mid-green leaves. Self-
branching, woody and upright habit.

Nina Wills
Wills, UK, 1961
(sport of 'Forget-me-not')
Single. T pink; S pale pink; C baby pink;
filament pink; style pale pink. Small, long-
lasting, freely borne flowers. Small, light
green leaves. Self-branching, upright
habit.

Normandy Bell
Martin, USA, 1961
Single. T pale pink; S pale pink with green tips; C pale mauve, paler at base, bright pink veins; filaments bright pink; style pale pink. Large, freely borne, bell-shaped flowers. Mid-green, medium-sized leaves. Lax habit.

Northumbrian Pipes [137]
De Graaff, Netherlands, 1983
(*F. magdalenae* × *F. panicultata*)
Single. T, S and C deep pink. Almost self-coloured, bell-shaped flowers, freely borne. Mid-green foliage. Vigorous, self-branching habit; needs careful shaping.

Northway
Golics, UK, 1976
('La Campanella' × 'Howlett's Hardy')
Single. T and S pale pink; T short and thick; S short and reflexed; C cherry red. Small flowers, freely borne. Small, light green leaves. Self-branching, upright but rather lax habit.

Nutshell
De Graaff, Netherlands, 1977
('La Campanella' × not known)
Single. T pink, short, fairly round; S pink, salmon pink underside; C orange-red; filaments light red; style pink. Compact, medium-sized flowers, freely borne. Mid-green leaves. Slow-growing, trailing habit. Suitable for hanging-basket.

Orange Cocktail
Handley, UK, 1972
Single. T light salmon, waxy; S light salmon, long and narrow, with yellow-green tips; C bright orange at centre and base, shading to cardinal red at edges; long and overlapping. Large, multicoloured flowers, profusely borne early in the season. Light to mid-green leaves. Rather lax habit. Needs staking if grown as bush.

Orange Crush [33]
Handley, UK, 1972
Single. T and S salmon orange; T waxy; S thick and pointed; C bright orange, pale at base; filaments pink; style pale pink. Medium-sized flowers, freely borne early in the season. Light green leaves. Upright, vigorous habit. Short stem joints, but needs regular pinching out.

Orange Flare [32]
Handley, UK, 1972
Single. T and S salmon orange, both short and thick; filaments orange; style salmon. Medium-sized flowers, freely borne early in the season. Strong, upright, self-branching growth. Best colour if grown in sun.

Orange Mirage
Tiret, USA, 1970
Single. T light salmon pink; S salmon pink with green tips; C dull orange salmon; filaments salmon pink; style light red. Freely borne, medium-sized flowers. Light green leaves. Vigorous, trailing habit. Suitable for hanging-basket.

Oranje Boven [30]
De Graaff, Netherlands, 1980
('Speciosa' × not known)
Single. T and S orange-red; S paler than T; C light orange. Long, slim flowers. Olive-green leaves. Upright but lax habit. Not easy to grow.

Oranje van Os [31]
Raiser unknown, Germany(?), date unknown
Single. T and S white with deep pink orange blush, both fairly long; S with green tips; C orange. Fairly large flowers, freely borne. Discovered by J. van Os growing in an experimental garden at Venlo.

Ortenburger Festival
Topperwein, Germany, 1973
Single. T and S deep red; S lighter red on underside; C dark violet, fading to violet-red, outspread; filaments and style pink. Medium-sized flowers, freely borne. Dark green leaves. Upright, self-branching habit.

Other Fellow [8]
Hazard and Hazard, USA, 1946
Single. T and S white; S with green tips; T fairly long; C coral pink, white at base; filaments and style white. Small flowers, freely borne. Mid-green, small leaves. Self-branching, upright habit.

Pablo Picasso
Steevens, Netherlands, 1968
Double. T and S pink; C violet, outermost petals pink, innermost with pink spots; filaments and style pink. Medium-sized flowers. Dark green, medium-sized leaves. Lax habit. Suitable for hanging-basket.

Pacquesa
Clyne, UK, 1974
('Pacific Queen' × 'Sheryl Ann')
Single. T and S deep red; T short; S
reflexed with crepey underside; C white
with trace of dark red veins. Fairly large
flowers, very freely borne. Almond-shaped
leaves. Vigorous, upright growth. Short
stem joints.

Papa Bleuss
Tiret, USA, 1956
Double. T and S pale pink and ivory on
outside; S reflexed and carmine pink on
inside; C deep violet, pink at base;
filaments bright pink; style white. Fairly
large flowers, freely borne. Mid-green
leaves with crimson veins. Upright but lax
habit. Suitable for hanging-basket; needs
staking if grown as bush.

Papoose
Reedstrom, USA, 1960
Semi-double. T and S scarlet; C dark
violet, cherry red at base; filaments and
style scarlet. Small flowers, very freely
borne. Mid-green, small leaves. Self-
branching, bushy habit, but rather lax.
Easy to grow. Hardy.

Party Frock [107]
Walker and Jones, USA, 1953
Single to semi-double. T dark pink; S red-
pink, becoming lighter towards tips and
shading to green, recurved; C soft blue
with pink spots, outermost soft pink;
filaments pink; style pale pink. Medium-
sized, freely borne flowers. Mid-green
leaves with red veins. Upright, vigorous
habit. Needs regular pinching out.

Patricia Ann
Clements, UK, 1982
Double. T and S white; S striped pink on
outside, pale pink on inside; C bright, deep
pink, shading to paler pink at base, dark
pink veins. Large flowers. Mid-green,
medium-sized leaves. Naturally trailing
habit. Suitable for hanging-basket.

Peggy King
Wood, UK, 1954
Single. T and S pink-red; C peony red.
Small flowers, freely borne. Mid-green,
small to medium-sized leaves. Upright,
selfbranching habit. Hardy.

Pepi
Tiret, USA, 1963
Double. T pink-red; S pink-red to dull
orange-red with pinkish-orange spots at
base; filaments carmine; style pink.
Medium-sized flowers, fairly freely borne.
Dull, dark green leaves. Vigorous, upright
habit.

Peppermint Stick [109]
Walker and Jones, USA, 1950
Double. T and S carmine; S upturned
with clear white stripe on each; C violet at
centre, outer petals carmine pink with
violet edges. Medium-sized flowers, very
freely borne. Medium-sized, darkish green
leaves. Upright, self-branching habit. Easy
to grow.

Peredrup
Brouwer, Netherlands, 1983
('Orange Mirage' × 'Orange Mirage')
Double. T pale pink and fairly long; S pale
pink; C deep pink with flesh-coloured
spots; filaments pink; style white with pink
trace. Medium-sized flowers, freely borne.
Upright, fairly vigorous habit. Needs
regular pinching out.

Peter Pan
Erickson, USA, 1960
Single. T and S pink; S upturned; C lilac.
Medium-sized flowers, freely borne.
Bright green leaves. Vigorous, trailing
habit. Suitable for hanging-basket.

Petit Point
De Graaff, Netherlands, 1977
('Frau Alice Hoffmann' × not known)
Single. T and S pink-red; S with green,
out-turned tips, deeper shade on
underside; C deep violet-red, light red at
base; filaments light red; style pink. Fairly
small flowers, freely borne. Mid-green
leaves. Vigorous, upright habit.

Phenomenal
Lemoine, France, 1869
Double. T and S scarlet; S quite wide; C
bluish-violet, paler at base, fine carmine
veins; petaloids with pink and cherry red
spots, fading the reddish-violet as flowers
age; filaments and style cherry red.
Medium-sized flowers, freely borne but
drop easily. Mid-green leaves. Vigorous,
upright growth.

Phyllis
Brown, UK, 1938
Semi-double. T and S waxy, light red with
cherry red blush; C pinkish cherry red;
filaments pinks; style pale pink. Smallish
flowers, freely borne early in the season.
Small to medium-sized, mid-green leaves.
Vigorous, upright habit. Easy to grow.

Pink Bon Accorde [64]
Thorne, UK, 1959
(sport of seedling of 'Bon Accorde')
Single. T and S pale pink; S deeper on
underside with green tips; C deep pink,
paler at base; filaments red-pink; style pale
pink. Small flowers, freely borne. Mid-
green leaves. Upright, self-branching
habit. Flowers are not as erect as those on
'Bon Accorde'.

Pink Darling
Machado, USA, 1966
Single. T dark pink; S pale pink, darker
underside; C soft lilac-pink, turning paler
towards centre; filaments light red; style
pale pink. Small flowers, freely borne.
Mid-green leaves. Vigorous, upright
growth. Needs regular pinching out.

Pink Dessert
Kuechler, USA, 1963
Single. T white; S white with pink blush
and green tips, darker pink on underside;
C white with pink blush shading to pale
pink; filaments pink; style pale pink. Large
flowers, freely borne. Upright, self-
branching habit.

Pink Galore [80]
Fuchsia-la Nursery, USA, 1958
Double. T, S and C pink, T and S slightly
darker than C; S upturned; T long;
filaments and style pale pink. Beautiful,
medium-sized flowers. Mid-green leaves.
Suitable for hanging-basket. Tender.

Pink Marshmallow [70]
Stubbs, USA, 1971
Double. T pale pink to white; S white,
green tips, pink blush on underside; C
white with pale pink blush and fine veins;
filaments pink; style white. Large flowers.
Light green leaves. Trailing habit.
Suitable for hanging-basket.

Pink Pearl
Bright, UK, 1919
Semi-double to double. T and S pale pink;
P deep pink with darker pink blush.

Medium-sized flowers. Mid-green,
medium-sized leaves. Upright, self-
branching habit.

Pink Temptation
Wills, UK, 1966
Single. T and S creamy white with a touch
of pink; S with green tips, upturned; C
light red-pink, light salmon pink as flowers
age, pale pink at base; filaments pink; style
pale pink. Fairly large flowers, freely
borne. Mid- to dark green leaves. Upright
habit.

Pixie
Russell, UK, 1960
(sport of 'Graf Witte')
Single. T and S carmine; S recurved;
C mauve, lighter at base, carmine veins;
filaments scarlet; style carmine. Medium-
sized flowers, very freely borne. Yellowish-
green leaves with red veins. Self-
branching, vigorous, upright habit. Hardy.

Polychinelle
Author unknown, Netherlands, year
unknown
Double. T and S white with pink blush;
T fairly long; short S deep pink on
underside, green tips; C dull purple, pink
at base; filaments light red; style pink.
Medium-sized flowers, freely borne. Mid-
green leaves. Self-branching, vigorous,
upright habit.

Postiljon [104]
Van der Post, Netherlands, 1975
Single. T white with pin blush; S creamy
white with green tips; C pink-violet, white
at base; filaments and style white. Fairly
small flowers, freely borne. Small, mid-
green leaves. Vigorous, self-branching
habit. Suitable for hanging-basket.

Powder Puff [118]
Tabraham, UK, 1976
Double. T and S red; C white. Small, full
flowers. Dark green leaves. Upright,
compact bush.

Prelude
Kennett, USA, 1958
Double. T white; S white, sometimes with
violet blush on underside, turned back
almost complete over tube; C white and
violet; four inner petals violet, ringed by
shorter white petals; C white as buds open
with inner petals becoming visible as
flowers age; filaments pink; style white.

Beautiful, large, freely borne flowers. Mid-green leaves. Vigorous, trailing habit. Suitable for hanging-basket.

President
Standish, UK, 1841
('Formosa Elegans' × *F. boliviana*)
Single. T and S bright red; C reddish-cerise, scarlet at base; filaments red; style pink, shading to cherry red. Medium-sized flowers, freely borne. Conspicuous, dark green leaves with reddish ting. Vigorous, upright, self-branching habit. Easy to grow. Leaves achieve best colour in sunny position.

President Leo Boullemier
Burns, UK, 1983
('Joy Patmore' × 'Cloverdale Pearl')
Single. T short, violet-red strips; S white, fairly long, pointed, curling upwards; C magenta-blue, turning pink as flowers age; filaments magenta-blue; style white. Bell-shaped flowers, freely borne. Dark green leaves. Vigorous, upright growth.

President Margaret Slater
Taylor, UK, 1973
('Cascade' × 'Taffy')
Single. T white, thin; S white with salmon pink blush on outside, deep salmon pink undersides, long and narrow, slightly upturned, green tips; C pinkish to pale violet with keep salmon pink blush; filaments and style pink. Medium-sized flowers, freely borne. Light to mid-green leaves with serrated edges. Vigorous, trailing habit. Suitable for hanging-basket.

President Stanley Wilson
Thorne, UK, 1969
('Brentwood' ['Rolla' × 'Duchess of Albany'] × 'Orange Drops')
Single to semi-double. T carmine, long and slim; S carmine shading to pale pink with green tips, held out from corolla; C pinkish-carmine. Long, sturdy, medium-sized flowers, freely borne. Vigorous, long-stemmed, trailing habit. Needs early pinching out.

Preston Guild [114]
Thornley, UK, 1971
('Dorothea Flower' × 'Hawkshead')
Single. T and S pure white; T very long; S fairly wide, curling over, but not hiding T; C violet-blue shading to white at base; long filaments; very long style. Small

flowers with long, narrow ovary. Mid-green, small leaves. Free-flowering, vigorous, upright habit.

Princessita
Niederholzer, USA, 1940
('Fandango' × 'Mrs Rundle')
Single. T and S white; C deep pink. Medium-sized flowers, freely borne. Mid-to dark green leaves. Vigorous, trailing habit. Suitable for hanging-basket.

Pumila [90]
Young, UK, 1821
Single. T and S crimson; C lilac-violet, crimson at base; filament and style crimson. Small flowers, freely borne. Mid-to darkish green leaves. Upright, dwarf bush. Hardy. This cultivar should not be confused with *F. magellanica* var. *pumila*.

Purperprincess
De Groot, Netherlands, 1975
Single. T and S deep, shiny red; C purple, red at base, red veins; filaments and style deep red. Medium-sized flowers. Dark green leaves. Dark red stems and flower stalks. Upright, bushy habit.

Pussy Cat [6]
Felix, Netherlands, 1978
('Leverkusen' × 'Checkerboard')
Single. T orange-pink with light reddish-blush, long, thick, ridged; S orange-pink with green tips, wide and pointed, stands out horizontally; C salmon; half filaments pink with petaloid at end, rest white; style pink, short; stigma cream, very large. Medium-sized flowers, freely borne. Mid-to darkish green leaves. Upright bush.

Puts Folly
Baker, UK, 1971
Single. T pale pink, think; S creamy white with pink blush, green tips, soft pink underside; C lilac-pink, paler at base, dark pink edges. Medium-sized flowers, freely borne. Mid-green leaves. Vigorous, self-branching, naturally trailing habit. Suitable for hanging-basket.

Radings Inge
Reiman, Netherlands, 1981
Single. Flowers of Encliandra type. T white; S deep pink; C orange. Small flowers. Small leaves. Upright, vigorous but lax habit.

Radings Michelle [122]
Reiman, Netherlands, 1980
Single. Encliandra type. T, S and C pink.
Very small flowers. Small leaves. Vigorous,
upright habit.

R. A. F.
Garson, USA, 1942
Double. T and S bright red; C deep pink
with cherry red spot and veins; filaments
and style cherry red. Medium-sized
flowers, freely borne. Mid-green, medium-
sized leaves. Upright, rather lax habit.

Rambling Rose
Tiret, USA, 1959
Double. T pale pinkish-green; S pink,
green tips, deep pink underside; C
reddish-pink, petaloids pink; filaments
pink; style, reddish-pink. Large, almost
self-coloured flowers, freely borne. Mid-
green, medium-sized leaves. Vigorous,
naturally trailing habit.

Ravensbarrow
Thornley, UK, 1972
('Hawkshead' × 'Gruss aus dem Bodethal')
Single. T and S scarlet; T short and thick;
S short; C violet, scarlet at base, short;
filaments and style scarlet. Small flowers,
freely borne. Small, dark green leaves.
Vigorous, upright habit.

Red Jacket
Waltz, USA, 1958
Double. T and S bright red; S upturned;
C white, remains white when flowers age;
style and filaments very long. Large, loose
flowers; long buds. Mid- to darkish green
leaves. Vigorous, free-flowering, trailing
habit. Suitable for hanging-basket.

Red Ribbons
Martin, USA, 1959
Double. T and S red; S very long and
curled; C white; filaments bright pink;
style pale pink. Large flowers, freely
borne. Mid-green leaves. Lax habit;
requires pinching out.

Red Spider
Reiter, USA, 1946
Single. T and S deep crimson; T long; S
narrow and recurved; C madder red with
crimson edge and veins. Medium-sized,
long flowers, freely borne. Mid-green
leaves. Vigorous, trailing habit. Suitable
for hanging-basket.

Regal [91]
Author not known, USA, year not known
Single. T, S and C madder red. Medium-
sized flowers, freely borne late in the year.
Dark green leaves with reddish veins.
Vigorous, upright growth, difficult to
train.

Reverend Doctor Brown
Taylor, UK, 1973
('Sophisticated Lady' × 'Citation')
Double. T pale pink, short and thick;
S pale pink on upperside, long, green tips, reflexed almost
completely over T; C white with small
pink veins; filaments pink; style pale pink.
Medium-sized, loose-petalled flowers,
very freely borne. Mid-green leaves. Self-
branching, vigorous, upright habit.

Rika [55]
Van der Post, Netherlands, 1968
('Mephisto' × 'Water Nymph')
Single. T and S creamy white with pink
blush; T fairly long and round; S long;
C orange-red. Fairly small flowers. Dark
yellow-green leaves. Upright habit. Needs
nipping out when young.

Ringwood Market
Clyne, UK, 1976
('Tristesse' × 'Susan Ford')
Single. T and S deep pink; C powdery
blue, fading to lilac, pink at base.
Medium-sized flowers, freely borne. Mid-
green, medium-sized leaves. Vigorous,
upright habit.

Robert Stolz
Nutzinger, Austria, 1971
Semi-double. T and S scarlet; C deep
violet, red at base, fading to violet as
flowers age; filaments dark pink; style
white. Small flowers, freely borne. Dark
green, oblong leaves with red central veins.
Self-branching, upright bush.

Ron Ewart
Roe, UK, 1981
('Bobby Shaftoe' × 'Santa Barbara')
Single. T white, short and thick; S white,
short and wide, turned upwards towards
T; C bengal pink with white glow at base.
Small, sturdy flowers, freely borne. Mid-
green leaves. Self-branching, upright
shrub.

Rose Bradwardine [52]
Colville, UK, 1958
Double. T and S dark violet-pink; C
lavender with pink spots; filaments and
style pink. Large, full flowers, freely
borne. Mid-green leaves. Self-branching,
vigorous, upright habit. Easy to grow.

Rose of Castile
Banks, UK, 1855
Single. T and S white; T greenish; S with
pink blush and green tips; C violet with
pink blush, white at base; filaments pink;
style white. Profuse, small to medium-
sized flowers. Mid-green, small leaves.
Vigorous, upright, self-branching habit.

Rose of Castile (improved)
Lane, UK, 1871
Single. T pale pink; S flesh-pink with
green tips and deep pink underside;
C violet with dark pink veins, turning
reddish-violet as flowers age; filaments
pink; style white to pink. Medium-sized
flowers, freely borne. Light to mid-green
leaves. Upright, vigorous habit. Easy to
grow.

Rose van der Berg
Author unknown, USA, year unknown
Single. T and S pink; S with green-white
tips and deep pink underside; C deep
violet-pink, paler at base; filaments light
red. Small flowers, freely borne. Small,
mid-green leaves. Upright, bushy habit.

Rosy Frills
Handley, UK, 1979
Double. T greenish-white; S outside pale
pink, inside pink, pale yellowish-green
tips; C deep pink to light red, red edges,
outer petals with salmon stripes. Large,
full, sturdy flowers, freely borne. Dark
green leaves with red veins. Lax habit.
Suitable for hanging-basket.

Royal Purple
Lemoine, France, 1896
Single to semi-double. T and S waxy deep
red; S bright red underside; C deep violet,
paler at base, red veins; filaments and style
cherry red. Fairly large flowers, freely
borne early in the season. Mid-green,
medium-sized leaves. Vigorous, upright
habit.

Royal Velvet
Waltz, USA, 1962
Double. T and S crimson; S recurved; C
deep violet with crimson spots; filaments
and style crimson. Large flowers, freely
borne. Mid-green leaves. Vigorous,
upright, self-branching habit.

Rufus
Nelson, USA, 1952
Single. T, S and C bright red. Medium-
sized, self-coloured flowers, freely borne.
Mid-green, medium-sized leaves.
Vigorous, upright habit.

San Leandro [66]
Brand, USA, 1949
Double. T and S deep carmine, lighter
underside; C magenta, dotted with
vermilion; filaments and style cherry red.
Large flowers, freely borne. Dark green,
medium-sized leaves. Vigorous, upright
habit. Can be grown in full sun.

Santa Cruz
Tiret, USA, 1947
Semi-double to double. T and S dark red;
C darker red; filaments and style dark red.
Large, almost self-colour flowers, freely
borne. Mid-green leaves with red veins.
Vigorous, upright habit.

Satellite
Kennett, USA, 1963
Single. T greenish-white; S white with
green tips; C dark red shading to bright
red with white strips from base to tip;
filaments pink; style white. Freely borne,
large flowers. Mid-green leaves. Upright,
bushy habit. Prone to botrytis.

Saturnus
De Groot, Netherlands, 1970
(*F. regia* var. *typica* × 'Frau Henriette
Ernst')
Single. T and S red; S fairly long and
standing up in older flowers; T short; C
pale violet with red veins, lighter at base,
turning violet as flowers ge; filaments and
style light red. Fairly small flowers, freely
borne. Mid-green, medium-sized leaves.
Upright, small bush.

Sealand Prince
Walker-Bees, UK, 1967
Single. T and S light red; S long and
upturned; C violet, fading to reddish-
purple. Medium-sized, bell-shaped
flowers, freely borne. Mid-green, smallish
leaves. Vigorous, upright habit. Hardy.

138 An Encliandra hybrid

139 and 140 *F. procumbens*

141 *F. magdalenae*

142 *F. crassistipula*

143 *F. paniculata*

144 *F. denticulata*

145 A species from section 5, Hemsleyella

146 *F. macrostigma*

147 *F. nigricans*

148 An Encliandra hybrid

149 'Sipke Arjen', an Encliandra hybrid

Sea Shell
Evans, USA, 1954
Double. T pink; S pink to white, recurved;
C pink with darker pink veins; filaments
pink; style white. Medium-sized flowers,
freely borne. Dark green leaves. Upright
habit.

Seventh Heaven
Stubbs, USA, 1981
Double. T greenish-white with green
stripes, short and thick; S white, pink
blush appearing as flowers age, long, wide
and recurved; C orange-red shading to
orange, red at base. Large, freely borne
flowers. Medium-sized leaves with red
veins. Trailing habit.

Shanley
Mrs Shutt Jr, USA, 1968
Single. T and S bright orange; C deeper
orange. Large, almost self-coloured
flowers, freely borne. Mid-green, large
leaves. Upright, vigorous bush.

Sierra Blue
Waltz, USA, 1957
Double. T and S white; T short; S pink at
base and edges, paler pink on underside
with green tips; C silvery blue with white
at base and pin veins, turning soft lilac as
flowers age; filaments pink; style white.
Large, full flowers, freely borne. Mid-
green leaves. Trailing habit. Suitable for
hanging-basket.

Silver Jubilee
Hobbs, UK, 1976
Double. T and S red; T short; S with
green tips and pink underside, wide, short
and recurve; C white with deep pink veins
in the centre; filaments deep pink.
Medium-sized to large flowers, almost
round, short petals, rosette-type; petaloids
same colour as petals. Pale green leaves
with yellowish tint and red stems. Bushy,
upright habit.

Silver Wings
Soo Yun Field, USA, 1980
Double. T and S red; T short; C violet-
pink with petaloids of same colour on each;
style pink. Long flowers. Mid-green leaves
with red central veins. Naturally trailing
habit. Suitable for hanging-basket.

Sipke Arjen [149]
Reiman, Netherlands, 1986
(*F. microphylla* × *F. thymifolia*)
Single. Encliandra type. T and S white;
T relatively long; S with touch of pink of
underside; C white; filaments and style
white. Small flowers. Mid-green leaves.
Upright habit. Named after Dr
S. A. Appel.

Sleigh Bells [73]
Schnabel, USA, 1954
Single. T and S white; S long and
upturned, pale green tips; C white with
fine pink veins, bell-shaped. Medium-
sized flowers, freely borne. Fairly small,
mid-green leaves. Stiff, upright and
vigorous habit. Requires nipping out.

Snowcap
Henderson, UK, c.1880
Semi-double. T and S scarlet; C white
with cherry red veins; filaments cherry
red; style pink. Smallish flowers, very
freely borne. Mid- to dark green leaves.
Upright, vigorous habit. Easy to grow.

So Big
Waltz, USA, 1955
Double. T dark pink, fairly long; S pale
pink, darker pink at base, long, upturned,
with green tips; C creamy white; filaments
pink; style pale pink. Large flowers, very
freely borne. Medium-sized leaves with
reddish stems. Long, pointed buds and
long stalks. Vigorous, naturally trailing
habit. Suitable for hanging-basket.

Sonata
Tiret, USA, 1960
Double. T and S greenish-white; S pink,
paler towards green tips; C white with pale
pink veins; filaments and style pale pink.
Large, full flowers, freely borne. Mid-
green leaves. Lax, trailing habit. Needs
staking if grown as shrub.

Son of Thumb
Gubler, UK, 1978
(sport of 'Tom Thumb')
Single. T and S cherry red; C lilac. Small
flowers. Growth and habit identical to
'Tom Thumb' (see below).

Sophisticated Lady
Martin, USA, 1964
Double. T and S pale pink; S quite long,
paler towards green tips; C creamy white;

filaments and style pink. Large flowers, freely borne. Mid-green leaves with crimson central veins. Trailing habit; long-stemmed.

South Gate
Walker and Jones, USA, 1951
Double. T pale pinkish-green; S pale pink with green tips, deeper pink underside, upturned; C pale pink, deeper pink blush and veins; filaments keep pink; style pale pink. Fairly large flowers, freely borne. Mid-green leaves. Vigorous, upright habit. Easy to grow.

Space Shuttle [3]
De Graaff, Netherlands, 1981
('Speciosa' × *F. splendens*)
Single. T soft red, long and slightly flattened; S pale green, base soft red, small; T and S have short hairs; C pale soft yellow, outside orange base and veins; ovary long and thin; filaments and style white. Freely borne, medium-sized flowers, appearing early in season. Heart-shaped, mid- to dark green leaves, whitish undersides; young leaves sometimes with reddish tint. Upright, rather lax growth. Requires regular pinching out.

Spring Bells
Kooijman, Netherlands, 1972
Semi-double. T and S bright red; C white. Medium-sized flowers, freely-borne. Leaves mid-to dark green. Vigorous, upright habit. Probably a sport of 'Snowcap' (see above), with slightly larger flowers and a longer flowering period.

Stad Elburg [50]
Van der Beek, Netherlands, 1982
(sport of 'Aunt Juliana')
Double. T crimson, medium length; S shiny crimson,upturned; C bright blue with red veins, paler at base, fading to redviolet as flowers age; filaments and style red. Large flowers, freely borne. Mid-green leaves with red central veins and red stems. Trailing, vigorous growth. Suitable for hanging-basket.

Stanley Cash
Pennisi, USA, 1970
Double. T and S white, green tips, short; C deep violet. Large flowers. Mid-green foliage. Semi-trailing habit.

Starlite
Waltz, USA, 1961
Double. T and S dull pink; S wide and pointed; C dark lilacpink. Medium-sized to large flowers with star-shaped centres and long styles, freely borne. Mid-green, large leaves. Naturally trailing habit.

Stella Ann
Baker-Dunnett, UK, 1974
Triphylla hybrid. Single. T long and poppy red; S coral red, green tips, fairly wide and open; C orange. Rounded flowers, freely borne. Olive-green leaves with red veins. Vigorous, upright habit.

Strawberry Delight
Gadsby, UK, 1969
Double. T and S crimson; C white with pink blush, heavily veined; filaments cherry red; style crimson. Medium-sized to large blooms, freely borne. Yellowish-green leaves with bronze tinge, turning green as leaves age. Upright, rather lax habit.

Streamliner
Tiret, USA, 1951
Semi-double. T and S crimson; T long and thin; S long, narrow and twisted; C pinkish-red to crimson, lighter at base, long. Long and fairly sturdy flowers, freely borne. Mid-green, medium-sized leaves. Fairly vigorous trailing habit. Suitable for hanging-basket.

String of Pearls
Pacey, UK, 1976
(*F. lycioides* × not known)
Single to semi-double. T pale pink; S recurved, pale pink. C pale pinkish-violet with lavender veins. Medium-sized flowers, very freely borne. Leaves small and pale green. Upright, vigorous habit; difficult to train.

Sugar Blues [117]
Martin, USA, 1964
Double. T and S white; S pink underside; C dark blue, fading to violet-blue. Large flowers, freely borne. Mid-green leaves. Trailing habit. Suitable for hanging-basket.

Suikerbossie (Sugarbush)
Brouwer, Netherlands, 1982
(*F. magellanica typica* × not known)
Single. T and S greenish-white with pink to red blush, green tips, pink-red

underside; C violet; filaments dark pink; style pink. Small flowers. Medium-sized to small leaves, lighter undersides, with red veins. Self-branching, upright habit.

Summer Snow
Waltz, USA, 1956
Semi-double. T and S white; S reflexed, green tips; C creamywhite, yellowish when buds unfolds. Medium-sized flowers, freely borne. Mid-green, medium-sized leaves. Lax, semi-trailing growth. Tender.

Sunny Smiles
Gadsby, UK, 1969
Single. T pale pink, long; S carmine pink, salmon pink undersides; C crimson with pink blush; filaments carmine; style pale pink. Largish flowers, freely borne early in season. Light green leaves. Upright, bushy habit.

Sunray
Milne, UK, 1872
Single. T scarlet; S deep pink, lighter at top, scarlet underside; C red-violet; filaments cherry red;style pink to cherry red. Small flowers. Foliage variable, various shades of light green, creamy white edges and red blush. Fairly vigorous, upright habit. Needs careful watering and a sunny position. Tender.

Susan Travis
Travis, UK, 1958
single. T and S pink; S with green tips; C magenta-pink, lighter at base; filaments pink; style pale pink. Medium-sized flowers, freely borne. Mid-green leaves. Upright, bushy habit. Hardy.

Suzanna
Van Der Grijp, Netherlands, 1968
('Dollar Princess' × not known)
Single or semi-double. T and S pink; S a bit darker; T short; C blue with fine red veins at base, fades to lilac-violet. Medium-sized flowers, freely borne. Leaves dark green. Vigorous, upright habit.

Swanley Gem
Cannell, UK, 1901
Single. T and S scarlet; C violet, light scarlet at base, scarlet veins, stands out horizontally; filaments and style scarlet. Medium-sized flowers. Dark green, sturdy leaves. Upright, busy habit.

Swanley Yellow [28]
Cannell, UK, 1900
Single. T and S orange-pink; T long; P rich orange-vermilion; filaments and style pink. Medium-sized flowers, freely borne. Bronze-green leaves. Upright, rather lax habit. Needs regular pinching out.

Sweetheart
Van Wieringen, Netherlands, 1970
Single. T and S white; S faint pink blush and green tips; C cerise, white a base; filaments light red; style whitish-pink. Profuse, medium to large flowers. Leaves mid-green. Self-branching, trailing, rather lax habit.

Sweet Leilani
Tiret, USA, 1957
Double. T pink; S pale pink, green tips, deeper pink underside; C pale lavender blue with pale pink spots; filaments pink; style pale pink. Large flowers, freely borne. Fairly light green leaves. Upright, rather lax growth. Stands up to heat well.

Swingtime
Tiret, USA, 1950
('Titanic' × 'Yuletide')
Double. T and S scarlet; C milky white with scarlet veins; filaments and style cherry red. Fairly large flowers, freely borne. Mid-green leaves. Vigorous, upright but rather lax habit. Suitable for hanging-basket.

Taddle
Gubler, UK, 1974
Single. T and S light red; T quite short; S wide, lighter towards green tips, reflexed to the tube in ripe flowers; C white with fine red veins. Medium-sized flowers, freely borne. Light green, medium-sized leaves. Vigorous, upright habit.

Taffeta Bow
Stubbs, USA, 1974
Double. T carmine pink, short; S carmine pink, quite wide and long, crepey towards base, erect on opening then curved; C violet. Large, open flowers, freely borne. Dark green leaves with crimson veins. Self-branching, vigorous, trailing habit.

Tangerine [100]
Tiret, USA, 1949
(*F. cordifolia* × not known)
Single. T dark pink, long; S light salmon

pink, green tips, held out from corolla; C bright salmon orange, turning to light red as flowers age; filaments pink; style white. Medium-sized flowers, freely borne. Mid-green leaves. Vigorous, upright growth. Needs regular pinching out to get good shape, but worth the effort. Needs warmth and sun.

Television
Walker and Jones, USA, 1950
Double. T and S white; S pale pink undersides; C deep orchid blue, violet-pink spots. Medium-sized flowers, freely borne. Mid-green leaves. Semi-trailing habit.

Temptation
Peterson Fuchsia Farms, USA. 1959
Double. T and S white; S long; C orange with white at base. Fairly long flowers, freely borne. Mid-green leaves. Upright, bushy habit.

Tennessee Waltz [106]
Walker and Jones, USA, 1951
Semi-double to double. T and S madder red; S reflexed; C lilac-pink with light madder blush; filaments and style light red. Medium-sized flowers, very freely borne. Mid-green leaves. Upright, self-branching, vigorous habit.

Texas Longhorn [103]
Fuchsia-la Nursery, USA, 1960
Semi-double to double. T and S scarlet; C white with cherry red veins; filaments pink; style cherry red. Large flowers. Mid-green leaves with reddish veins. Trailing habit. Not easy to grow.

The Doctor [29]
Castle Nurseries, UK, 1934
Single. T pale pink, fairly long; S pink, deeper on underside, reflexed; C salmon pink; filaments bright pink; style pale pink, long. Medium-sized flowers, freely borne. Mid-green leaves. Upright, rather lax, bushy habit.

The Phoenix
Tiret, USA, 1967
Double. T and S pink; C lilac with notched edge. Large, full flowers, freely borne. Mid-green leaves. Vigorous trailing habit. Suitable for hanging-basket. Grow out of full sun or buds will not open.

Tiffany [10]
Reedstrom, USA, 1960
Double. T and S white; S upturned, light pink undersides; C white. Large flowers, freely borne. Dark green leaves, making beautiful background for flowers. Vigorous trailing habit. Suitable for hanging-basket.

Ting-a-Ling
Schnabel-Paskesen, USA, 1959
Single. T, S and C white; filaments pale pink; style white. Fairly large, dish-shaped flowers, freely borne. Mid-green leaves. Vigorous, upright, bushy habit. Prone to botrytis and needs to be nipped out regularly.

Tinker Bell
Hodges, USA, 1955
Single or semi-double. T pink; S white shading to pink near green tips, pale pink underside, long, narrow and reflexed over tube; C white with pink veins; filaments pink; style pale pink. Fairly large, long flowers, freely borne. Pale green leaves. Lax, bushy habit.

Tolling Bell
Turner, UK, 1964
Single. T and S carmine; C mauve-violet, pink at base, carmine veins; filaments and style carmine. Small flowers, freely borne. Mid-green leaves. Vigorous, upright habit.

Tom Thumb
Baudinat, France, 1850
Single. T and S carmine; C mauve-violet, pink at base, carmine veins; filaments and style carmine. Small, rather loose, flowers freely borne. Self-branching, upright but dwarf, bushy habit. Hardy.

Toos
Van Suchtelen, Netherlands, 1980
(seedling of 'Bon Accorde')
Single. T cream; S pale pink, green tips; C pale violet-pink; filaments pink; style pale pink. Medium-sized flowers, freely borne and held out horizontally. Mid-green leaves. Upright, vigorous habit.

Torch [15]
Munkner, USA, 1963
Double. T pinkish-creamy white; S pale pink with green tips; pale salmon pink underside; C pale violet; outer petals with orange, pink and violet spots; filaments pale pink; style white. Medium-sized

flowers, freely borne. Light to mid-green leaves. Upright, vigorous shrub. Needs regular pinching out.

Tour Eiffel
De Graaff, Netherlands, 1976
('Frau Alice Hoffmann' × not known)
Single. T and S salmon pink; T round; S salmon pink underside, held downwards; C violet-pink, salmon pink at base; filaments and style pink. Medium-sized flowers, freely borne. Bronzegreen leaves with red central vein and stems. Fairly vigorous, somewhat lax bush.

Tourtonne [67]
Van Suchtelen, Netherlands, 1968
('Leverkusen' × 'Water Nymph')
Single. Self-colour red; C with a touch of violet; T very long. Fairly large flowers, freely borne. Darkish green leaves. Vigorous, upright habit. Does best in sun. Tender.

Trail Blazer
Reiter Jr, USA, 1951
Double. T and S crimson; T long; C reddish-violet; filaments and style red. Fairly large, long, almost self-coloured flowers, freely borne. Mid-green serrated leaves. Self-branching, vigorous habit. Suitable for hanging-basket.

Trailing King [27]
Brown, USA, 1936
Single. T and S white; C orange. Small flowers, freely borne. Bronze-coloured leaves. Vigorous, trailing habit. Suitable for hanging-basket.

Trailing Queen
Kohene, Germany, 1896
Single; T and S red; C dull red. Medium-sized, almost selfcoloured flowers, very freely borne. Bronze-red leaves. Vigorous, trailing habit. Suitable for hanging-basket.

Traudchen Bonstedt
Bonstedt, Germany, 1905
(*F. triphylla* × not known)
Triphylla hybrid. Single. T, S and C cream to salmon pink; T long; C short. Light green leaves, lightly covered with bronze hairs and reddish undersides. Free-flowering, upright bush. Tender.

Tresco
Tresco Abbey Gardens, UK, date not known
Single. T and S pale pink; S with green tips; C violet, pink at base; filaments pink; style red. Small flowers, freely borne. Longish leaves mid-green. Vigorous, upright, bushy habit. Hardy.

Tristesse [21]
Blackwell, UK, 1965
('Lilac Lustre' × not known)
Double. T and S pale pink; S with green tips; C pale lilacblue; filaments and style pink. Medium-sized flowers, freely borne. Mid-green, small to medium-sized leaves. Self-branching, upright habit. Easy to grow.

Troika [113]
De Graaff, Netherlands, 1976
('La Campanella' × not known)
Double. T pink, paler in warm conditions; S white; C pale blue to lilac-pink; filaments pink; style white. Medium-sized to large flowers, freely borne. Mid-green leaves. Upright, bushy and vigorous habit. Needs care in winter.

Tropicana
Tiret, USA, 1964
Double. T greenish-white; S pale salmon pink, paler near green tips, deeper pink underside; C orange; filaments pink; style white to pink. Large flowers, freely borne. Light green, longish leaves. Vigorous, trailing habit. Suitable for hanging-basket.

Tropic Sunset
Antonelli, USA, 1964
('Autumnale' × not known)
Double. T and S carmine; C violet with pink spots; filaments and style pink. Medium-sized flowers, freely borne. Small, reddish-bronze leaves with green tips and red stems. Self-branching, vigorous, trailing habit. Suitable for hanging-basket.

Trumpeter
Reiter, USA, 1946
(*F. triphylla* × not known)
Triphylla hybrid. Single. T, S and C bright red; T long and thick; C darkens as flowers age. Bluish-green leaves. Naturally trailing, free-flowering and rather slow-growing habit. Suitable for hanging-basket.

Tsjiep [54]
De Graaff, Netherlands, 1981
('Mephisto' × 'Countess of Aberdeen')
Single. T and S cream with pink blush;
T slightly curved; S with green tips; C
orange, lighter at base; filaments light red;
pistil pale pink. Small flowers, very freely
borne. Medium-sized leaves, paler on
undersides. Fairly vigorous, upright but
dwarf habit. The name is pronounced
'cheep'.

Tumbler
Tolley, UK, 1974
Single. T and S flesh pink; T long; S
upturned and twisting (pin-wheel type);
C geranium red and pink. Medium-sized,
spindle-shaped flowers, freely borne.
Small to medium-sized, mid-green leaves.
Long, think branches and trailing habit.

Tuonela [110]
Blackwell, UK, 1969
Double. T and S pale pink; S with green
tips and deeper pink underside; C pale
lavender blue with pink veins; filaments
pink; style white. Fairly large flowers,
freely borne. Mid-green, largish leaves.
Upright, bushy and vigorous habit.

Twiggy
De Graaff, Netherlands, 1980
(*F. magellanica* × *F. lycioides*)
Single. T and S bright red, long and slim;
S strongly pointed and held at upward
angle; C mauve with red veins; filaments
and pistil light red. Small flowers of the
spider type, freely borne. Dark red, grape-
size berries. Light green, medium-sized
leaves. Long, thick stems. Naturally
trailing habit. Suitable for hanging-basket.

Typhoon
Rijff, Netherlands, 1983
('First Kiss' × 'Pink Bon Accorde')
Single. T pale pink; S pale pink, deeper on
underside, green tips; C bright red, deeper
red inside. Dull, mid-green leaves. Self-
branching.

U.F.O.
Handley, UK, 1972
Single. T pinkish-white; S white with
greenish tips and rather pink undersides,
reflexed to stem; C lavender violet, white
at centre of each petal; filaments pale pink;
style white to pale pink. Medium-sized,
dish-shaped flowers, freely borne in
clusters. Fairly small, mid-green leaves.

Self-branching, upright, vigorous and
bushy habit. Easy to grow.

Uncle Charley
Tiret, USA, 1949
Semi-double. T and S pink; C lavender
blue, fading to lilac. Medium-sized, bell-
shaped flowers, freely borne. Mid-green
leaves. Upright, vigorous habit.

Unique
Hazard and Hazard, USA, 1930(?)
Single. T pinkish-white, short; S white,
pink underside, wide; C pale violet, deeper
at edges and fading to white at base;
filaments soft pink; style white. Medium-
sized flowers, freely borne. Light green
leaves. Upright, vigorous, bushy habit.

Upward Look
Gadsby, UK, 1968
('Bon Accorde' × 'Athela')
Single. T and S carmine and short; S with
green tips; C pale violet-blue; filaments
and style pink. Fairly small, upright
flowers, very freely borne. Medium-sized,
light green leaves. Vigorous, upright,
bushy habit.

Valerie [37]
Mitchinson, UK, 1981
('Norman Mitchinson' ×
['Simonside' × 'Lindisfarne'])
Single. T pink with red stripes, relatively
short, average thickness; S white with
green tips, fully reflexed; C violet with
pink blush at base of each petal. Medium-
sized flowers, freely borne. Mid-green
leaves. Upright, vigorous growth. Best
colour in shade.

Vanessa Jackson
Handley, UK, 1980
Single. T salmon red, average length and
thickness; S salmon orange, long and
standing out well from the corolla; C
salmon orange, long and trumpet shaped,
fading to orange-red then to cardinal red.
Large, elegant flowers, freely borne. Mid-
green to bronze leaves. Self-branching,
trailing habit. Suitable for hanging-basket.

Vanity Fair
Schnabel-Paskesen, USA, 1962
Double. T greenish-white; S white with
pink blush, reflexed with green tips; C pale
pink; filaments pale pink; style white.
Large, full flowers, freely borne. Large,
mid-green leaves. Upright, vigorous,
bushy habit.

Venus
De Groot, Netherlands, 1972
(*F. regia* var. *typica* × 'Jamboree')
Single to semi-double. T and S pink; T
fairly short; S gracefully erect; C violet
with red spots at base; filaments and style
pink. Medium-sized to small flowers. Mid-
green, medium-sized leaves. Upright
habit.

Vielliebchen
Wolf, Germany, 1911
('Charming' × *F. magellanica* var. *gracilis*)
Single. T and S shining red; C keep violet
fading to redviolet; filaments pink; style
pink-red. Small to medium-sized flowers,
freely borne. Smallish, mid-green leaves.
Upright, bushy habit.

Vincent van Gogh [123]
Van der Post, Netherlands, 1984
Single. T pink, long; S pink with some
green and green tips, underside pale pink;
C pink; filaments and style pink. Small,
almost self-coloured flowers. Medium-
sized, mid-green leaves. Trailing habit.

Violet Bassett-Burr [9]
Holmes, UK, 1972
Double. T short, greenish-white and pink;
S white, green tips, pink at base and with
fine pink lines, reflexed and completely
covering T; C pale lilac, lighter at base;
filaments pink; style white. Large, full
flowers, freely borne. Dark green leaves.
Upright, vigorous bush. Needs regular
pinching out.

Violet Gem
Niederholzer-Waltz, USA, 1949
Semi-double. T and S carmine; C deep
violet. Large, spreading flowers, freely
borne. Darkish green, medium-sized
leaves. Fairly vigorous, upright growth.

Viva Ireland
Ireland, USA, 1956
Single. T and S pale pink; C soft lilac-
violet with flesh-pink spots. Medium-sized
flowers, very freely borne. Mid- to darkish
green, long, narrow leaves. Rather lax,
self-branching, bushy habit.

Vobeglo [95]
De Groot, Netherlands, 1974
('Pallas' [*F. regia* var. *typica* × 'Bon
Accorde'] × 'Frau Henriette Ernst')
Single. T and S pink; T short; C violet-
lilac, darker at edges, fine red veins;

filaments pink; style pale pink. Fairly
small, erect flowers, freely borne.
Smallish, mid-green leaves. Dwarf shrub
with short stem joints.

Voodoo
Tiret, USA, 1953
('Maxine's Purple' × unknown seedling)
Double. T and S dark red; T short; S long,
wide and erect; C dark violet. Large
flowers, fairly freely borne. Darkish green,
medium-sized leaves. Upright, vigorous
and self-branching habit.

Vrouwtje
De Groot, Netherlands, date unknown
Single. T and S red; T small; C violet,
fading to violet-red. Fairly small flowers,
freely borne. Small, mid-green leaves.
Upright habit.

Walsingham
Clitheroe, UK, 1979
('Northumbrian Belle' × 'Blush o' Dawn')
Semi-double. T and S palest pink to off-
white; S pink undersides and held out
horizontally; C pale lilac. Beautiful,
sturdy, bell-shaped flowers. Long, pointed
and serrated leaves. Upright, self-
branching habit. Prone to botrytis.

Walz Bergtop
Waldenmaier, Netherlands, 1982
Single. T and S red-pink, shiny, bright red
when grown in sun, with green tips;
C lilac-violet. Small to medium-sized
flowers; buds held high; flowers between
erect and horizontal; long-lasting and
profuse. Dark green leaves with paler
undersides. Upright, vigorous and self-
branching habit.

Walz Brandaris
Waldenmaier, Netherlands, 1982
('Chang' × not known)
Single. T orange-red, thick; S orange-pink
with cream-coloured tips, held out
horizontally; C orange-red,orange at base
and with darker edges; filaments and style
pink. Sturdy, medium-sized flowers, freely
borne. Upright, rather lax growth. Stands
up to sun well.

Walz Bruintje
Waldenmaier, Netherlands, 1983
('Achievement' × 'Achievement')
Single. T pink-red; S pink-red but rather
paler than T; C red with orange tinge.
Fairly small, profuse flowers borne over a
long period. Dark green leaves, lighter

undersides. Upright and vigorous, somewhat lax growth. Suitable for hanging-basket or as small bush.

Walz Epicurist
Waldenmaier, Netherlands, 1981
('Fascination' × 'Vogue')
Single. T and S pink; S reflexed; C blue on opening, fading to lilac, more fan-shaped than bell-shaped. Flowers medium-sized and freely borne. Dark green leaves, lighter undersides. Upright, vigorous growth.

Walz Estafette
Waldenmaier, Netherlands, 1981
('Walz Bruintje' × 'Walz Bruintje')
Double. T long, white, thickening at top; S white with touch of pink and green tips, fairly long and recurved; C violetred, four inner petals under four outer petals in mature flowers. Mid-green leaves. Naturally trailing habit. Suitable for hanging-basket. This F2 of 'Achievement' manifest recessive qualities already thought lost – i.e., the four petals on small stems so that the long flower has three levels.

Walz Floreat [75]
Waldenmaier, Netherlands, 1981
('Normandy Bell' × 'Normandy Bell')
Single. T and S white with a touch of pink; S recurved; C pale blue with touch of lilac, fading to pale lilac, slightly flared. Small flowers, freely borne. Mid-green leaves, lighter undersides. Vigorous, self-branching, dwarf shrub.

Walz Freule
Waldenmaier, Netherlands, 1982
Single. T pink; S pink with green tips, recurved; P pale bluelilac first, fading to lilac with pink-red veins. Medium-sized flowers, very freely borne. Medium-sized, light green leaves. Trailing, vigorous habit. Suitable for hanging-basket.

Walz Gigolo
Waldenmaier, Netherlands, 1982
('Swingtime' × 'Walz Bruintje')
Double. T pink; S pink, slightly recurved; C lilac-red with orange-red spots at base and red vines. Medium-sized, longlasting flowers, freely borne. Mid-green leaves, lighter undersides. Fairly lax and vigorous habit.

Walz Meermin
Waldenmaier, Netherlands, 1984
('Speciosa' × 'Walz Bruintje')
Single. T pink, maturing to red; S yellow-green, inside turning red as flowers age, slightly reflexed; C pale pink, darkening as flowers age. Fairly small flowers, freely borne and conspicuous, produced throughout flowering period. Medium-sized leaves. Upright growth. Can withstand sun, but colours turn more red.

Walz Parasol
Waldenmaier, Netherlands, 1984
('Walz Floreat' × 'Golden Glow')
Single. T and S salmon pink; S held out horizontally; C salmon pink, darker than T and S. Fairly large, sturdy, bell-shaped flowers, freely borne. Dark yellow-green leaves. Fairly vigorous, stiff trailing habit. Does best in full sun.

Walz Toorts
Waldenmaier, Netherlands, 1981
('Leverkusen' × not known)
Triphylla type. Single. T fairly long, pink-red; C orange-red, larger than in 'Leverkusen' and held horizontally. Medium-sized flowers, profusely borne throughout season and, in the greenhouse, also in winter. Drops berries with stalks spontaneously. Dark green, medium-sized leaves. Upright, vigorous growth. Requires regular pinching out. Fairly hardy.

Walz Vuurtoren
Waldenmaier, Netherlands, 1982
Single. T pink-orange, fairly long; S pink-orange, underside pink-white with deep pink spots, recurved; C orange. Medium-sized flowers, freely borne. Emerald green leaves. Upright, rather lax growth. Requires regular pinching out. Grow in full sun.

Walz Waardin
Waldenmaier, Netherlands, 1984
('Normandy Bell' × 'Tuonela')
Single to semi-double. T white-pink, long; long S white, crepey pink on inside, long and held horizontally; long C pale blue-lilac-pink. Large flowers, freely borne. Mid-green leaves, lighter on undersides. Naturally trailing habit. Suitable for hanging-basket.

Walz Waterval
Waldenmaier, Netherlands, 1984
('Normandy Bell' × 'Mrs W. Rundle')
Single. T white, long and thickening at
top; S white, pale pink underside, long and
held out horizontally and recurved; C red;
half filaments clearly visible outside
corolla. Medium-sized, conspicuous
flowers, freely borne. Mid-green leaves.
Self-branching, naturally trailing habit.
Requires regular pinching out. Do not
grow in full sun.

Warton Crag
Thornely, UK, 1963
('Jamboree' × not known)
Single. T short, thick and flesh-pink; S
creamy white, thick, green tips, thick,
crepey, creamy white petaloids appear
when flowers open; C pink. Unusual
flowers, freely borne. Dark green leaves.
Upright, bushy habit. Prefers shade.

Water Nymph [39]
Story, UK, 1859
Single. T and S creamy white; C orange-
red. Medium-sized flowers. Vigorous
bush.

Waxen Beauty
Clyne, UK, 1974
('Ting-a-Ling' × ('La
Campanella' × 'Flirtation Waltz'))
double. T greenish-white with pink
shading, waxy; S greenish-white, slightly
reflexed; C white, paler pink in centre.
Medium-sized flowers, freely borne.
Medium-sized, almond-shaped leaves.
Vigorous, bushy habit.

Westergeest
De Graaff, Netherlands, 1979
Single. T and S pale salmon orange;
T round; S with green tips, held out
horizontally and recurved; C salmon pink,
darker pink at edges; filaments pink; style
pale pink. Fairly small flowers, freely
borne. Light green leaves. Upright, fairly
vigorous habit. Needs regular pinching
out.

Westminster Chimes
Mrs I. Clyne, UK, 1976
('La Campanella' × 'Liebriez')
Semi-double. T deep pink-red; S pink-red
shading to pale pink, green tips, outspread
but not reflexed; C violet-blue, turning
magenta as flowers age, pink at base. Fairly

small flowers, very freely borne, becoming
fluted and spreading as flowers age. Small
to medium-sized mid-green leaves. Rather
lax habit, naturally trailing.

Whirlaway [68]
Waltz, USA, 1961
Semi-double. T greenish-white; S white
with a touch of pink, very long and with
green tips; C white with a touch of pale
pink, turning pinker as flowers age;
filaments pink; style white. Large flowers,
freely borne. Mid-green, long leaves.
Vigorous but lax, upright growth. Does
best in greenhouse. Requires regular
pinching out.

White Galore
Fuchsia-la Nursery, USA, 1968
Double. T, S and C off-white with a faint
trace of pink. Large flowers, fairly freely
borne. Trailing habit.

White Joy
Burns, UK, 1980
('Joy Patmore' × 'Eden Lady')
Single. T and S white with pale pink
blush; T short; S fairly wide and held out
horizontally; C white. Medium-sized,
bellshaped flowers, freely borne. Mid-
green leaves. Upright, bushy habit. Short-
jointed stems.

Whiteknight's Ruby [62]
J. O. Wright, UK, 1976
(*F. triphylla* × *F. procumbens*)
Triphylla hybrid. Single. T quite long
(about 2cm) shading from cardinal red to
violet; S small (about 1cm), violet;
C violet; filaments and style violet;
rudimentary filaments; stigma in four
parts. Dark, elliptical, velvety leaves with
red veins, red undersides and red to pink
stems with darker spots. Self-branching,
upright bush.

White Pixie
Merrist Wood, UK, 1968
(sport of 'Pixie')
Single. T and S carmine; C white with
pink veins; filaments carmine; style
carmine pink. Small flowers, freely borne.
Yellow-green leaves with crimson veins.
Upright, bushy habit. Hardy.

White Spider [72]
Haag, USA, 1951
Single. T pale pink; S pink with green
tips, long and curling upwards; C white

with pink veins; filaments pink;style pale pink. Medium-size flowers, appearing early in season and freely borne. Mid-green leaves. Vigorous, upright bush. Not easy to grow.

Willie Tamerus [43]
Tamerus, Netherlands, 1981
Single. T pale salmon pink, long; S salmon pink on upperside, shading to pale pink, green tips, somewhat darker on underside, long and fairly narrow and graceful, held out horizontally; C orange-red, salmon orange at base; filaments pink; style pale pink. Medium-sized, graceful flowers. Light green, fairly large leaves. Naturally trailing habit.

Wings of Song
Blackwell, UK, 1968
Double. T and S bright pink-red; S long and upturned; C violet-red with pink veins; filaments and style pink. Fairly large flowers, freely borne quite late in the season. Mid-green leaves with reddish veins. Vigorous, self-branching naturally trailing habit. Suitable for hanging-basket.

Winston Churchill [16]
Garson, USA, 1942
Double. T and S pink; S green tips and bright pink undersides; C violet-blue, fading to pale violet, pink veins; filaments and style cherry red. Medium-sized flowers, freely borne. Mid-green, small to medium-sized leaves. Upright, self-branching, bushy habit. Fairly tender.

Witchingham
Clitheroe, UK, 1981
('Nancy Lou' x 'The 13th Star')
Double. T and S bright pink; S long and reflexed; C white. Medium-sized flowers, freely borne early in the season. Mid-green leaves. Medium-sized shrub with upright but rather lax habit. Does best in shade.

Cultivars by Suitability and Colour

	Hanging-basket	Standard or shrub	Triphylla	Variegated leaf	White	Red	Orange	Red-violet	Pink	Pink-violet, Pink-red	White-violet	Pink-white	Red-white	Winter-hardy	Single	Semi-double	Double	Self-branching	Easy to Grow	Dwarf	Requires winter temp. of 10°C	Tolerates shade	Sun and/or warmth	Greenhouse
A																								
Abbé Farges		•						•							•									
Achievement		•						•							•									
Aika	•									•					•								•	
Alaska	•			•												•								
Alice Hoffmann		•									•		•		•				•					
Alison Ewart		•							•						•			•						
Alison Ryle		•							•						•								•	
Ambassador	•	•						•										•						
Amelie Aubin	•	•											•											
Andenken an Heinrich Henkel		•	•			•									•							•	•	
Andromeda		•						•							•									
Angela Leslie		•							•								•	•						•
Angel's Flight	•	•									•						•	•						
Annabel		•			•												•							
Ann H. Trip		•			•										•									
Applause	•	•				•									•									
Aquarius		•						•								•								
Arcadia				•											•									
Archie Owen	•											•					•		•					
Army Nurse		•														•			•					
Athela		•						•							•									
Auntie Jinks	•					•											•	•						
Aunt Juliana	•					•											•	•						
Autumnale	•	•	•																				•	
B																								
Baby Chang	•	•				•									•					•				
Balkonköningin	•							•							•									
Barbara		•						•							•								•	
Baronesse van Dedem		•						•							•									
Baroque Pearl		•									•						•							
Beacon		•						•							•				•					
Beacon Rosa		•							•						•				•	•			•	
Belle de Lisse	•	•													•		•							
Belle de Spa	•	•			•										•								•	
Belsay Beauty	•						•							•										
Berba	•											•				•	•				•			
Berbanella																								
Berba's Trio		•								•		•		•										
Bergnimf		•			•										•		•							
Bernadette		•			•												•				•	•		
Beth Robley	•												•			•							•	
Bicentennial	•					•										•	•							
Billy Green		•	•				•								•									
Black Prince		•				•									•		•							
Blanche Regina	•								•						•		•							

	Hanging-basket	Standard or shrub	Triphylla	Variegated leaf	White	Red	Orange	Red-violet	Pink	Pink-violet, Pink-red	White-violet	Pink-white	Red-white	Winter-hardy	Single	Semi-double	Double	Self-branching	Easy to Grow	Dwarf	Requires winter temp. of 10°C	Tolerates shade	Sun and/or warmth	Greenhouse
Blue Pearl	•									•							•							
Blue Ribbon	•	•									•						•		•					
Blush o' Dawn	•	•								•							•							
Bobby Shaftoe		•		•														•	•					
Boerhaave	•				•										•			•						
Bon Accorde		•									•				•									
Bon Bon	•	•			•												•							•
Border Queen		•						•							•	•								
Border Reiver		•							•						•								•	
Bornemann's Beste		•	•												•						•			
Bouffant	•												•		•									
Bountiful		•										•					•							
Bow Bells		•											•		•				•					
Brandt's 500 Club	•	•													•									
Bridesmaid		•										•			•									
Brilliant		•						•						•	•				•					
Brenda		•										•					•	•						
Brookwood Joy	•	•								•							•							
Brunette		•											•		•									
Bunny		•							•							•								
Buttercup		•					•								•							•		
C																								
Caledonia	•	•				•									•			•						
Callaly Pink		•							•															
Cambridge Louie		•								•														
Cara Mia	•	•											•			•								
Cardinal	•	•				•										•								
Cardinal Farges		•											•			•								
Carillon van Amsterdam		•				•									•			•						
Carmel Blue		•									•				•			•						
Carmen Maria	•	•							•						•			•						
Carnival	•	•											•		•									
Caroline		•							•						•									
Cascade	•	•											•		•									
Celador		•							•								•							
Celia Smedley		•																	•				•	
Chang		•					•														•		•	
Chartwell		•										•		•					•				•	
Checkerboard		•											•	•					•				•	
Checkmate		•							•					•				•						
Chillerton Beauty		•							•					•										
China Lantern		•	•							•					•									
Cicely Ann	•	•																					•	
Citation		•												•										
Cliff's Hardy		•						•						•	•									
Cliff's Unique		•								•							•							

	Hanging-basket	Standard or shrub	Triphylla	Variegated leaf	White	Red	Orange	Red-violet	Pink	Pink-violet, Pink-red	White-violet	Pink-white	Red-white	Winter-hardy	Single	Semi-double	Double	Self-branching	Easy to Grow	Dwarf	Requires winter temp. of 10°C	Tolerates shade	Sun and/or warmth	Greenhouse
Cloverdale		•						•							•			•		•				
Cloverdale Jewel		•							•						•			•						
Cloverdale Pearl		•										•			•			•	•			•		
Coachman	•	•					•								•									
Come Dancing	•	•							•								•							
Constance		•							•					•			•		•					
Contramine		•									•				•									
Corallina	•	•						•							•				•					
Cornelis Steevens	•							•						•										
Coquet Bell		•							•						•									
Countess of Aberdeen		•										•			•									
Crackerjack	•								•						•				•					
Cross Check	•								•						•									
Crystal Stars		•		•					•										•					
Curly Q	•								•						•									
Curtain Call	•	•				•									•									
D																								
Daisy Bell	•	•	•						•						•								•	
Danny Boy		•		•												•								
Dark Eyes		•						•								•								
Dark Secret		•							•							•								
Dark Spider	•	•						•									•							
Dee Copley		•						•									•	•						
Delice	•	•							•								•							
Delta Beauty	•								•						•									
Delta Pearl												•												
Deltaschon		•											•											
De Pleiaden		•										•												
Derby Imp	•	•						•							•									
Diana Wills		•							•								•	•						
Dilly Dilly	•	•							•								•		•					
Dirk van Delen		•						•							•									
Display		•						•							•			•	•					
Dollar Princess		•						•									•		•					
Dominyana		•	•	•	•											•								•
Drame		•						•						•		•			•					
Dr S.A. Appel		•								•					•									
Dulcie Elisabeth		•						•										•	•				•	
Duke of York		•						•						•	•									
Dusky Beauty		•						•							•					•				
Dusky Rose	•								•							•	•							
Dutch Firebird	•	•			•										•									
Dutch Flamingo	•	•							•						•									
Dutch Mill		•						•							•									
E																								
Earl of Beaconsfield	•	•				•									•									

	Hanging-basket	Standard or shrub	Triphylla	Variegated leaf	White	Red	Orange	Red-violet	Pink	Pink-violet, Pink-red	White-violet	Pink-white	Red-white	Winter-hardy	Single	Semi-double	Double	Self-branching	Easy to Grow	Dwarf	Requires winter temp. of 10°C	Tolerates shade	Sun and/or warmth	Greenhouse
El Camino		●											●			●	●							
Eleanor Leytham		●							●						●									
Elfriede Ott		●	●						●						●								●	
Elizabeth	●	●							●						●									
Ellen Morgan		●								●						●	●							
El Matador	●							●											●					
Elsie Mitchell		●							●							●	●					●		
Emile de Wildeman		●								●														
Empress of Prussia		●				●									●				●					
Estelle Marie		●									●				●									
Eternal Flame							●									●								
Eusebia		●									●					●								
Evensong		●			●										●									
F																								
Falling Stars		●					●								●									
Fanfare	●	●	●												●									
Fenna		●	●		●	●									●									
Fiery Spider	●						●								●									
Filigrain		●						●							●									
Fiona	●	●									●				●									
First Kiss		●										●			●				●					
First Succes		●							●						●									
Flash		●				●									●								●	
Flashlight		●							●						●					●				
Flimflam		●							●						●									
Flirtation		●							●							●	●							
Flirtation Waltz		●										●			●									
Flora		●				●									●									
Floral City		●								●					●									
Florentina	●	●							●						●									
Flower Dream	●			●												●	●						●	
Flying Cloud	●	●							●						●									
Forget-me-not		●							●						●									
Formosissima		●								●					●									
Foxtrot		●					●							●										
François Villon	●	●											●		●									
Franz Noszian		●							●							●			●					
Frau Henriette Ernst									●						●				●					
Frau Ida Noack		●							●						●									
Frederike		●											●		●				●					
Frosted Flame	●	●											●		●									
G																								
Galadriel		●											●		●								●	
Gartenmeister Bonstedt		●	●	●			●								●						●			
Gay Fandango	●	●						●											●					

	Hanging-basket	Standard or shrub	Triphylla	Variegated leaf	White	Red	Orange	Red-violet	Pink	Pink-violet, Pink-red	White-violet	Pink-white	Red-white	Winter-hardy	Single	Semi-double	Double	Self-branching	Easy to Grow	Dwarf	Requires winter temp. of 10°C	Tolerates shade	Sun and/or warmth	Greenhouse
Gay Parasol		•								•							•	•						
General Monk		•						•							•									
Genii		•	•					•							•								•	
Georgana		•						•									•							
Glitters		•				•									•									
Golden Dawn		•					•								•								•	
Golden Glow	•	•					•								•								•	
Golden La Campanella	•			•							•				•				•					
Golden Lena	•			•								•			•									
Golden Marinka	•			•	•										•						•			
Golden Moonlight Sonata	•			•					•						•			•						
Golondrina	•	•			•									•	•			•						
Grasmere		•	•		•										•			•						
Greenpeace		•							•						•									
Groenekan's Glorie		•				•									•									
Gruss aus dem Bodethal		•						•							•					•				
H																								
Hanna		•												•			•	•						
Harebell		•								•						•							•	
Harriet	•										•						•							
Harry Gray	•	•		•											•							•		
Heather Hobbs		•											•		•		•							
Heidi Ann		•							•								•	•						
Hellas		•												•			•		•					
Hendrikje Stoffels	•									•					•				•					
Henri Poincaré	•	•						•							•									
Heron		•						•						•			•							
Heydon											•				•							•		
Hiawatha		•								•					•									
Hidcote Beauty	•	•									•				•									
Highland Pipes		•							•						•									
Hindu Belle		•											•		•									
Hobson's Choice		•						•							•									
Hula Girl	•												•				•							
Hummeltje		•							•						•			•		•				
Hurrycane										•														
I																								
Iced Champagne		•						•								•								
Igloo Maid		•	•	•													•							
Impudence		•											•		•									
Ina		•											•		•									
Indian Maid	•	•				•									•									
Ingram Maid		•		•											•								•	
Iris Amer		•																						
Isis		•						•							•			•						

240

	Hanging-basket	Standard or shrub	Triphylla	Variegated leaf	White	Red	Orange	Red-violet	Pink	Pink-violet, Pink-red	White-violet	Pink-white	Red-white	Winter-hardy	Single	Semi-double	Double	Self-branching	Easy to Grow	Dwarf	Requires winter temp. of 10°C	Tolerates shade	Sun and/or warmth	Greenhouse
J																								
Jack Ackland	•	•							•						•									
Jack King		•							•								•							
Jamboree		•								•							•							
Jan Bremer	•	•			•										•									
Janny Appel		•						•							•									
Jean Ewart		•						•							•									
Je Maintiendrai		•			•	•									•									
Jessimae																								
Joan Gilbert		•						•									•							
Joan Pacey		•						•							•			•						
Johanna Roemerman		•											•			•								
Joker	•									•														
Joy Patmore		•										•			•				•					
Julie Horton	•							•							•									
K																								
Kaboutertje		•			•										•					•				
Karina		•				•									•									
Kathy Louise	•					•											•							
Kegworth Carnival	•										•													
Keukenhof		•			•										•									
Kiwi	•	•									•				•									
Kokarde		•						•								•							•	
Komeet		•				•									•									
Komeet v. Halley	•	•									•				•									
Kon Tiki	•	•										•			•									
Koralle		•	•				•														•			
Kwintet		•			•										•									
L																								
La Bergere	•				•											•								
La Campanella	•	•									•						•		•					
Lace Pettycoats		•										•		•										
Lady Boothby	•	•				•							•	•										
Lady Isobel Barnett		•						•							•									
Lady Kathleen Spence		•						•							•									
Lady Thumb		•											•		•					•				
Laga		•									•				•									
Lakeland Princess		•									•				•									
La Neige	•	•			•											•	•							
La Rosita	•	•						•									•							
Lazy Lady	•	•				•												•						
Le Berger	•	•			•																			
Lena	•	•									•				•									
Lena Dalton		•						•									•			•				
Leonora		•						•							•									
Leverkusen		•	•		•										•								•	

	Hanging-basket	Standard or shrub	Triphylla	Variegated leaf	White	Red	Orange	Red-violet	Pink	Pink-violet, Pink-red	White-violet	Pink-white	Red-white	Winter-hardy	Single	Semi-double	Double	Self-branching	Easy to Grow	Dwarf	Requires winter temp. of 10°C	Tolerates shade	Sun and/or warmth	Greenhouse
Liemers Lantaern	●	●							●									●	●			●		
Lilac Lustre		●						●										●						
Lilac Queen		●											●					●						
L'ingénue		●								●					●									
Lisa	●									●								●						
Little Beauty		●								●					●								●	
Liz		●										●						●						
Lochinver		●								●								●						
Loeky		●								●					●				●	●				
Lolita	●	●													●						●			
Lord Lonsdale		●				●									●									
Lottie Hobby		●			●										●									
Loveliness	●	●									●				●									
Lunters Roem		●									●							●						
Lynn Ellen		●								●								●						●
M																								
Madame Cornelissen		●											●	●		●								
Machu Picchu	●	●				●								●	●								●	
Magic Flute	●	●										●												
Major Heaphy		●			●										●									
Mandarin	●	●							●						●									
Mantilla	●	●	●		●																	●	●	
Marco Boy		●										●										●		
Margaret		●						●							●									
Margaret Roe		●						●							●									
Marinka	●														●									
Maori Maid	●														●									
Marjon Wit		●						●							●								●	
Marlies		●												●				●						
Marie Punselie	●	●						●							●									
Marin Glow		●									●				●					●				
Mary		●	●			●									●									
Mary Fairclo		●							●						●									
Masquerade	●								●								●							
Mazda	●	●			●																		●	
Meadowlark	●												●		●									
Medusa	●												●											
Melody		●						●								●				●				
Menna		●		●													●			●				
Mephisto		●		●										●		●			●					
Mercurius		●						●							●									
Merry Mary	●												●				●							
Mevr Goyaerts	●														●	●								
Mia van der Zee		●						●							●									
Micky Goult		●						●							●									
Mieke Meursing		●							●						●				●					

242

	Hanging-basket	Standard or shrub	Triphylla	Variegated leaf	White	Red	Orange	Red-violet	Pink	Pink-violet, Pink-red	White-violet	Pink-white	Red-white	Winter-hardy	Single	Semi-double	Double	Self-branching	Easy to Grow	Dwarf	Requires winter temp. of 10°C	Tolerates shade	Sun and/or warmth	Greenhouse
Mimi Kubischka		●											●				●							
Minirok	●								●															
Minirose		●													●	●				●				
Miss California	●	●										●				●		●						
Mission Bells		●						●					●			●		●						
Molesworth	●												●					●						
Monstera	●			●													●							
Montezuma	●							●									●							
Moonraker		●										●					●							
Morgenrood		●											●		●									
Morning Glow		●							●							●	●		●					
Morning Kiss		●						●									●						●	
Morning Light	●								●								●							●
Moth Blue	●							●									●							
Mountain Mist		●									●						●					●		
Miss Lovell Swisher		●					●									●								
Mrs Popple		●						●						●		●								
Mrs W.P. Wood		●									●					●								
Mrs W. Rundle	●								●							●								
Multa	●							●								●			●					
Muriel	●							●							●									
N																								
Nancy Lou		●										●					●							
Native Dancer	●							●							●									
Nellie Nuttall		●										●			●									
Nellie Wallace	●											●				●								
Nicolaas Aalhuizen		●						●							●									
Nina Wills		●							●						●									
Normandy Bell	●	●						●							●									
Northumbrian Pipes		●									●				●									
Northway	●	●								●					●									
Nutshell	●									●					●									
O																								
Orange Cocktail	●										●				●									
Orange Crush		●					●								●									
Orange Flare		●					●								●								●	
Orange Mirage	●						●								●									
Oranje Boven	●	●							●						●									
Oranje van Os		●					●								●									
Ortenburger Festival		●						●							●									
Other Fellow		●										●			●									
P																								
Pablo Picasso	●								●								●							
Pacquesa	●	●											●		●				●	●				
Papa Bleuss	●							●							●				●					
Papoose		●						●							●				●	●				

243

	Hanging-basket	Standard or shrub	Triphylla	Variegated leaf	White	Red	Orange	Red-violet	Pink	Pink-violet, Pink-red	White-violet	Pink-white	Red-white	Winter-hardy	Single	Semi-double	Double	Self-branching	Easy to Grow	Dwarf	Requires winter temp. of 10°C	Tolerates shade	Sun and/or warmth	Greenhouse
Pathetique	•												•				•							
Patricia Ann	•									•														
Party Frock		•							•							•								
Peggy King		•							•							•								
Pepi		•							•											•				
Peppermint Stick		•				•											•							
Peredrup	•							•							•									
Peter Pan	•								•						•									
Petit Point		•						•							•									
Phenomenal	•	•						•									•							
Phyllis		•			•									•	•									
Pink Bon Accorde		•							•						•									
Pink Darling		•							•						•									
Pink Dessert		•										•			•								•	
Pink Galore	•								•								•					•		
Pink Marshmallow	•			•								•					•							•
Pink Pearl		•							•						•									
Pink Temptation	•	•										•			•									
Pinch Me	•									•					•									
Pixie		•							•						•									
Polychinelle		•								•						•		•						
Postiljon	•									•					•			•						
Powder Puff	•								•							•								
Prelude	•									•						•								
President							•																•	
President Leo Boullemier																								
President Margaret Slater		•								•					•								•	
President Stanley Wilson	•									•					•									
Preston Guild		•								•					•						•			
Purper Princess		•						•							•							•		
Pussy Cat	•					•									•								•	
Puts Folly	•														•				•					
R																								
R.A.F.	•									•					•									
Radings Inge		•													•									
Rambling Rose	•	•							•										•					
Ravens Barrow	•	•						•							•								•	
Red Jacket	•												•			•								
Red Ribbons	•												•			•								
Red Spider	•				•										•			•						
Reverend D Brown	•	•										•					•	•						
Regal	•	•			•										•									
Rika		•											•		•									
Ringwood Market		•								•					•			•						
Robert Stolz		•						•							•			•						
Ron Ewart		•								•					•									

244

	Hanging-basket	Standard or shrub	Triphylla	Variegated leaf	White	Red	Orange	Red-violet	Pink	Pink-violet, Pink-red	White-violet	Pink-white	Red-white	Winter-hardy	Single	Semi-double	Double	Self-branching	Easy to Grow	Dwarf	Requires winter temp. of 10°C	Tolerates shade	Sun and/or warmth	Greenhouse
Rose Bradwardine		•								•							•	•	•					
Rose of Castile		•									•				•	•			•					
Rose of Castile (improved)		•							•						•	•			•					
Rose van der Berg		•							•						•									
Rosy Frills		•										•					•							
Royal Purple		•						•							•	•								
Royal Touch	•	•							•								•							•
Royal Velvet		•				•											•							
Rufus		•			•										•									
Ruth King	•	•							•								•							
S																								
Santa Cruz		•			•												•						•	
Satellite		•												•		•								
Saturnus		•						•								•								
Sealand Prince		•						•						•		•								
Sea Shell		•						•									•							
Seventh Heaven	•	•			•												•							
Shanley		•					•										•							
Sierra Blue	•	•									•						•							
Silver Jubilee		•										•					•							
Spike Arjen		•		•													•	•						
Sleigh Bells		•										•			•									
Snowcap		•												•			•		•					
So Big	•								•								•							
Sonata	•	•		•													•							
Son of Thumb		•							•						•									
Sophisticated Lady	•	•															•							•
South Gate		•							•								•							
Space Shuttle		•					•										•							
Spring Bells		•										•				•								
Stad Elburg	•	•						•									•	•	•					
Stanley Cash	•	•									•						•							
Starlite		•										•				•	•							
Stella Ann		•	•		•												•							
Strawberry Delight		•		•					•								•							
String of Pearls		•							•								•					•		
Sugar Blues	•	•											•						•					
Suikerbossie		•						•									•							
Summer Snow	•	•		•													•							
Sunny Smiles	•	•							•								•							
Sunray		•		•				•							•						•			
Susan Travis		•						•						•		•								
Suzanna		•						•								•								
Swanley Gem		•						•								•								
Swanley Yellow		•					•									•								
Sweetheart		•								•						•		•						

245

	Hanging-basket	Standard or shrub	Triphylla	Variegated leaf	White	Red	Orange	Red-violet	Pink	Pink-violet, Pink-red	White-violet	Pink-white	Red-white	Winter-hardy	Single	Semi-double	Double	Self-branching	Easy to Grow	Dwarf	Requires winter temp. of 10°C	Tolerates shade	Sun and/or warmth	Greenhouse
Sweet Leilanie	●	●							●								●						●	
Swingtime	●	●											●				●		●					
T																								
Taffeta Bow	●							●									●							
Tangerine		●					●											●			●		●	
Television	●	●										●					●							
Temptation		●											●		●									
Tennessee Waltz		●						●							●			●	●					
Texas Longhorn	●	●											●											
The Doctor	●	●										●			●									
The Phoenix	●	●						●							●									
Theseus	●	●				●									●									
Tiffany	●	●		●													●						●	
Ting-a-Ling		●		●											●									
Tinkerbell	●										●					●								
Tolling Bell		●											●		●									
Tom Thumb		●						●						●	●					●				
Toss		●								●					●									
Torch		●							●								●							
Tour Eiffel	●	●							●						●									
Tourtonne		●	●												●						●		●	
Trail Blazer	●	●				●											●							
Trailing King	●	●								●					●									
Trailing Queen	●	●				●									●									
Traudchen Bonstedt		●	●					●													●		●	
Tresco		●				●								●	●									
Tristesse		●						●									●	●	●					
Troika	●							●									●							
Tropicana	●											●					●							
Tropic Sunset	●	●		●					●								●						●	
Trumpeter	●	●						●							●									
Tsjiep		●											●							●				
Tumbler	●									●					●							●		
Tuonela		●								●						●								
Twiggy	●									●					●									
Typhoon		●								●					●				●					
U																								
U.F.O.		●									●				●									
Uncle Charley		●						●										●						
Uncle Steve	●							●											●					
Unique		●								●					●									
Upward Look		●						●							●									
V																								
Valerie		●								●					●									
Vanessa Jackson	●					●									●				●			●		
Vanity Fair		●										●						●						

246

	Hanging-basket	Standard or shrub	Triphylla	Variegated leaf	White	Red	Orange	Red-violet	Pink	Pink-violet, Pink-red	White-violet	Pink-white	Red-white	Winter-hardy	Single	Semi-double	Double	Self-branching	Easy to Grow	Dwarf	Requires winter temp. of 10°C	Tolerates shade	Sun and/or warmth	Greenhouse
Venus		●						●							●									
Vielliebchen		●						●							●									
Vincent van Gogh	●	●							●						●									
Violet Bassett-Burr		●									●						●							
Violet Gem		●						●										●						
Viva Ireland	●	●							●						●									
Vobeglo		●							●						●				●					
Voodoo		●						●									●							
Vrouwtje		●						●							●									
W																								
Walsingham		●									●				●		●							
Walz Bergtop	●	●							●						●							●		
Walz Brandaris		●					●								●									
Walz Bruintje	●	●				●									●									
Walz Epicurist	●	●							●						●									
Walz Estafette	●	●											●		●									
Walz Floreat	●	●									●				●		●			●				
Walz Freule	●	●							●						●		●							
Walz Gigolo	●	●				●												●						
Walz Meermin	●							●							●								●	
Walz Parasol		●						●							●								●	
Walz Toorts		●	●			●									●						●			
Walz Vuurtoren		●				●									●									
Walz Waardin	●	●							●						●							●		
Walz Waterval	●												●				●					●		
Warton Crag		●											●											
Water Nymph		●											●						●					
Waxen Beauty		●		●																				
Westergeest		●				●									●			●						
Westminster Chimes	●							●								●								
Whirlaway	●			●												●								
White Galore	●			●														●						
White Pixie												●	●	●										
White Spider	●	●										●		●										
Willie Tamerus	●	●				●								●										
Wings of Song	●							●								●	●							
Winston Churchill		●									●					●	●				●			
Witchingham													●											

Fuchsia Societies

Australia
Australian Fuchsia Society
PO Box 97
Norwood
South Australia 5067

Canberra Geranium & Fuchsia Society
PO Box 930
Civic Square
ACT 2608
Liaison Officer: Laurienne Atkinson

Waverley Garden Club Fuchsia Group
11 Padua Court
Glen Waverley
Victoria 3150
President: Kenneth C. McLister

Western Australian Fuchsia Society
6A Poolya Road
City Beach
Western Australia 6015
Editor: Mrs Helen Martin-Beck

Austria
Osterreichische Fuchsienfreunde
Wienerstrasse 216
A–8051 Graz
Secretary: Frau Elisabeth Schnedl

Belgium
Les Amis du Fuchsia
24 rue du Moulin
6239 Pont-à-Celles
Contact: Michel Cornet

De Vlaamse Fuchsiavrienden
25 Hoge Akker
2130 Brasschaat
President: Dr Oscar Defeu

De Vrije Fuchsiavrienden
92 Lijkveldestraat
2778 St Pauwels
Contact: Erna Van Wiele

Canada
British Columbia Fuchsia and Begonia Society
2402 Swinburne Avenue
North Vancouver
British Columbia V7H 1L2
Contact: Lorna Hechenson

Greater Victoria Geranium and Fuchsia Society
PO Box 5266
Postal Station B
Victoria
British Columbia V8R 6N4

Denmark
Dansk Fuchsia Club
Frugtparken 1
2820 Gentofte
Secretary: Mrs Merete Printz

Ethiopia
Horticultural Society of Ethiopia
PO Box 1261
Addis Ababa

France
Section Fuchsia
Société Nationale d'Horticulture de France
84 rue de Grenelle
75007 Paris

Société Franco-européenne de Fuchsiasphilie
1 rue de la Convention
93120 La Courneuve
President: Bruno Fournier

Germany
Deutsche Dahlien,
Fuchsien und Gladiolen Gesellschaft
Drachenfels-Strasse 9a
D–5300 Bonn 2
Contact: Elisabeth Göring

Deutsche Fuchsien Gesellschaft
Pankratiusstrasse 10
Grossförste
D–3208 Giesen
Secretary: Hans-Peter Peters

Netherlands
Nederlands Kring van Fuchsiavrienden
73 Mauritshoek
2988 EC Ridderkerk
Secretary: Maria Rijkaart van Cappellen

New Zealand
National Fuchsia Society
18 Churton Drive
Churton Park
Wellington 4
President: E. D. Sweetman

Canterbury Horticulture Society,
Fuchsia Circle
25 Albert Terrace
St Martins
Christchurch 2

Norway
Norsk Fuchsia Selskap
Nyboveien 8C
N–3400 Lier
Contact: Mrs Joan Haugland

South Africa
South African Fuchsia Society
Box 537
Alberton 1450
Secretary: Mrs Roos Breytenbach

Sweden
Fuchsiasallkapet
Östermalmsgaten 68
S-114 50 Stockholm
Secretary: Agneta Westin

Switzerland
Schweizerischer Fuchsienverein
Fuchsia-Gartnerie Angst
CH–8196 Wil/Zurich

United Kingdom
British Fuchsia Society
20 Brodawel
Llannon Llanelli
Dyfed
Secretary: R. Williams

United States
American Fuchsia Society
County Fair Building
9th Avenue & Lincoln Way
San Francisco
CA 94122

National Fuchsia Society
11507 East 187th Street
Arlesia
CA 90701

Northwest Fuchsia Society
PO Box 133071
Bitter Lake Station
Seattle
WA 98133–0071

Oregon Fuchsia Society
336 South East 63rd Street
Portland
OR 97215

Zimbabwe
Fuchsia Society of Zimbabwe
PO Box GD 115
Greendale
Harare

Fuchsia Nurseries

Belgium
Kwekerij Sterkex
Dorp 24
2430 Olen
tel: 014–211828

Joseph Vassart
12 rue du Joki
6071 Châtelet

Denmark
Villy Mougaard
Bjerringholmveg 14
Batum
18800 Viborg

Heinz Jochimsen
Skolevej 2
DK6862 Tistrup

France
Adam Philippe
14 Lot de la Devrie
35450 Val d'Ize

Ghislaine Barrere
Les 4 Coins
Ch. d'Estandens
Beaumont sur Leze
31190 Auterive

Jacques Briant
49480 Saint-Sylvain-d'Anjou

Bureau Savennières
49170 Saint-Georges-sur-Loire

Despalles
5 rue d'Alésia
75005 Paris

Gaubin
155 rue de la Mairie
La Riche
37000 Tours

Millerioux
7 rue Alexandre Prachais
95590 Presles

Plantations Modernes
182 rue due Faubourg
St Denis
75010 Paris

Kerisnel
29250 Saint-Pol-de-Leon

Seillade
10 rue de la Forêt
Avrainville
91630 Marolle-en-Hurepoix

Tourly
17 rue Danton
18000 Asnitres-les-Bourges

Germany
Rudolf & Clara Baum
Scheffelrain 1
7250 Leonberg
tel: 07152–27558

Reinhard Heinke
Gartenbau
Eichholzstrasse 2
4600 Dortmund-Lichtendorf
tel: 02304–40321

Gärtnerei Hermann Ermel
Krupfalzstrasse 1
6719 Zellertal 1
tel: 06355–639

Gartenbau Wener Behre.
Haneburthwinkel 23–27
300 Hannover 51 (Buchholz)
tel: 0511–690682

Gartenbau Heinrich Breuckmann
Leinschede 22
5970 Plettenburg 2
tel: 02391–51791

Netherlands

Gerben Calkhoven
Brakenbeltsweg 30
7440 AG Nijverdal
tel: 05486–13813

Giesen Fuchsias
Nieuwe Kerkweg 24
7031 HH Neiuw Wehl
tel: 08347–81784

Kwekerij M. de Groot en Zoon
Lijsterbeslaan 8
8181 GV Heerde
tel: 05782–1694

Aloys & Diny Hetterscheid
Doesburgseweg 12A
6941 SJ Loil
tel: 08362–23712

Tuincentrum A. G. de Keyzer
Hogeweg 29
6621 BN Dreumel
tel: 08877–1672

Tuincentrum 'De Tuinier' Kuperus BV
Zuiderdwarsvaart 97
9203 HK Drachten
tel: 05120–14164

Limburgs Tuincentrum
Rijksweg-Zuid 250
6161 BZ Geleen
tel: 04494–46006

Fuchsias Mathijissen
Wolfhoeksestraat 9
6662 PH Reeth-Elst
tel: 08819–72003

Kwerkerij Frans & Nelly Noten
Veestraat 6
5595 GG Leende
tel: 04906–1421

Kwekerij 'Overhagen'
Biljoen 9
6883 JH Velp
tel: 085–620884

Kwekerij 'Eeuwige Lente' J. A. Penning
Langestraat 53
4542 ZG Hoek (Z-VL)
tel: 01154–1468

Kwekerij C. Spek Jr
Eerste Hoornerveenseweg 7
8181 LW Heerde
tel: 05782–3604

Kwekerij Verheugd
Alendorperweg 40
3451 GN Vleuten
tel: 03407–1736

Gebr. van 't Westeinde
Westhofsezandweg 3
4444 SM's Heer Arendskerke
tel: 01106–1219

Kwekerij Zeelenberg
Sionsweg 10
2286 KK Rijswijk
tel: 015–131–31

De Zweetdruppel
Le Zandwijkje 6b
7913 VM Hollandscheveld
tel: 05284–1893

Zwette Fuchsia
Zettewei 68A
8269 ED Scharnegoutum
tel: 05150–18986

Switzerland

E. & A. Angst van der Leek
Gärtnerei
CH 8196 Wil/Zurich

United Kingdom

Arcadia Nurseries
Brasscastle Lane
Nunthorpe
Middlesborough
Cleveland TS8 9EB
tel: 0642 310782

B. & H. Baker
Bourne Brooke Nurseries
Greenstead Green
Halstead
Essex CO9 1RJ
tel: 0787 472900

R. J. Blythe
Potash Nurseries
Cow Green
Bacon
Stowmakret
Suffolk IP14 4HJ
tel: 0449 781671

Chingford Nurseries
20 Chingford Mount Road
South Chingford
London E4
tel: 081 531 7041

Goulding's Fuchsias
West View
Link Lane
Bentley
Ipswich
Suffolk IP9 2DP
tel: 0473 310058

High Trees Nurseries
Buckland
Reigate
Surrey RH2 9RE
tel: 0737 47217

F. H. Holmes
Mariwood
Hulver
Beccles
Suffolk NR34 7US
tel: 0502 76647

Jackson's Nurseries
Clifton Campville
near Tamworth
Staffordshire B79 0AP
tel: 0827 86307

Lechdale Garden and Fuchsia Centre
Fairford Road
Lechlade
tel: 0367 52372

C. S. Lockyer (Fuchsias)
Lansbury
70 Henfield Road
Coalpit Heath
Bristol BS17 2VZ
tel: 0454 772219

Kathleen Muncaster Fuchsias
18 Field Lane
Morton
Gainsborough
Lincolnshire DN21 3BY
tel: 0427 2329

R. & J. Pacey
Stathern
Melton Mowbray
Leicester LE14 4HE
tel: 0949 60249

J. V. Porter
12 Hazel Grove
Southport
Lancashire
tel: 0704 33902

J. Ridding
Fuchsiasvale Nurseries
Stanklyn Lane
Summerfields
Kidderminster
Worcester DY10 4HS
tel: 0562 69444

John Smith & Son
Hilltop Nurseries
Thornton
Leicestershire
tel: 0530 21331

A. P. & E. V. Tabraham
St Mary's
Isles of Scilly
tel: 0720 22759

Travis Fuchsias
394 Brindle Road
Bamber Bridge
Preston PR5 6AP
tel: 0772 36609

Further Reading

American Fuchsia Society, *The Third Fuchsia Book*, 1962

Beckett, Kenneth A., *Plants Under Glass*

Berry, P. E., 'Studies in Fuchsia' in *Annals of the Missouri Botanical Garden*, 1982

Boullemier, L. B., *Fascinating Fuchsias*, privately published, Northampton, 1973

Boullemier, L. B., *The Checklist of Species, Hybrids and Cultivars of the Genus Fuchsia*, Cassell, London, 1991 (revised edition)

Breedlove, D. E., *The systematics of Fuchsia, section Encliandra (Onagraceae)*, University of California, 1969

Bruin, E. de, *Een kas i:: eigen tuin*, Thieme & Cie, Zutphen

César, J. *Les Fuchsias*, Editions Dargaud, Neuilly sur Seine, 1981

Clapham, S., *Fuchsias for House and Garden*, David & Charles, Newton Abbot, 1982; Universe Publishing Co., New York, 1982

Deelen, D. van, *Fuchsias*, Misset, Doetinchem, 1967

Ewart, Ron, *Fuchsia Lexicon*, Blandford Press, London, 1992 (revised edition)

Fessler, A., *Fuchsien für Haus und Garten*, Kosmos, Stuttgart, 1980

Fessler, A., *Fuchsias voor huis en tuin*, vert. door dr. J. E. van der Laane, Thieme & Cie, Zutphen, 1980

Garner, R. J., *The Grafter's Handbook*, Cassell, London

Gaucher, M., *Les Fuchsias, d'ombre et de luminaire*, La Maison Rustique, Paris, 1979

Goulding, E. J., *Fuchsias*, Bartholomew, Edinburgh, 1973

Graafland, Christiaan, *Alles over broeikassen*, Helmond BV, Helmond

Grzimek, B., *Enzyklopädie des Tierreiches, Entwicklungsgeschichte der Lebeswesen*, Kindler Verlag AG, Zürich, 1972

Hayden, Nickey, *Bezig zijn met kweken in kas en back*, Helmond BV, Helmond

Jennings, K. and Miller, V. V., *Growing Fuchsias*, Croom Helm, London, 1979; Timber Press, Portland, Oregon, 1982

Laan, J. E. van der, *Fuschsias, het hele jaar door*, Thieme & Cie, Zutphen, 1974

Manthey, G. *Fuchsien*, Ulmer, Stuttgart, 1983

Munz, P. A., *A Revision of the Genus Fuchsias (Onagraceae)*, California Academy of Sciences, 1943

National Fuchsia Society Inc., *The New A to Z on Fuchsias*, 1976

Nederlandse Kring van Fuchsiavrienden (Dutch Circle of Fuchsia Lovers), *Lijst van in Nederland aawezige species en cultivars*, 1977, 1979, 1982, 1985

Porcher, F. *Le Fuchsia*, Libraire Centrale d'Agriculture et de Jardinage, 1874
Proudley, B. and V., *Fuchsias in Colour*, Blandford Press, Poole, 1975
Puttock, A. G., *Lovely Fuchsias*, John Gifford, London, 1959
Puttock, A. G., *Pelargoniums and Fuchsias*, Collingridge, London, 1959
Robinson, G. W., *The Cool Greenhouse*, Penguin Books Ltd, Harmondsworth, Middlesex
Saunders, E., *Wagtail's Book of Fuchsias* volumes i, ii, iii and iv
Thorne, T., *Fuchsias for All Purposes*, Collingridge, London, 1959
Tomlinson, V., *Growing Fuchsias in Southern Africa*, Galaxie Press, Salisbury, Zimbabwe, 1976
Travis, J., *Fuchsia Culture*, privately published, Bamber Bridge, Lancaster
Wells, G., *Fuchsias: A Wisley Handbook*, Cassell/Royal Horticultural Society, London, 1985
Wilson, S. J., *Fuchsias*, Faber & Faber, London, 1974 (revised edition)
Witham Fogg, H. G., *Begonias and Fuchsias*, John Gifford, London, 1971
Witte, J. *Handboekje voor de kennis en het kweken van lievelingsbloemen*, volumes ix and x: 'The Fuchsia', Stemberb, The Hague, 1882
Wood, W. P., *A Fuchsia Survey*, Williams & Norgate, 1959
Wright, J. O., *Hardy Fuchsias*
Wright, J. O., *Fuchsia: A Garden History*
Zee-Kruseman, M. van der, *Recente aantekeningen*

Photographic Credits

(the numbers refer to illustration numbers)

H. Aalhuizen-Nijhuis (37, 47 and 121); Dr S. A. Appel (22, 24, 129, 133, 136 and 144); J. G. van de Beek (11, 60 and 143); L. Bögemann (18 and 20); C. van Brunschot (27); P. van der Craats (5, 39, 76 and 140); F. van den Elshout (2, 6, 7, 16, 31, 38, 41, 42, 43, 44, 46, 49, 57, 62, 63, 64, 74, 83, 93, 97, 101, 106, 107, 110, 111, 123, 128, 130, 138, 139, 148, 149); H. J. de Graaff (3 and 105); M. Grijsen-Sellink (52, 69, 71, 81, 91 and 118); W. J. Luiste (8, 10, 12, 13, 21, 25, 26, 32, 45, 61, 68, 79, 80, 82, 87, 89, 92, 94, 102, 112 and 125); J. de Nie (17, 40, 73 and 78); J. W. N. W. van der Post (1, 9, 19, 23, 30, 33, 34, 35, 36, 50, 51, 53, 54, 55, 56, 58, 65, 67, 70, 72, 75, 84, 85, 86, 88, 90, 95, 96, 104, 108, 109, 113, 114, 115, 116, 117, 120, 124, 132, 134, 137, 141, 142, 145 and 147); D. Reiman-Dietiker (126 and 127); T. Spakman (4, 14, 15, 28, 39, 77, 99 and 103); P. C. Venema-Hollestelle (59 and 122); and A. van Wijk (48, 66, 98, 100, 119, 131 and 135).

List of Colour Plates

(the numbers refer to illustration numbers)

Species

General Index

(numbers in **bold** type refer to numbers of colour plates)

Index of Cultivars

(page numbers in *italics* refer to line illustrations;
numbers in **bold** refer to numbers of colour plates)

Index of Species

(numbers in **bold** type refer to numbers of colour plates)